THE STORY OF THE NATIONS

OCTAVO, ILLUSTRATED. PER VOL., $1.50

THE EARLIER VOLUMES WILL BE

THE STORY OF GREECE. By Prof. Jas. A. Harrison

THE STORY OF ROME. By Arthur Gilman

THE STORY OF THE JEWS. By Prof. Jas. K. Hosmer

THE STORY OF CHALDEA. By Z. A. Ragozin

THE STORY OF NORWAY. By Prof. H. H. Boyesen

THE STORY OF GERMANY. By S. Baring-Gould

THE STORY OF SPAIN. By E. E. and Susan Hale

THE STORY OF HUNGARY. By Prof. A. Vámbéry

THE STORY OF CARTHAGE. By Prof. Alfred J. Church

THE STORY OF THE SARACENS. By Arthur Gilman

THE STORY OF ASSYRIA. By Z. A. Ragozin

THE STORY OF THE MOORS IN SPAIN. By Stanley Lane-Poole

THE STORY OF THE NORMANS. By Sarah O. Jewett

THE STORY OF PERSIA. By S. G. W. Benjamin

THE STORY OF ALEXANDER'S EMPIRE. By Prof. J. P. Mahaffy

THE STORY OF ANCIENT EGYPT. By Geo. Rawlinson

THE STORY OF THE GOTHS. By Henry Bradley

For prospectus of the series see end of this volume

G. P. PUTNAM'S SONS   NEW YORK AND LONDON

BUST OF A GERMAN, BY TRADITION, HERMANN.
(The Capitoline Museum, Rome.)

THE

STORY OF GERMANY

BY

SABINE BARING-GOULD, M.A.

AUTHOR OF "GERMANY PRESENT AND PAST," "CURIOUS MYTHS OF THE MIDDLE AGES," ETC.

WITH THE COLLABORATION OF

ARTHUR GILMAN, M.A.

AUTHOR OF "THE STORY OF ROME," "A HISTORY OF THE AMERICAN PEOPLE," ETC.

NEW YORK

G. P. PUTNAM'S SONS

LONDON : T. FISHER UNWIN

MDCCCXXXVII

Press of

G. P. PUTNAM'S SONS

New York

PREFACE.

GERMANY is the heart of Continental Europe, and influences have gone forth from her which have deeply affected every one of her neighbours. The present volume traces the life of this powerful nation from the time when imperial Rome was baffled by her valiant Hermann down to the hour when France fell before her, and the idea of Empire (which had been a delusion and a terrible embarrassment since the crowning of Charlemagne) became, under William the First, a power making for peace and strength.

The absorbing story begins with pictures of the surgings of the nations,—the Huns, the Sclavs, the Goths, the Saxons, the Franks; it tells of the throes by which the heroes of old brought the great people to its independent life; recounts the struggles of the various Teutonic families among themselves, and of all of them with their neighbours; and brings up vividly the power of an idea, as it shows the strife and perplexities arising from the Imperial spectre, as well as the dire contest that followed the schism of the Church and in a short time involved all Christendom in disputes touching the highest interests of humanity.

The reader of the story of Germany is thus

brought face to face with problems of the deepest moment, with which men of deadly earnestness were struggling through the ages, putting forth all the power of their intellect and the force of their vigorous bodies, intensified by the deep-seated religious convictions which they nourished in their hearts.

The story of such a people as the Germans could not fail to possess intense interest for anyone; but for us of another branch of the Teutonic family, it has the additional charm that it is the history of our blood-relations. On their experience we have built, and to the light of their example we look for guidance; in their triumphs we rejoice; to the grandeur of the genius of their poets and prose writers, of their scientists and theologians, we look with pride and admiration, congratulating ourselves that we, too, are Teutons. We stood with their Hermann, as he said to the Roman Varus, "No farther!" just as we stood with the barons before King John on the field of Runnymede.

It has been the endeavour in preparing the following pages to keep before the mind this unity of the Teutonic peoples, as well as to indicate the steps by which the idea of Empire has progressed to the present German Unity.

A. G.

Cambridge, *May 1st,* 1886.

CONTENTS.

LIST OF ILLUSTRATIONS.

The larger proportion of the illustrations in this volume are based upon the excellent designs in the comprehensive and authoritative "Deutsche Geschichte," by L. Stacke, to the publishers of which, Messrs. Velhagen & Klasing, of Bielefeld, we desire to express our cordial acknowledgments.

May 1, 1886.   G. P. PUTNAM'S SONS.

I.

THE FIRST GERMANS.

(B.C. 113–102.)

In the year 113 before Christ was born, the inhabitants of Northern Italy were startled to see multitudes of savage men sitting on their great shields, shooting down the snow slopes of the Alps upon them. They had fair hair, thick and long ; some had shaggy red hair. They were tall, strong men ; their eyes were blue. They wore the heads of wolves and bears and oxen on their helmets, the latter with the horns ; and others again had the wings of eagles spread, and fastened to their iron caps. Who were these? They belonged to two different races, and spoke different languages ; and though both were fair-haired, yet one set of men was taller, sturdier than the other.

These invaders called themselves the Cimbri and Teutones. They had lived side by side in the Swiss valleys till the valleys could no longer support them, and then they burst their way over the snowy passes to conquer and colonize the sunny plains of Italy.

At the present day the mountains of Switzerland

will not support all its inhabitants. The men go out as masons, and waiters, and pastry cooks, and clock and watchmakers, and the girls as nurses and cooks. In those days they went out only in one way—to fight and conquer themselves new homes.

If you were to travel through Switzerland to-day you would find that in one canton French is spoken, in the next German; that in the town of Freiburg, French is spoken in the lower and German in the upper town. This is because two distinct races live together in Switzerland now, as they did 113 years before Christ. The French-speaking people represent the Cimbri and the German-speaking people represent the Teutones. The Welsh call themselves Cymri, which is the same as Cimbri. They belong to the same great Keltic family. The Germans call themselves Deutsch, which is the same as Teut-ones.

The Romans sent armies against these warriors who came down on Italy from the snowfields, but the Cimbri and Teutones defeated them. They fought with desperation; starvation was behind in their mountain valleys; they must conquer or die. They destroyed the villages they came upon, they took and burnt the cities, they overran the plains. They killed the horses they took, and hung their captives to trees as sacrifices to Wuotan, the god of the air, after whom Wednesday (Wuotans-tag) takes its name. Italy was filled with dismay. If the Cimbri and Teutones had known how to profit by the terror they inspired, and by their victories, they would have soon taken Rome; but they turned to

ROMANS AND CIMBRI IN COMBAT.

the West, and poured along the beautiful Riviera road into the south of what we now call France. This gave the Romans a little breathing time; a great army was assembled, and placed under the command of their best general, Marius. He pursued the wild men into Gaul, and formed a strongly fortified camp on the Rhone. Thence he watched them. His soldiers were at first too much afraid of these great men with their animals' heads,—their faces peering out of the jaws of wolf and bear,—to be trusted to meet them in battle, but after awhile they became accustomed to the sight. The wild warriors despised the Roman soldiers, and as they ate up the produce of the land where they settled, they divided, and the Cimbri went off again, like a swarm of bees, back through Switzerland and Tyrol into Italy. Then the Teutones also turned to go back into Italy. When they did this, Marius came out of his camp and followed them. At the right moment he fell on the Teutones near Aix, and in a tremendous battle completely defeated them.* Marius drove the men back to their camp. "Then," says the historian, "the Teutonic women rushed to meet them with swords and cudgels, uttering hideous howls; they drove back their flying countrymen, upbraiding them as cowards; they assailed the pursuers as enemies, beating down the swords of the Romans with their bare hands, and allowed themselves to be hacked to pieces rather than yield."

In the mean time the Cimbri were in the valley of

---

* See "The Story of Rome," pp. 181, 182.

A GERMAN CAVALRY-MAN. (ROMAN RELIEF.)

the Adige, coming down by Botzen and Trent into Italy. As the river incommoded them, they rolled great rocks into it, and hewed down pines and threw them across and made a great dam, so as to enable themselves to wade across.

Marius left the battle-field of Aix and came with his army across the northern plains of Italy, and caught the Cimbri near Verona. He planted his own men so that the blazing August sun should shine in the faces of the enemy, and that the wind should carry the dust and sand into their eyes. The first ranks of the Cimbri had tied themselves together with ropes, so as to bear as a compact mass upon the Romans; but this arrangement was a failure, the dead men falling, dragged down the living. The Romans gained a complete victory; and the poor Cimbric women, when they saw their husbands and brothers slain, ran themselves through with swords, or hung themselves to the poles of their wagons, rather than become the slaves of the conquerors.

Such was the end of this great invasion of Italy. It is interesting to us, because this is the very first time we hear of the Teutons or Germans. Their first appearance was in 113, and the two great defeats took place in 102 before Christ.

II.

WHAT WAS OLD GERMANY LIKE?

GERMANY, you must understand, is divided into Upper and Lower Germany. Upper Germany is a hilly country; Lower Germany is a dead, sandy flat. In primeval times, when the Germans first colonized the country, it was covered with vast forests of oak and pine, and where there was much rolled stone, with birch. Out of the forests rose the mountain ranges of South or Upper Germany, like islands. In Lower Germany there were many bald patches of heathery waste, and marshy tracts strewn with lakes. The great rivers rolled through the valleys and plains, changing their courses and heaping up piles of rubble.

The great valleys were first colonized where the richest pasture land was, and only little by little did the inhabitants thin the forest and creep up among the hills.

Was it one great family of races—the German—that occupied the vast northern plains and the valleys among the hills? That we cannot think. Over the northern plains are found strewn great burial mounds, containing within them passages made of stones set on end, and huge stones above.

The peasants call them Huns' graves. They are not, however, the graves of Huns, but belong to an unknown race which occupied the shores of the Baltic and the Northern Sea before the Germans came into the land. In the South there are no such graves, but there are other traces of a people strange to the Germans, and these are the names of rivers and mountains, such as Pegnitz, the river on which Nürnberg stands, and Karwendel, a mountain in the Bavarian highlands, and the Scharnitz pass. These point to a Sclav population, that is, one related to the modern Russians, and Poles, and Bohemians. But there is another trace of an earlier people in Germany besides mounds and names. It is found in the old laws of the German tribes. By these laws we learn that there was a race of serfs,—conquered people who tilled the land,—and the pure-blooded conquerors were not allowed to intermarry with them. If a German did so, then he lost his rights as a free man, and all his children were slaves. That law remains to some extent in force still in Germany, but it has lost its original meaning. Now a prince cannot marry out of the princely families. If he does, his wife is not regarded as a princess, and his children have only their mother's rank. Originally this law, which is found among all the old races of Germany, was passed to keep the grand Teutonic blood pure.

However, if you travel in Bavaria, or Baden, you will see that the greater number of peasant men and women have hazel eyes and dark hair. That shows they are not pure-blooded Germans;

they have flowing in their veins the blood of the conquered race.

The Germans were so called from the spears they carried. The name means Spear-men, but they called themselves Deutschen, or, as the Romans rendered the name, Teutones. This name comes from an old German word that simply means "the People."

ANCIENT GERMAN DWELLINGS. (ROMAN PERIOD.)

They were divided into a great many tribes, of which we must mention the principal.

The Chatti lived in Hesse, and have never moved thence. The present Hessians are the lineal descendants of the old Chatti.

The Saxons lived in Holstein and the Angles in Schleswig. They have spread since the veil first rises on their history. The Saxons and Angles in-

vaded Britain, and the English, or Anglo-Saxon
people, are their descendants.

South and east of the Saxons lived the Suevi, or
Swabians. They have shifted far to the south and
Saxons now occupy their lands. To them belonged the branches of the Marcomanni, or Marchmen, who lived on the Rhine at first, the frontier of

the Kelt, and also the Longobards,
who were on the Middle Elbe.
Later, these latter deserted their
home and conquered the North of
Italy, which is called after them,
Lombardy. The Goths lived or-
iginally near the sources of the
Vistula. Akin to them were the
Vandals and the Burgundians.

What is remarkable is, that the
races in the South had very different ways of living from those in
the North. The Suevi were a warlike race. They had no settled
homes, no fixed fatherland. The
land was divided among them by
lot every year, and so changed
owners annually. One part of the people went out
yearly to war, and the rest remained at home and
tilled the ground. Those races which were in the
North had, however, the land given to the great
men, who lived on their farms, ruling their serfs ;
and they handed on their lands to their sons. Even
to this day the different systems show. In Westphalia, for instance, you will see fine farm-houses,

SAXON COLONIST WITH
CAPTIVE WEND.

as in England, the same in Holstein, and the fields are hedged about. But in the South it is not so. The farm-houses are all gathered together in little villages, and you cannot see a hedge anywhere.

The old inhabitants of Germany were divided

A GERMAN COUNCIL. (ROMAN PERIOD.)

into two great classes, the free and the enslaved. The free were divided into the greater and lesser nobility, and they alone were allowed to bear arms.

The old German religion was very like that of the Norwegians. They regarded Wotan as the chief of the gods. He had one eye in his forehead, which was the sun. He was the god of the heaven, and the air, and men and horses were sacrificed to him by being hung up in trees. The German peasants still remember him, but do not think of him any more as a god. They tell of a Wild Huntsman, who is heard of a night galloping over the forest tops, blowing his horn, with fire-breathing dogs going before him, and a white owl fleeting on spread wings with eyes like moons.

Another of their gods was Donar, whom the Norsemen called Thor. He is the Thunderer, and is armed with a hammer, which he flings at his enemies; but it always returns to his hand. After him the Germans call Thursday (Thor's-day), Donner's-tag.

Among the goddesses were Freyja, from whom we get the name of Friday (in German, Frei-tag), and Hertha, the goddess of the earth. Another was variously called Hulda, Bertha, or Hörsel. She was a kind goddess, loving children, and was really the moon. She was represented as taking to her the souls of all little children who died, and nursing them. These were the stars, and the moon and the stars were supposed to be the gentle Hulda, with her crowd of little children's souls gathered in heaven about her. She was also called Nothburga, the "helper in need." You shall hear how old heathen stories linger on to the present day. In Tyrol there was, in the 14th century, a peasant girl called Nothburga, who was so good that she came to be regarded as a saint. The old traditions about the goddess were still hanging about in men's minds, and they came to associate them with this peasant girl, who chanced to bear the name of the moon-goddess; so when they made pictures of her, they represented her with a silver

GERMANS ON THE RHINE.

crescent.　Then, when they had forgotten all about the goddess, they invented a story to account for the silver crescent in the pictures, and they told how S. Nothburga had one day thrown up her sickle into the sky whilst reaping, and that there it had hung.

III.

HOW HERMANN MET THE ROMANS.

(A.D. 9.)

ABOUT fifty years after the defeat of the Cimbri and Teutones the Romans came a second time into contact with the Germans. Julius Cæsar, one of the greatest and most famous of Roman generals, was governor of Gaul. The Marchmen had crossed the Rhine under their prince, Ariovistus, or, as he would be called by his own people, Arbogast, and established themselves in Burgundy. Julius Cæsar drove them back over the Rhine, which he also crossed repeatedly ; but his successors, Drusus and Tiberius, were the first to subjugate a portion of Germany between the Rhine and the Weser.

There was a tribe called the Cherusci, occupying the south of what is now Hanover. Their chief, named Hermann, had been taken to Rome during the time of Drusus, probably as a hostage. He had carefully studied his Latin lessons there, but he never forgot the words that he had been taught at his mother's knee, and was always proud that he was a German. As he read history, he learned how the Romans had achieved their power, and he seems

to have thought that his own people might accomplish noble deeds if only they would unite and
stand as one nation before the world.

Hermann saw that the Romans were rich and had
colonies all over the world, but he knew that they
were gay and pleasure-seeking, and lived to a great
extent in cities, where every sort of dissipation
abounded. As he looked towards his German

CÆSAR.

woods he reflected up-
on the difference be-
tween his captors and
the active and liberty-
loving people who
dwelt there in humble
village homes, where
love bound the father
to the mother and
united the children to

both, and where, as a great Roman writer said
(casting reproach upon his own countrymen and
women), it was not fashionable to do wrong, and
no one smiled at vice. As he grew up these feelings became stronger.

After a time Hermann returned to Germany, and
found the people ready to listen to his advice and
follow his leadership. In the course of events the
Romans sent a general, named Varus, to look after
their interests and assert their power. He knew
how Hermann had been educated and, little suspect-
ing the hot thoughts that were welling up in his
patriotic heart, ventured to take him as his coun-
sellor and guide. Hermann saw that his moment

GERMAN HORSEMEN FIGHTING ROMAN LEGIONS.
(From the Column of Antoninus, in Rome.)

had come, and took advantage of this circumstance
to draw Varus and his great army into the hilly region of the Teutoberger Forest, where he rightly
thought that the numbers and the strong bodies
of his fellow-countrymen would be more than a
match for the better drilled and heavily-armed co-
horts of the invaders.

It was the autumn of the year 9 A.D. There
were no roads, and Varus was obliged to cut down
trees to make a way for the slow march of his army.
Almost before he knew it he found himself in a
trap.   To add to his dismay and confusion a great
storm arose.   The mountain torrents, swollen by the
rain, overflowed their banks ; and whilst the Romans, encumbered by their baggage and by hosts of
camp-followers, and wearied by the toilsome way,
passed in irregular columns through the wet marshes
and narrow valleys, the thunders of the German war-
cry suddenly burst upon them from all the hills
around, and they were struck down by showers of ar-
rows that seemed to drop from the clouds.   Panic-
stricken, and not knowing which way to turn, they
halted, and were, as in a moment, surrounded by the
hosts of their assailants, who were perfectly at home
in the most intricate passes.

All day long the battle raged, and then the invaders tried, under cover of darkness, to throw up a
protecting earthwork, but they were too much worn
to accomplish anything.   Hundreds were lost in the
morasses ; their eagles were taken from them ; they
were entirely without provisions, and it was plain
that there was no safety but in retreat.   The only

ROMAN SOLDIERS DESTROYING A GERMAN VILLAGE.
(From the Column of Antoninus, in Rome.)

question was which direction they should take. Inch by inch they gave way, but very few escaped to tell the story of the fight in the terrible German forests.

Varus, who had marched into the treacherous fastnesses as if bound on a holiday excursion, threw himself on his own sword in despair, and when the news reached the great emperor, Augustus, that his army had been destroyed,—the army of the proudest people in the world, the people who were then chief among the nations,—he clothed himself in mourning, let his hair and beard grow, and cried again and again in the bitterness of his heart, "Varus, Varus, give me back my legions!" The capitol was stirred as it had been when, after "tearful Allia," the Gauls threatened the city, for the people thought that the victorious Germans would surely march that way.* Hermann had no such plans; he did not fight for conquest, but for freedom; he had the first vision of a united Germany. He had won independence for his native land, and had put a stop to Roman conquest in one quarter of the globe. He had given the nations of German blood an example that was to bear fruit on the peaceful field of Runnymede, when the English barons wrung the Magna Charta from King John; for it was from the region in which Hermann fought that our ancestors came, and we may take pride in him and in the great statue erected in his honor hundreds of years after his day

---

* For some account of the terrible victory of the Gauls over the Romans at the river Allia, see "The Story of Rome," pp. 101, 136.

STATUE SUPPOSED TO REPRESENT THUSNELDA.
(In Florence.)

by the princes of Germany on the culminating point
of the Teutoberger Alps.

Hermann's wife was Thusnelda, daughter of an
old chief named Siegast, who was friendly to the
Romans. She was renowned for her beauty as well
as for great patriotism. Her spirit was rather like
that of her husband than that of her father, for
Siegast had treacherously warned Varus to be on
his guard against Hermann, and when opportunity
came he even delivered up his daughter to her country's enemies. The feelings of the Germans was
strong against such a man, so strong, in fact, that
Siegast was attacked, and only found safety by flee-
ing to the enemy. A few years later Thusnelda and
her son adorned a triumphal procession in Rome.

It may well be imagined that Hermann was
strengthened in his hatred of Rome by the loss of
his wife and son ; and when, five years after the defeat of Varus, another army was sent against the
Germans, he met it with a strong force and effectually resisted it. Once and again the attempt to conquer the land failed, and at last the effort was abandoned. When there was no longer fear from that
quarter Hermann suffered the fate of many others
who have striven to do good for their fellow-citizens.
Like Camillus, Manlius, and the Gracchi among the
Romans, his motives were not understood. His
own people rose against him, and at the early age of
thirty-seven he fell by the hands of his near relations. It was reserved for a Roman historian to
speak his praises and for after ages to raise his monument. Tacitus says that it was his honour to have

successfully met the arms of Rome in the pride of its imperial power, and to have had his pæans chanted in the songs of his countrymen. He became the typical War-man, the " Man of Hosts," the deliverer of Germany, and he was remembered by our own Anglo-Saxon ancestors after they had removed to the British Isles. Hermann and Thusnelda stand out as the representatives of the true love between husband and wife, for which the early Germans were celebrated.

After this the Romans held possession of a very small portion of the soil of Germany, which they called the Titheland. It lay between the Danube, the Main, and the Rhine, and was protected by a moat and wall, with towers at intervals. The wall was a mound with palisades at the top. The traces are still to be seen, and are called by the people " The Devil's Walls."

IV.

THE FIERCE HUNS APPEAR.

(375–452.)

In the year 375 a great change began in the positions of the peoples who were settled in Germany. A game of puss-in-the-corner was played there on a very large scale, and with no laughter, but many tears.

The cause of this was the appearance of the Huns.

The Huns, or Calmucks, wandering shepherd tribes, were natives of the North of Asia, and inhabited the vast plains between Russia and China. They had no houses. They lived in tents, in which they also stabled their horses. From being constantly on horseback their legs were crooked. They were short men, broad shouldered, with strong, muscular arms; had coarse, thick lips, straight, black, wiry hair, little, round, sloe-like eyes, yellow complexions, and sausage noses. They were filthy in their habits; their horrible ugliness, their disgusting smell, their ferocity, the speed with which they moved, their insensibility to the gentler feelings, made the Goths, with whom they first came in contact, believe they were half demons. They ate,

GERMAN CAPTIVE. (ROMAN PERIOD.)
(From Statue in Vatican Museum.)

drank, slept on horseback. Their no less hideous wives and children followed them in waggons. They ate roots and raw meat. They seemed insensible to hunger, thirst, and cold.

In the year 375 after Christ they crossed the Volga in countless hordes, and poured down on Germany. The East and West Goths, unable to resist their numbers and savagery, deserted their lands on both sides of the Dnieper, and, crossing the Danube, descended into the Roman empire with the entreaty that they might be accommodated with lands there.

At last these barbarians spread over Dacia, which has since been called after them Hungary, where they were well content to ramble over the grassy plains that reminded them of their Asian steppes. But about the middle of the fifth century there rose among them a prince of very remarkable character, called by the Romans Attila, and by the Germans Etzel, but who was best pleased to be called "The Scourge of God." This man murdered his own brother, so as to unite the sovereignty of the Huns under himself. He is introduced in the Nibelungen Lied, the great national epic poem of Germany. Kriemhild, the widow of Siegfried, and daughter of a king of the Burgundians, was married to Attila. Her dearly loved husband, Siegfried, had been murdered treacherously by order of her brother, the Burgundian king, Gunther, who was jealous of him. When Kriemhild became Queen of the Huns she persuaded Attila to invite her brother and all his nobles to Buda, and, unsuspicious of evil, they accepted the invitation.   But the queen meditated revenge for the slaying of her dear Siegfried, and when her brother and the nobles were banqueting her guards fell on them.   There was a furious fight, the palace caught fire, and Kriemhild saw her brother, and all those who had counselled and assisted in the murder, perish by sword and flame. After that she died herself.   The story is only possibly founded on fact.   History tells us nothing about this deed of revenge.

BOUNDARY WALL.   (ROMAN PERIOD.)

In the year 451 Attila broke up his camp at Buda and marched West, at the head of an enormous host of Huns.   They overran the South of Germany, crossed the Rhine, and resolved to conquer their way to the Atlantic.   Those who could not escape were either killed or had to join the army.   But the Franks, the West Goths, the Burgundians, and the Romans united in one great host under the general Aetius, and withstood the onslaught of the Huns in the plains of Chalons on the Marne.   The battle was furious, and ended in the

defeat of the Huns.   Attila was forced to retire
with the loss of half his men, and the Western Empire was saved.

Next year Attila descended into Italy, but retreated toward his own country and died through
the bursting of a blood-vessel, A.D. 453.

V.

THE MIGRATIONS OF THE TRIBES.

YOU may well imagine that the arrival of the Huns was like the introduction of a wasp into a bee-hive. It created an enormous commotion, and many of the German races changed their habitations.

About the middle of the third century the numerous German tribes had united into great confederacies. The most important of these were—1. The Allemanni; 2. The Franks; 3. The Saxons; 4. The Goths.

1. The Allemanni were so called from the custom of those in the South to own land in common. To this day, in Switzerland and Baden, there is much common land belonging to the parishes, as well as forest and quarry, and this goes by the name of the Allmend. The Allemanni lived in the South of Germany, in the Black Forest, and in German Switzerland, and in Würtemberg, about the Lake of Constance.

2. The Franks occupied the banks of the Rhine and the Main, to Nürnberg. The Ripuarian Franks lived on the Rhine, the Salic Franks on the river Saal.

3. The Saxons spread over a great part of North

GERMAN SKIRMISHERS (GEFECHT'S-ERÖFFNER). (ROMAN PERIOD.)

Germany, taking the places vacated by the Lombards and the Burgundians.

4. The Goths were divided by the Dnieper into the East Goths (Ostrogoths) and the West Goths (Visigoths), and were the most cultured of the German peoples. They had been converted to Christianity by a bishop named Ulphilas, who translated the Bible into old Gothic, and his translations of the Gospels, written in silver letters on a purple ground, is still preserved, and is one of the treasures of the library of Upsala in Sweden.

The appearance of the Huns in Germany created the utmost confusion. As already said, the Ostrogoths crossed the Danube and entered the Roman Empire. After awhile they made themselves masters of Italy, under the famous King Theoderic.

The Visigoths, or West Goths, descended on the South of Gaul, and made Toulouse their capital. The Vandals left their old home between the Elbe and Oder, invaded Spain, crossed over to Africa, and formed a kingdom on the north coast, with Carthage as their capital. The Angles and a portion of the Saxons took ship in 449 for Britain, which they conquered. The Longobards, or Lombards, deserted the old watery, peaty region about the Middle Elbe and descended on the North of Italy. The Burgundians left their homes between the Oder and the Vistula, and formed the Burgundian kingdom between the Rhone, the Saône, and the range of the Jura.

As the Germans deserted the cold, sandy plains of North Germany, the Sclavs from the north-east crept

MARCUS AURELIUS PARDONING GERMAN CHIEFS.
(Triumphal Arch at Rome.)

after them, and occupied all Pomerania, Mecklenburg, and Oldenburg.

Those German peoples who had left Germany settled down in their new countries among populations more civilized than themselves, and so they gradually acquired their habits, and lost their own language and peculiar institutions, even their German appearance and characters. Thus they disappeared, sinking into, and becoming absorbed by, the people they conquered, and the Burgundians, Goths, Vandals, and Lombards disappear completely. The Franks, who had spread into Northern Gaul, gave to it the new name of France, but ceased on its soil to be Germans.

VI.

CLOVIS, KING OF THE FRANKS.

(481–511.)

THE Franks had extended themselves over the north of Gaul. They had a capital at Tournay, but they had gained power over what we now call Normandy. There was none to resist them. Government in Gaul had fallen into confusion since the fall of the Roman Empire. The Salic Franks came from what is now called Lower Franconia, and take their name from the river Saal, which flows into the Main. It is a bare and not a productive country, and so a portion of the Franks pushed their way into Belgium, and Flanders, and Normandy. I am using, you must understand, modern names. Thirty years after the battle of Chalons the Franks were not united into one nation ; there were several tribes of their name, independent one of another. In the year 481 Clovis became king of the Salic Franks in Belgium. The French call him Clovis, the old Germans, Clodwig, which is the same as the modern German Ludwig, and the French, Louis. He was fifteen years old when he became king, a proud, cunning, ambitious man, but with some natural good qualities. He determined to extend his power, so he led his men against the Roman governor of Soissons, drove him out, and took the place, which he thenceforth made his capital. He and his people were pagans, and when they took a town they plun· dered the churches. On one of his expeditions he took Rheims, and when the spoil of the Cathedral was brought out and spread before the king and his nobles, the bishop of the place, Remigius, came to Clovis, and entreated that one beautiful chalice might be spared from the plunder, for the service of the altar. Clovis replied that by their rules all the spoil was divided into lots, and then lots were drawn for each division. However, if the chalice came to him, he would return it to the bishop, who had written him a kind letter, full of good advice, when he was made king. But as S. Remigius urged his request very earnestly, the king turned to his chiefs and asked them to grant him the goblet over and above his proper share. All consented but one man, who suddenly swung his axe, and brought it down on the precious cup, saying, " No ! I will not consent ; all shall share alike." The king bore the affront without a word. The man had acted within his right.

A year after Clovis held a grand parade, at which his nobles were to show their equipments. After having passed all in review, and examined their arms, the man came who had refused to give up the chalice. He was a truculent, ill-conditioned fellow, and his harness was rusty and dirty, and when he showed the king his battle-axe it was not clean. Then Clovis threw it down, and when the man

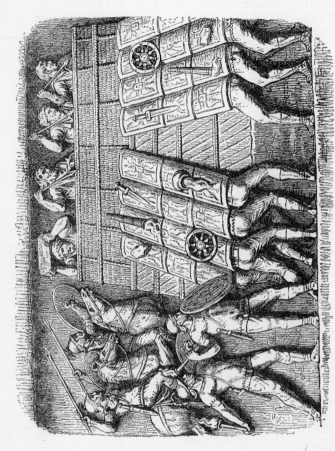

ROMANS BESIEGING A GERMAN FORTRESS.
(Column of Marcus Aurelius at Rome.)

stooped to pick it up the king raised his axe and cleft his skull, saying, "Thus didst thou to the chalice of Rheims." It was an act of revenge, but the king was careful to act within his right. The man was bound to appear at the parade with all his equipments in perfect order.

Clovis heard that Gundebald, King of Burgundy, had a niece called Clothild, at Geneva. Gundebald had murdered her father and her brothers, who stood in his way to the throne. Now Clovis was a very crafty man, and he wanted to pick a quarrel with Gundebald, so as to get hold of Burgundy. So he resolved to marry Clothild and make her quarrel his own ; but he did not want to marry her if she was not very beautiful. So he gave his ring to a friend, a Roman, called Aurelian, and told him to go in disguise to Geneva, and see Clothild, and if she were really beautiful to give her his ring and get hers in exchange. Aurelian dressed himself in rags, and went to Geneva, and knocked at her door and begged for food. Clothild at once invited him in, and brought water, and began herself to wash his travel-stained feet. Whilst she was thus engaged Aurelian stooped and whispered into her ear, "Lady, I must speak to you in secret." Then he showed her the ring, and said, "Clovis, King of the Franks, asks for you in marriage." Clothild considered a moment, then drew off her own ring and gave it to Aurelian. "Go back," she said, "to your master, and tell him if he takes me he must carry me away as fast as he can fly, for my uncle has a friend called Aridius, now away, who will advise him not to give

me to Clovis." Then Aurelian hasted back to
Soissons, and Clovis sent to Gundebald and asked
for the hand of his niece. Gundebald, glad to be
rid of her, consented that she should go. So Clothild started from Geneva. Clovis had sent a sort of
waggon richly decorated for Clothild to travel in.
She went in it some little way, and then became
uneasy. She got out and said to the Frank lords
who attended her, " I pray you give me a horse and
let us leave the waggon in the road, and ride at full
gallop, night and day, till we get out of Burgundy."

She was right. After the consent had been given
Aridius returned to Metz, where Gundebald was,
and the king told his friend what he had done.
Then Aridius exclaimed, " This is no bond of friend-
ship, but the beginning of strife. Send troops at
once in pursuit and bring your niece back."

The king did so, but was too late. They came
on the deserted waggon, but Clothild had escaped.
The consequences were what Aridius had predicted.
Clovis made war on Gundebald and made him his
tributary. Clothild bore a son to Clovis. She was
a Christian, and she begged her husband to let the
child be baptized. He consented, but the boy died
soon after. " There," exclaimed Clovis, " that is
what comes of baptism." After some time she bore
him another, and had much ado to get this one baptized. Soon after this boy also fell ill, and Clovis
was very angry. But when the child recovered he
began to think that perhaps Christian baptism was
not as dangerous as he had supposed. Clothild
was a very pious woman, and she often spoke to her

husband about Christ, but he did not seem to pay much heed to her words.

At last, in the year 496, the Allemanni,—that is, the Germans of the Black Forest and Switzerland, and the Vosges—burst into the territories of the Franks, and Clovis marched against them and met

GERMAN PRIESTESSES FOLLOWING THE ARMY.
(Column of Marcus Aurelius at Rome.)

them in the plain of Tolbiac, now called Zulpich, near Cologne. He had with him Aurelian, whom he had made Duke of Melun. The battle was going ill ; the Franks were wavering and Clovis was anxious. Then Aurelian, who rode near him, suddenly exclaimed, " My lord, there is no hope for us now but in the God of Queen Clothild." When Clovis heard this he dropped the reins, and holding up his hands to heaven cried, " Christ Jesus, whom

Clothild believes in, I have called on my gods, and
they have withdrawn from me. Help thou me!"
Then the tide of battle turned: the Franks recovered confidence and courage ; and the Allemanni,
beaten, and seeing their king slain, surrendered
themselves to Clovis.

When Clovis was on his way back he came to
Rheims, where the old bishop, Remigius, was, who
had written good advice to him when he was a boy,

GERMAN BODY-GUARD OF THE LATER CÆSARS.
(Column of Trajan, Rome.)

and who had asked for the chalice. The king was
touched by the danger he had been in, and thank-
ful for the victory. His wife came to him to
strengthen his good resolutions, and he resolved to
become a Christian. We have a very interesting
and curious account of the baptism of King Clovis,
written by Hincmar, who was Bishop of Rheims
some years after the death of Remigius, and who
probably took it from an account by an eye-witness.
"The bishop," he says, "went in search of the
king at early morning to his bed-chamber, in order
that he might communicate to him the truths of

the Gospel before his mind was occupied with secular cares. The chamberlains received him with
great respect, and they went into the chapel of S.
Peter near the palace. When the bishop, the king,
and the queen had taken their places on the seats
prepared for them, the bishop began his instructions
on the way of salvation. Meanwhile, preparations
were being made along the road from the palace to
the baptistery; curtains and valuable stuffs were
hung up; the houses on both sides of the street
were dressed out; the baptistery was sprinkled with
balm and all kinds of perfume. The procession
moved from the palace; the clergy led the way,
carrying the Gospels, the cross, and the banners,
and singing hymns. Then came the bishop, leading the king by the hand; after him the queen;
lastly the people. On the road the king is said to
have asked the bishop if that was the kingdom of
heaven promised him. 'No,' answered the prelate,
'it is the beginning of the road to it!' When the
king bared his head over the baptismal water, the
bishop thus addressed him: 'Bend thy head, Sicam-
brian,* adore what thou hast burned, burn what
thou hast adored!'" Three thousand Frankish
men, together with women and children, were baptized the same day.

Though Clovis had joined the Christian Church
he was but a poor Christian. He led a life of war,
and was brought under no other Christian influence

---

* Clovis belonged to the tribe of Sicambri, which was in the Frank
confederation.

than that of his wife, and he did not think it manly to give ear to her best advice.

The Ripuarian Franks had their capital at Cologne, and their king was Siegbert. Clovis sent to the king's son this message: "Your father is old, and lame of a leg. When he is dead I will be your friend, and you shall be king." That stirred up the young man to kill his father treacherously one day, as the old man was walking in a beech wood. Then he sent a messenger to Clovis to say that his father was dead, and that he would send him some of the old king's treasures. But when the wicked son was showing the messenger of Clovis the precious things in the treasure-house, he came to a great battle-axe. "See," said the young man, "this was my father's weapon."

"And so does it avenge its master!" said the messenger, and he brought it down on the young man's head, and clove it.

After that, the realm of the Ripuarian Franks fell to Clovis, as well as that of the Salic Franks, and Burgundy and a large portion of Gaul.

He died in 511, at Paris, which he had made his capital; and he left behind him a great Frank kingdom, which was divided between his four sons.

VII.

THE MAYORS OF THE PALACE.

(751–768.)

THE successors of Clovis, called, after an earlier Frank king, Merovingians, were weak creatures. They left the management of their kingdom to their Mayors of the Palace, and only showed themselves to their people once a year, at the March parliament, riding on a car drawn by oxen, after an old Frank custom, wearing their fair hair down to their waists, combed out and adorned with crowns. As they did nothing but eat and drink and enjoy themselves they went by the name of the sluggard kings, and all the real power was in the hands of the Mayor of the Palace for the time being.

Among these mayors, Pepin of Heristal made himself conspicuous. His home was near Spa, in the pretty woodland country about Liege. He made the office hereditary in his family. His heroic son, Charles Martel, or the Hammer, was still more famous, because he utterly routed the Arabs in a great battle at Tours in 732, who had conquered Spain and the south of France, and threatened the whole of France.

His sons, Pepin the Short and Karlomann, succeeded him, but Karlomann resigned his authority into his brother's hands, and, tired of fighting, entered a monastery. Pepin had much to do ; the Saxons, Bavarians, and Arabs were all menacing or revolting, and he had to fly from one part of the kingdom to another, defending its frontiers, and getting no help from the stupid sluggard king at Paris. At last, impatient of the farce, he sent this question to the Pope : " Who is king, he who governs or he who wears the crown ? " " He who governs, of course," answered the Pope. " That is myself," said the little man with a great will ; " so the sluggards shall go to sleep forever," and he sent the last of them, Childeric III., into a monastery. Then his nobles put their shields together, and the little man was seated on a chair, on their shields, and they marched with him thus, shouting and raising their shields as high as they could, thrice, round the parliament, and then he was anointed by S. Boniface, Archbishop of Mainz, A.D. 752. Pepin did not forget that he owed a debt of gratitude to the Pope for the answer he had given to his question, and when, shortly after, the Pope sent to complain of the trouble occasioned by the Lombards, Pepin crossed the Alps, chastised the Lombards, took from them all their territory about Rome and gave it to the Pope, to belong to him and to the bishops of Rome forever. That was the beginning of the Papal sovereignty. " The States of the Church," as they were called, remained under the sovereignty of the Popes till 1871.

Pepin died in 768, and left behind him two sons,
Charles and Karlomann. The latter died a few years
after, and then, with the consent of the great nobles,
Charles became sole king.

INVESTITURE OF A BISHOP BY A KING.
(From a Codex in St. Omer.)

VIII.

THE GERMANS HEAR THE GOSPEL.

WHERE should you suppose that the earliest Irish manuscripts are to be found? Not in Ireland, but in Switzerland and Germany. The reason of this is that the Irish were the first preachers of the Gospel in Germany. In the 6th and 7th centuries a perfect passion to do missionary work fired the monks of Ireland. In dreams and ecstasies they thought they saw the barbarous Germans crying to them from the gloom of their sombre pine woods to come over and bring them light. Then they got into rude boats of wicker-work covered with tanned hides, and paddled, or were blown across, to England. They traversed England and took boat again, and pushed up the Rhine, and Scheldt, and other rivers, till they found places where the people were all heathens, and there they established themselves and taught. In 590 S. Columbanus appeared at the court of Guntram, King of Burgundy. He came from Ireland, and he established himself at Luxeuil, under the Jura, and when he was driven out he settled himself at Bobbio, in North Italy. His disciple, S. Gall, made himself a home in Switzerland, in a forest, where he had difficulty to hold his own against the bears. He preached at Bre-

TREATY OF ALLIANCE BETWEEN GERMAN TRIBES.
(Column of Antoninus, Rome.)

genz at the head of the Lake of Constance, and threw the idols he found there into the lake. Another Irishman, called Fridolin, planted himself at Seckingen, an island in the Rhine, under the slopes of the Black Forest. Another, Beatus, made himself a home in a cave in the face of a precipice, above the Lake of Thun. Another, Fintan, who had been carried off by pirates and taken to Belgium, escaped from them, mounted the Rhine, and made Rheinau, near Schaffhausen, the place whence he taught the heathen. Foilan and Ultan, two Irish brothers, established themselves on the Meuse. Kilian, Colman, and Totnan made Würzburg the centre from which they taught, and there Kilian was martyred. Frigidian went further, and died at Lucca. Fursey preached among the Franks at Lagny, a little north of Paris.

Thus it was that Christianity was brought among the Allemanni and the Franks. The Saxons were still heathen ; so were the Frisians, who occupied the present Holland.

But though Christianity was brought into the heart of the land, and here and there a bishopric was established, everything was in disorder in those disturbed days, and in some places Christianity died out for want of a succession of missionaries ; and in others, those who were Christians, and even bishops and priests, were under no discipline, had received little instruction, and lived very little better than heathens.

Then it was that S. Boniface, or, as he was called in his Devonshire home, Winifred, sailed from Ports-

A JUDGMENT OF GOD.

(Title-Page of Missal in Bamberg Library.)

mouth for Germany, with a band of devoted men. He found that the little Christianity there was among the Germans was of very poor quality. So he went to Rome to ask the Pope to authorize him to bring some order into the German church. Furnished with authority, and consecrated and appointed Archbishop of Mainz, and having received the name of Boniface, " Good-doer," from the Pope, he returned to Germany, and sent home to England for helpers. Many came, men and women, and he planted them where were most suitable centres. At Geismar, in Hesse, stood a huge old oak, dedicated to the god Donnar. The heathens made pilgrimages to this oak, and even converted Christians regarded it with religious awe, and told wonderful stories about it, and visited it to hear oracles from its dark whispering branches. One day when there was a great assembly at this oak on a festival of Donnar, Boniface went boldly to the place, unattended by armed men, but with an axe in his hands, and before all the pagan crowd began to hack at the tree. They drew back in dismay, expecting lightning to fall and consume him. Boniface did not rest till the oak was cut down, and fell with a crash. Then the heathen recognized the powerlessness of their gods, and their faith in them fell with the oak.

Boniface did not content himself with preaching. He said that the only way in which the Germans could be made good Christians was to civilize them; accordingly, he established schools and monasteries where he could. The monks taught, but did not teach only; they drained the morasses, felled the trees, ploughed the soil, sowed corn, planted fruit trees, and carried on various trades. Those whom they converted they settled in cottages round their monasteries, and so, in time, these settlements grew into towns.

When Boniface was old he went to carry the Gospel to the heathen Frisians. The pagans fell upon him and murdered him in the year 755, A.D.

GERMANY CAPTIVE.

IX.

A MAN OF MARK.

(768–814.)

WE come now to one of the greatest men of all
times, Charles the Great, son of Pepin the Short, a
man who has left his mark on history for all times.
Charles—(called by the French Charlemagne)—was
great in many ways, whereas most great men are
great in one or two. He was a great warrior, a
great political genius, an energetic legislator, a lover
of learning, and a lover also of his natural language
and poetry at a time when it was the fashion to
despise them. And he united, and displayed, all
these merits in a time of general and monotonous
barbarism, when, save in the Church, the minds
of men were dull and barren.

From 769 to 813, in Germany and Western and
Northern Europe, Charlemagne conducted thirty-
two campaigns against the Saxons, Frisians, Bavarians, Avars, Slavs, and Danes; in Italy, five
against the Lombards; in Spain, Corsica, and Sardinia, twelve against the Arabs; two against the
Greeks; and three in Gaul itself, against the Aqui-
tanians and Bretons. In all, fifty-three expeditions in forty-five years, amongst which those he

Kaiolus imparw

magnus Annis 14.

CHARLEMAGNE.
(From the painting by Dürer.)

undertook against the Saxons, the Lombards, and
the Arabs were long and difficult wars.

The kingdom of Charles was vast; it comprised
nearly all Germany, Belgium, France, Switzerland,
and the North of Italy and of Spain. He had, in
ruling this mighty realm, to deal with different
nations, without cohesion, and to grapple with their
various institutions and bring them into system.

The first great undertaking of Charles was against
the Saxons. They were still heathen, and were a
constant source of annoyance to the Franks, for
they made frequent inroads to pillage and destroy
their towns and harvests.

In the line of mountains which forms the step
from Lower into Upper Germany, above the Westphalian plains, is one point at which the river Weser
breaks through and flows down into the level land,
about three miles above the town of Minden. This
rent in the mountains is called the Westphalian
Gate. The hills stand on each side, like red sandstone
door-posts, and one is crowned by some crumbling
fragments of a castle; it is called the Wittekindsberg, and takes its name from Wittekind, a Saxon
king, who had his castle there. Wittekind was a
stubborn heathen, and a very determined man. In
772 Charles convoked a great assembly at Worms,
at which it was unanimously resolved to march
against the Saxons and chastise them for their incursions. Charles advanced along the Weser,
through the gate, destroyed Wittekind's castle,
pushed on to Paderborn, where he threw down an
idol adored by the Saxons, and then was obliged to

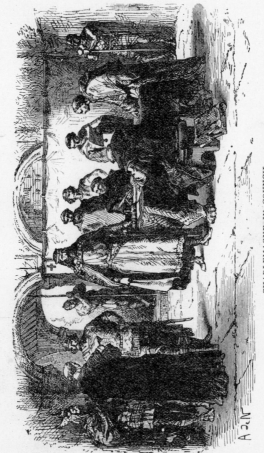

CHARLEMAGNE IN COUNCIL.

return and hurry to Italy to fight the Lombards, who had revolted. Next year he invaded Saxony again. He built himself a palace at Paderborn, and summoned the Saxon chiefs to come and do homage. Wittekind alone refused, and fled to Denmark. No sooner had Charles gone to fight the Moors in Spain than Wittekind returned, and the Saxons rose at his summons, and, bursting into Franconia, devastated the land up to the walls of Cologne. Charles returned and fought them in two great battles, defeated them, erected fortresses in their midst, and carried off hostages. Affairs seemed to prosper, and Charles deemed himself as securely master of Saxony as Varus had formerly in the same country, and under precisely the same circumstances. Charles then quitted the country, leaving orders for a body of Saxons to join his Franks and march together against the Slavs. The Saxons obeyed the call with alacrity, and soon outnumbered the Franks. One day, as the army was crossing the mountains from the Weser, at a given signal the Saxons fell on their companions and butchered them.

When the news of this disaster reached Charles he resolved to teach the Saxons a terrible lesson. Crossing the Rhine, he laid waste their country with fire and sword, and forced the Saxons to submit to be baptized, and accept Christian teachers. Those who refused he killed. At Verdun he had over four thousand of the rebels beheaded. At Detmold, Wittekind led the Saxons in a furious bat-

.tle, in which neither gained the victory. In another battle, on the Hase, they were completely routed.

Then Wittekind submitted, came into the camp of Charles, and asked to be baptized. A little ruined chapel stands on the Wittekindsberg, above the Westphalian Gate, and there, according to tradition, near the overturned walls of his own castle, the stubborn heathen bowed the neck to receive the yoke of Christ. Charles' two nephews, the sons of Karlomann, were with Desiderius, the Lombard king, and Desiderius tried to force the Pope to anoint

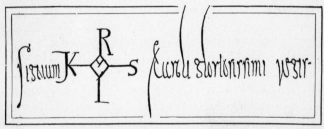

CHARLEMAGNE'S SIGNATURE.

them kings of the Franks, to head a revolt against Charles. When the great king heard this he came over the Alps into Italy, dethroned Desiderius, and shut him up in a monastery. Then he crowned himself with the iron crown of the Lombard kings, which was said to have been made out of one of the nails that fastened Christ to the cross.

Duke Thassilo of Bavaria had married a daughter of Desiderius, and he refused to acknowledge the authority of Charles. He also stirred up the Avars who lived in Hungary to invade the Frankish realm. Charles marched against Thassilo, drove him out of Bavaria, subdued the Avars, and converted the country between the Ems and Raab—that is, Austria proper—into a province, which was called the East March, and formed the beginning of the East Realm (Oesterreich), or Austria.

Charles also fought the Danes, and took from them the country up to the river Eider.

When we consider what continuous fighting Charles had, it is a wonder to us that he had time to govern and make laws; but he devoted as much thought to arranging his realm and placing it under proper governors as he did to extending its frontiers.

Charles constituted the various parts of his vast empire—kingdoms, duchies, and counties. He was himself the sovereign of all these united, but he managed them through counts and vice-counts. The frontier districts were called marches, and were under march-counts, or margraves. Count is not a German title; the German equivalent is graf, and the English is earl. The counties were divided into hundreds; a hundred villages went to a vice-count. He had also Counts of the Palace, who ruled over the crown estates, and send-counts (missi), whom he sent out yearly through the country to see that his other counts did justice, and did not oppress the people. If people felt themselves wronged by the counts they appealed to these send-counts, and if the send-counts did not do them justice they appealed to the palatine-counts.

Every year Charles summoned his counts four times, when he could, but always once, in May, to meet him in council, and discuss the grievances of the people. As the great dukes were troublesome, because so powerful, Charles tried to do without them, and to keep them in check. He gave whole principalities to bishops, hoping that they would be supporters of him and the crown against the powerful dukes.

He was also very careful for the good government of the Church. He endowed a number of monasteries to serve as schools for boys and girls. He had also a collection of good, wholesome sermons made in German, and sent copies about in all directions, requiring them to be read to the people in church. He invited singers and musicians from Italy to come and improve the performance of divine worship, and two song-schools were established, one at Gall, another at Metz. His Franks, he complained, had not much aptitude for music; their singing was like the howling of wild beasts, or the noise made by the squeaking, groaning wheels of a baggage waggon over a stony road. Charles was particularly interested in schools, and delighted in going into them and listening to the boys at their lessons. One day when he had paid such a visit he was told that the noblemen's sons were much idler than those of the common citizens. Then the great king grew red in the face and frowned, and his eyes flashed. He called the young nobles before him and said in thundering tones: "You grand gentlemen! you young puppets! You puff yourselves up with the thoughts of your rank and wealth, and suppose you have no need of letters! I

tell you that your pretty faces and your high nobility are accounted nothing by me. Beware! beware! Without diligence and conscientiousness
not one of you gets anything from me."

Charles dearly loved the grand old German poems
of the heroes, and he had them collected and
copied out. Alas! they have been lost. His stupid son, thinking them rubbish, burnt them all.
The great king also sent to Italy for builders, and
set them to work to erect palaces and churches.
His favorite palaces were at Aix and at Ingelheim.
At the latter place he had a bridge built over the
Rhine. At Aix he built the Cathedral with pillars
taken from Roman ruins. It was quite circular,
with a colonnade going round it; inside, it remains
almost unaltered to the present day.

He was very eager to promote trade, and so far
in advance of the times was he that he resolved to
cut a canal so as to connect the Main with the
Regnitz, and thus make a waterway right across
Germany, from the Rhine to the Danube, and so
connect the German Ocean with the Black Sea.
The canal was begun, but wars interfered with its
completion, and the work was not carried out till
the present century, by Louis I., of Bavaria.

Charles was a tall, grand-looking man, nearly
seven feet high. He was so strong that he could
take a horseshoe in his hands and snap it. He ate
and drank in moderation, and was grave and dig-
nified in his conduct.

In the year 800 an insurrection broke out in
Rome against Pope Leo III. Whilst he was riding

in procession his enemies fell on him, threw him from his horse, and an awkward attempt was made to put out his eyes and to cut out his tongue. Then, bleeding and insensible, he was put in a monastery. The Duke of Spoleto, a Frank, hearing of this, marched to Rome and removed the wounded pope to Spoleto, where he was well nursed and recovered his eyesight and power of speech. Charles was very indignant when he heard of the outrage, and he left the Saxons, whom he was fighting, and came to Italy to investigate the circumstance. He assumed the office of judge, and the guilty persons were sent into prison in France. Then came Christmas Day, the Christmas of the last year in the eighth century of Christ. Charles and all his sumptuous court, the nobles and people of Rome, the whole clergy of Rome, were present at the high services of the birth of Christ. The Pope himself chanted the mass; the full assembly were wrapt in profound devotion. At the close the Pope rose, advanced towards Charles with a splendid crown in his hands, placed it upon his brow, and proclaimed him Cæsar Augustus. " God grant life and victory to the great emperor ! " His words were lost in the acclamations of the soldiery, the people, and the clergy.

Charles was taken completely by surprise. What the consequences would be to Germany and to the Papacy, how fatal to both, neither he nor Leo could see. So Charlemagne became King of Italy and Emperor of the West—the successor of the Cæsars of Rome.

When Charles felt that his end was approaching he summoned all his nobles to Aix, into the church he had there erected. There, on the altar, lay a golden crown. Charles made his son, Ludwig, or Louis, stand before him, and, in the audience of his great men, gave him his last exhortation: to fear God and to love his people as his own children, to do right and execute justice, and to walk in integrity before God and man. With streaming eyes, Louis promised to fulfil his father's command. "Then," said Charles, "take this crown, and place it on your own head, and never forget the promise you have made this day."

A few months later, Charles died (814). He was buried robed in full imperial raiment, with a crown on his head, the purple mantle over his shoulders, girded with his great sword, the book of the Gospels on his knees, seated on a marble throne, and with a pilgrim's pouch at his side. He was buried under the dome of the church at Aix, and there to this day may be seen the great stone that covers his tomb, with nothing engraved on it but Carolo Magno. In the year 1165 the tomb was opened, and the body found as thus described.

SILVER PIECES OF CHARLEMAGNE.

X.

THE HOLY ROMAN EMPIRE.

BEFORE we go any further with the history of Germany it is necessary that we should get some clear idea of the empire of which Charles the Great was constituted head when the Pope on Christmas Day crowned him in S. Peter's Church at Rome.

The old Roman Empire, of which Augustus had been the first imperial head, had fallen into decrepitude, and Constantine had transferred the capital from Rome to Byzantium. Since his death many emperors had succeeded to the title, but none had been able to maintain the Empire in its ancient integrity and splendour.

Before Constantine the Empire had been heathen, Rome and her princes had been enemies of the Church, drunk with the blood of the saints. But from the conversion of Constantine onward Rome and Christianity had formed so close an alliance that the names Roman and Christian had become almost synonymous. The emperors presided at councils of the Church, and protected the faith with edicts and with the sword. Thus the Empire, which had once been the bitterest foe of the Gospel, now became inseparably connected with its

profession.   The Empire became holy, and a special sanctity was thought to be attached to the
emperor as temporal head of the great Christian
body.   " The successor of Mahomet inherited alike
the temporal and the spiritual functions of the
prophet.   In the Mahometan system, Church and
State needed not to be united, because they had
never been distinct.   But closely as the Roman
Empire and the Christian Church became united,
one might almost say identified, traces still remained of the days when they had been distinct
and hostile bodies.   The bishop's commission was
divine, proceeding neither from the prince nor from
the people.   Of such an organization the emperor
might become the patron, the protector, the exter-
nal rule, but he could not strictly become the
head." *

Italy was overrun by the Lombards.   The emperors in Constantinople became weaker, less able
to maintain their dignity and to protect their dominions.   At last the imperial crown rested on the
head of a woman, Irene, who had raised herself to
power by deposing and blinding her own son.   That
a woman should occupy the throne of Augustus was
preposterous to the nations of the West, already
indignant at the weakness of the emperors in Byzantium.   And then, Charles seemed to the eyes
of those in Italy the grandest and most suitable
figure to fill the imperial throne.   The coronation
of Charles was a revolt, a justifiable revolt of the

---

* Freeman : Historical Essays.   " The Holy Roman Empire."

West against the feeble "rois fainéants" of the East. As Pepin had been declared by the Pope the true sovereign instead of the sluggard Merovingians, so now the Pope declared the son of Pepin true emperor, instead of the sluggard Byzantines.

Thenceforth, in the eyes of the West and of the Church in the West, Charlemagne and his successors, who were crowned by the Pope, were regarded as the true emperors of the Christian world, the true successors of Augustus and Antoninus, as the true temporal heads of the Holy Roman Empire.

Not every king of Germany was emperor, but only such as were crowned by the Pope. The Pope claimed to be the spiritual head of the Church, the viceroy acting for Christ in His kingdom. Before His death Christ said: "He that hath no sword, let him sell his garment and buy one." Then the disciples said to Him, "Lord, behold, here are two swords." And He said unto them, "It is enough." Upon this text a theory was founded that Christ gave to His Church, and to the Pope as the spiritual head of His Church, the two swords of spiritual and temporal power, but that, as it was inexpedient for the Pope in his spiritual capacity to wield the sword of temporal menace, he delegated it to a temporal sovereign, and that thus the Pope in sacred matters remained the spiritual ruler, whilst the emperor exercised the delegated authority in temporal matters. The Pope cut off with the sword of excommunication, and the emperor with the sword of justice. You must bear this theory well in mind, or you will never get a right notion of what is meant by the Holy Roman Empire, and if you do not lay hold of this you lose the key to the history of Germany in the Middle Ages.

ST. MICHAEL, THE PATRON SAINT OF THE EMPIRE.
(Sculpture in the Cathedral of Bamberg, 12th Century.)

XI.

A KING PIOUS BUT NARROW.

(814–840.)

Louis, the son of Charles the Great, resembled his father in size, but in that only. He was a narrow-minded and irresolute man, giving way to his violent passions and then being filled with remorse; a man sincerely desirous of doing what was right, but without self-control. He had not the genius of his father to manage the great empire he had founded. One instance of his character will show the sort of man he was. Louis had a nephew, Bernard, son of his elder brother, Pepin, whom Charles the Great had made King of Italy. He was suspicious of Bernard and ordered him to appear before him at Chalons. Pepin was dead, and Bernard was dangerous, or might be, as a rival. Bernard hesitated, so Louis got his wife, the Empress Irmgard, to send Bernard his solemn assurance that he would be allowed to come and go in safety. Relying on this promise Bernard came to court, when Louis caused his eyes to be torn out in so barbarous a manner that he died a few days after. That was in April, 818. A little later the Empress Irmgard fell ill and died. Louis was passionately attached to her, and her death brought home to him the crime he had committed, and he was stung with remorse. Grief for what he had done never left him, and it made him earnest in his prayers and efforts to do good, so that he was given the name of "The Pious."

His next wife was Jutta, daughter of a certain Welf, the Count of Bavaria, a clever woman, who at once did all in her power to reconcile the friends of the murdered Bernard. Louis had three sons by his first wife, Irmgard. Their names were Lothair, Pepin, and Louis. By Jutta he had another, Charles, who was his favorite. Before Louis married Jutta he divided his great empire into three parts, one for each of his sons by Irmgard; but when Charles was born, he wanted to make a change, and divide it into four, so that Charles might have a share. This made the three elder angry, and they rebelled against their father, seized him, and brought charges of witchcraft against their step-mother, Jutta. But this outraged the feelings of the great nobles, and the people murmured threateningly. Lothair was obliged to let his father go. In his rage, however, he took the town of Chalons, which held to his father, burned it, and murdered the son and daughter of Duke Bernard, of Septimania, who was the adviser of his father and guardian of the little Charles. The poor girl was at school in a convent. He fastened her up in a wine cask and threw her into the river.

Lothair's brothers, Pepin and Louis, were jealous

ELECTION OF A KING.
(Heidelberg MS.)

of him, and they leagued against him, under the
pretext that they could not countenance his conduct to their father.   Thereupon, a new division of
the empire was made, between Pepin, Louis, and
Charles, to the exclusion of Lothair.

The weak-minded emperor was thenceforth powerless.   The rest of his reign was spent in vain en-
deavors to reconcile his quarrelsome sons.   After
the death of Louis the Pious, which took place
in 840, war broke out between the brothers, of
whom, fortunately, there was now one less, for
Pepin had died.   But Pepin had left a son, with the
same name, who inherited his kingdom of Aquitaine.   Louis—called, to distinguish him from his
father,   " The German "—and Charles wanted to
snatch Aquitaine from him, but he was supported
by Lothair, his other uncle.

A great battle was fought in 841 at Fontenay, in
Burgundy, between Louis and Charles, united
against Lothair.   A hundred thousand men fell,
and Lothair was defeated.   He fled to Aix, where
he melted up the great silver tables of Charlemagne into coin, and with bribes and promises
stirred up the Saxons to a general revolt.   In view
of this danger Charles and Louis met at the head of
their armies near Strasburg, and made a solemn
alliance.   The words of the oath have been preserved.   Louis and his soldiers took it in Romance,
Charles and his in German ; and the former is the earliest specimen we have of the French language, which
was thus forming out of a mixture of the Gaulish,
Latin, and German dialects, which were melting up

and fusing in the country we now call France. This was in 842.

Next year a treaty was concluded between all three brothers at Verdun, by which Lothair was granted the imperial crown, and the Netherlands, the Rhine country, Burgundy, and Italy, which was called after him—Lotharingia. That portion of his kingdom which afterwards came to be held together was called by the French Lorraine. Louis the German was given all Germany east of Lotharingia, and Charles, who was nicknamed " The Bald," had as his share all France west of Lotharingia.

Thus, through the Treaty of Verdun in 843, Germany became an independent kingdom, and its history detaches itself from that of France.

XII.

A NEW SYSTEM OF GOVERNMENT.

As you have already heard, the North Germans
had always been in the habit of holding lands and
handing them on to their sons. This was not the
case in South Germany; there, no one had as much
land as he could put his foot on. The land was
held to belong to the community, and was parcelled
out every year in lots among the various house-
holders who made up a village. This was all very
well in a rude state of society, but it was most in-
convenient after agriculture had been introduced,
and it was modified in various ways.

The Frank monarchs combined the principle of
the North German and the South German tenure.
They proclaimed that all the land belonged to the
crown, but the crown gave it back to the land-
holders on certain conditions, to have and to hold,
from generation to generation, so long as they fulfilled these conditions. These land-holders were
the nobles,—barons. These barons, in like manner,
parcelled up their land into farms and let the farms
to farmers on the same condition, to have and to
hold, from generation to generation, not to be dis-
possessed so long as they fulfilled the conditions.

The conditions were these: the farmers were bound to furnish so many fighting-men, and so much food to the baron, and to work for him so many days in the year. The baron on his part had his castle, and he was bound to furnish the king with so many fighting-men and to administer justice on the land of his barony. He was responsible to the count, and the count to the king. When a baron died without a son, his barony fell back to the crown, and was given away to another. The count had to see that the barons administered justice; and the send-counts appointed by Charlemagne went about the country seeing that the counts did their duty. This was the feudal system. Every man was bound by duties, and no man could call anything his own unless he discharged his duties.

In the south of Germany, the nobles did not like this new system at all. Welf, Count of Bavaria, had a son, Henry. Louis the Pious, who had married Jutta, Welf's daughter, offered to give Henry some land on the new principle; but the old Bavarian forbade his son to take it. However, Jutta persuaded her brother to do as the emperor offered, which was that he should have and hold as much land as he could run a gold plough round whilst the emperor slept. When the old Welf heard that his son had done this he was so offended that he hid himself for the rest of his days in the Black Forest.

You see by this feudal system no man could sell his property out and out; he could only sell it subject to the king's consent, and subject to the duties it entailed, or pawn what he got from it, without freeing himself from the responsibilities.

We shall see later how the towns were governed on the same principle.

XIII.

TROUBLE COMING.

(840–911.)

THE successors of Louis the German were Charles the Fat, Arnulf, and Louis the Child.

One day Charles the Great was looking from his window by the sea, when he saw some white sails on the far horizon, shimmering along like sea-gulls. Those who were in the room with him heard him sigh heavily. " Sire, what troubles you?" He pointed to the white sails. " I see a coming trouble there," he answered. The sails belonged to the Northmen. After the death of Louis the Pious, the incursions of the Northmen became indeed a trouble. In France, as you know, they conquered and formed Normandy. They made sad havoc in England, and Alfred had hard battles to fight before he could drive them back ; but there also they founded a kingdom in Northumbria. Charles the Fat was too lazy to meet and fight the Northmen ; he bought them off with gold. This created general disgust ; a great assembly of the nobles and people was held at Tribur on the Rhine, and he was declared incapable of governing and was deposed. His brother's son, Arnulf, succeeded him. He was a good king, very courageous and active, but was cut off by poison after a short reign. He was succeeded by his son Louis, aged six. Under him Germany went through many years of suffering. The Magyars, or Hungarians, invaded the country nearly every year, ravaging it, plundering the churches, burning the towns, and butchering or carrying away into captivity the unhappy people. The Germans fought on foot with long two-handed swords, or with balls covered with spikes which were attached by chains or thongs to a stick, and which they swung about and brought down on the heads of their enemies. The Hungarians were mounted on fleet horses and were armed with bows, so that the Germans could not come to close quarters with them. Then the great vassals took advantage of the fact that the king was a child to enlarge their own dominions and reduce his power. "Woe to thee, O land, when thy king is a child," said Solomon of old, and Germany experienced the truth of his saying. One little anecdote of the times may be quoted. Ulric, Count of Linzgau, was carried away a prisoner by the Hungarians. His beautiful wife remained behind. She believed him to be dead. Years passed and she heard nothing of him. She refused to marry again, but lived quietly in her castle, doing good to all who were near. One day a poor beggar came to her door, dressed in rags, with bare and bleeding feet, and hair almost white. The countess at once came down to give him food, when, with a cry, he threw his arms round her neck and kissed her. The attendants rushed to interfere, but he waved them away with his hand, and the tears ran down his brown, furrowed cheeks. "Let me hold her to my heart once more. I have suffered blows and famine these many years, and had no love. I am Ulric, your lord."

The young king died in 911, before he had come of age to rule, and with him ended the race of Charlemagne in Germany.

XIV.

HOW HENRY THE FOWLER RULED.

(919–936.)

FROM the time of the death of Louis the Child the crown ceased to be in the family of the great Charles. The great vassals elected the king. Though the kingship was not hereditary, it was usual to elect the son or some near relative of the late emperor, so long as a suitable person was found in the family to hold the office. Also the kings, during their lives, did what they could to insure the succession to their own families. By this change one great advantage was gained: the Germans made sure that they should be governed by able princes; but, on the other hand, this great disadvantage came of it, that the vassals were able to make themselves too powerful, and to rule almost quite independently of the emperor in their own lands. The kings were obliged to bribe and favour the great nobles to secure them to vote for their sons, and so the central power of the crown was weakened and the unity of Germany dissolved. It must be remembered that the German kings claimed also to be kings of Italy, and, by virtue of their coronation by the popes, to be emperors of Rome. So they were crowned twice, once at Aix—in aftertimes at

Frankfort, as kings of Germany—afterwards at Rome as emperors. So they were ever distracted from what should have been their chief care,—to bring Germany into unity and subjection,—by the craze that they were the descendants of the emperors of Rome, and by their efforts to re-establish the great old Empire, not now as a pagan power, but, as they called it, a Holy Roman Empire. When Pope Leo III., on Christmas Day, 800, crowned and proclaimed Charles the Great as emperor, he did, without knowing it, the greatest mischief he could to Germany. He diverted the ambitions of the kings of Germany for seven hundred years from their proper duties at home, and sent them wild-goose hunting in Italy.

The first king who was chosen, after the death of Louis, was Conrad, a Frank duke. He got into contest with Henry, the young Duke of Saxony. Archbishop Hatto, of Mainz, sent Henry a present of a necklace for his throat, made of twisted gold formed to act like a spring, so that he could pass it over his head and it would close tight on his throat. Henry put it on, and the gold shrank so tight as nearly to throttle him. He had never seen a spring coil before, and the chain had to be broken off him. He was very angry, and declared that the bishop wanted to strangle him by this ingenious artifice. So he entered some of the bishop's lands with an army ; thereupon the emperor marched to protect the archbishop. A battle was fought and the Franks were defeated. Then a peace was patched up. Not long after Conrad died, without leaving any sons. On his death-bed he called to him his brother Eberhard, and said : "My hours are numbered. I know that no man is worthier to take the throne than my enemy, Henry of Saxony. Do not you think of yourself in opposition to the general good. We Franks have might, and strong cities, and all that royal splendour requires; but something more than that is needed: great prudence and wisdom, and that Henry has. When I am dead take him the crown and the sacred lance, the gold armlets, the sword, and the purple mantle of the old kings, and so make Henry your friend. Tell him and the princes that my dying advice is, that he should succeed me."

Directly Conrad was dead, the electors met and chose Henry. They sent Eberhard and others to announce his election to him, and found him out bird-catching, with a hawk on his wrist, in the Harz Mountains. He was thenceforth called "The Fowler." He obeyed the call of the nation without delay. The error he had committed in rebelling against the state he firmly resolved to atone for by his conduct as emperor. Of lofty stature, although slight and youthful in form, with a handsome face, a clear eye, and a pleasant smile, his very appearance won hearts to him. Besides these personal advantages, he was intelligent, eager for knowledge, and had much good sense. His wife, Bertha, was an excellent woman, who wove and spun, and there are seals remaining that represent her spinning, seated on her throne as an empress.

His first idea was how to protect the land from that incessant plague, the Hungarian incursions.

He formed his plan, which was not liked by his
nobles at first, because they did not understand
what he aimed at. He bought peace of the Hun-

THE HEERBANN—CALLING OUT THE MILITIA.
(Heidelberg MSS.)

garians for nine years by promising them a yearly
tribute. But this was not through cowardice; he
wanted to gain time. During those nine years he
occupied himself in building strong fortresses dot-

ted about along the frontiers, and filling them with munitions of war and well-trained soldiers. These were called burgs, and were placed under the command of counts, called burgraves. Hitherto the Germans had not lived in walled towns, and had a great dislike to doing so. Henry ordered that out of every nine freemen who lived on their lands, one should be always on guard in the burg, and that the other eight should support him. By degrees, the Germans on the frontier saw what protection these burgs gave them, and they gathered about them, and closed walls round their collection of houses, and formed the walled towns of Germany.

When the nine years were elapsed, and Henry stopped the tribute, he was ready for the Hungarians. They sent to him as usual the tenth year for the money, but he threw a dead mangy dog at their feet, and told them that was all they should have from him and his Germans for the future. The ambassadors returned with fury in their hearts, and the Hungarians poured over the frontier in two enormous hordes. They found themselves troubled with the strong burgs, which they could not take, and which menaced their rear if they advanced. Moreover, Henry's men were full of confidence, for they could always fall back within walls if they found the Hungarians too strong for them. Henry had a great banner painted of St. Michael trampling on the dragon, with wings of blazen gold, and had it carried before his army. A furious battle was fought near Merseburg, and thirty thousand Hungarians were killed. The remainder fled. The terror of the Hungarians now equalled that with which they had formerly inspired the Germans. In their belief, the Angel Michael was the German god of victory, and they made golden wings like those borne by the angel on the banner and fastened them to their own idols, in hopes thereby of making them like Michael. From the fact that Henry had been the builder or founder of so many cities that grew up about his burgs, he got the name of Henry "the City Builder," as well as "the Fowler."

Another institution of Henry's was the knighthood. There were at that time a good number of freemen, younger brothers of those holding land, who hired themselves at different courts, or who robbed on the highways. They did not know exactly what to do with themselves; there were not then many openings for men, and they were too proud to serve as foot soldiers. Henry offered those who had been robbers a free pardon, and invited the rest to come and serve the empire. They were to be called knights,—that is, servants of the crown,—and he organized them into a body of mounted cavalry, and imposed on them certain conditions, which made the rank of a knight one of honour. The story goes that Henry and some of his nobles were discussing the proofs required to show that a soldier deserved this rank. Then said Henry, "First, he must not, by word or deed, wrong the Mother Church." "Nor," added the Count Palatine Conrad, "nor hurt the Holy Roman Empire." Then Berthold of Bavaria said

" He must not be a liar." " Nor," said Hermann of Swabia, " have injured a weak woman." " No, nor run away in battle," said Conrad of Franconia. So these were made the laws of knighthood, to be true to church and country, true in everything, gentle to women, and courageous.

XV.

THE HUNGARIANS BURST IN AGAIN.

(936–973.)

TWENTY-TWO years after the Hungarians had been defeated at Merseburg they once more burst into Germany. They were so numerous that they boasted that their horses would drink the rivers dry and stamp the towns to dust. They pushed up the Danube to where the river Lech joins it, and there turned south and followed up this river to the great and wealthy city of Augsburg. They had been disappointed of spoil. They had traversed long tracts of rubble of white limestone with willows sprouting between the stones; no rich towns, only poor villages, few and far between. They were hungry for spoil, and they knew that Augsburg would furnish abundance. Augsburg stood on the great trade road from Italy into the heart of Germany. It was full of merchants who were as wealthy as princes. It was an old Roman town, and had, no doubt, at one time been surrounded by walls. At this time it had a very prudent bishop, named Ulric. For some time he had suspected mischief was brewing, before others were aware of the danger, and he persuaded the citizens to rebuild their walls.

These were fortunately finished just before the Hungarians attacked the place. As soon as Ulric heard that they were coming he sent to his brother, who was Count of Kyburg,* and to Duke Burkhard

HENRY II. AND CUNIGUNDE BUILD CHURCHES.
(From an Illuminated MS. in Bamberg.)

of Swabia, to fly to his aid, and they hastily came into the city with their men before the barbarians appeared. There was a moat round the walls and the river Lech had been made to send a stream into it. This puzzled the Hungarians, and they stood

---

* The family of the Count of Kyburg became extinct in 1264, and their possessions passed first into the hands of the counts of Hapsburg and then to the House of Austria, one of the present titles of the Austrian emperor being Count of Kyburg.

OTTO II. AND HIS SPOUSE BLESSED BY CHRIST.
(From an Ivory Carving in the Hotel Cluny.)

looking at the water and the walls beyond. Then
their chiefs whirled their long whips and slashed at
their men to drive them into the ditch, and force
them through. A gigantic Hungarian stood on the
bank blowing a horn. Then, all at once, a gate was
opened in the walls, a bridge was dropped, and out
rushed the weavers of Augsburg, armed with pikes,
fell on the enemy, surrounded and killed their king,
and went back in triumph, carrying the shield of the
king with them. Ever after, to this day, the shield
has been preserved by the guild of the weavers.
The Hungarians were detained outside Augsburg,
unable to take it, and unwilling to leave it, till Otto,
the emperor, the son of Henry, had collected an
army and come swiftly upon them in the rear.
Then a great battle was fought, on the 10th of August, 955. The sun was blazing, and very hot. The
great bare plain of rolled white limestones was glar-
ing. The fight was a desperate one. Those in the
city sallied out and helped the emperor. For some
time the fate of the day was uncertain. Indeed, the
German troops were wavering, when the day was
turned by the heroism of the gallant Conrad of
Franconia, the brother-in-law of the emperor. But
he who saved the fortunes of the day was himself
slain. Unable to bear the heat of the sun, which
made his helmet burn his head, he took it off for a
moment, and at that instant an arrow pierced his
neck. A hundred thousand Hungarians fell; others
plunged, mad with fear, into the river, to escape
the pursuit of the Germans, and the stream swept
them away and drowned them, and along its course

HENRY II. RECEIVES FROM GOD THE CROWN, HOLY LANCE, AND IMPERIAL
SWORD.
(From Henry's Missal.)

for many miles, among the willows and rushes and rolled stones, dead Hungarians were washed up in great numbers. Those who managed to get over the river were hunted in the bushes with pitch-forks and flails, and killed by the peasants without mercy like wolves. Never again did the Hungarians venture an invasion of Germany.

Otto I., called the Great, was the son of Henry the Fowler. He succeeded him in 936. He was a very fine man. Wittekind, an historian of the times, says: " His demeanor was full of majesty. His white hair waved over his shoulders. His eyes were bright and sparkling. His beard was of extraordinary length."

He was crowned at Aix, with great splendour, in the grand circular church Charlemagne had built. The gigantic crown of Charles the Great, the sceptre, the sword, the gold-embroidered mantle, and the sacred lance were used. This lance was supposed to have been that employed by the centurion to pierce the side of our Lord ; and it was one of the things always put into the hands of the king when he was crowned. It is now at Vienna, in the treasury of the Emperor of Austria. Otto was seated on the throne of Charles the Great, which was covered with plates of gold. He was anointed by the Archbishop of Mainz, and the great dukes and princes stood about him, invested with honorary offices in the palace. The Duke of Lotharingia was his chamberlain, the Duke of Franconia his carver, the Duke of Swabia his cup-bearer, the Duke of Bavaria his marshall, or master of the stables. Edith,

OTTO III. AND REPRESENTATIVES OF NOBLES AND CLERGY.
(From an Illustrated Codex Title-Page.)

the daughter of Edmund, King of England, his wife, was crowned with him. When the dukes went home from the coronation they were pleased with the state, and thought to copy it, so they appointed counts under them to be butlers, and servers, and chamberlains, and marshals to them. Then those of the bishops who were princes did the same, and made these offices hereditary in certain noble families on their lands. Our word constable means count of the stables, and a sheriff is a count of a shire (shire-graf).

If there were some pomp and state observed by Otto I. there was more introduced into the court by his son, Otto II., who married Theophania, a Greek princess, accustomed to the elaborate ceremonial of the court at Constantinople. Never had the Germans seen any one so lovely as this beautiful princess. She appeared among them as a being from another world. When she arrived, we are told that the trappings of her horse were enriched with feathers and gold, her Greek dress was encrusted with jewels and embroidered over with pearls, and her hair was confined in a golden net. Yet all this splendor was outshone by the beauty of her features and the brilliancy of her eyes. She did, however, something better than introduce mere ceremonial. She brought in a love of letters, and she polished and refined the somewhat rough and boorish manners of the court. Otto I. was crowned King of the Lombards at Milan, and emperor at Rome.

Otto II., and his son, Otto III., died after short reigns, and with Henry II., called "the Saint," a great-grandson of Henry I., the Saxon dynasty came to an end.

XVI.

SOME TRIALS OF A KING.

(1053–1106.)

THE first king of the race of the Salic Franks
was Conrad II. He and his son, Henry III., were
good sovereigns, holding the reins of government
with a firm hand. Unhappily for Germany, the latter died in the vigor of manhood, and his son Henry
was proclaimed king, at the age of six. We have
come now to one of the saddest periods in the history of Germany.

Agnes, the empress mother, a good woman, was
left by Henry guardian of his infant son, and regent
during his childhood. She had not sufficient
strength of character for what was required of her.
She sought to rule the turbulent spirits of the age
by gentleness and persuasion.

Charles the Great had made some of the archbishops and bishops secular princes, that is, he had
given them dominions over which they might reign
like sovereigns, and he did this in the hope that
they would stand by the throne against the violent
and ambitious dukes. But his scheme answered
badly. The archbishops of Cologne and Mainz
were sovereigns, raising armies, making laws, im-

posing taxes, exercising the power of life and death. Consequently, their minds were turned as much, if not more, to the advancement of their power as princes than to their duties as bishops. Indeed, it came to this, that they kept bishops under them, like curates, to do all their sacred functions, and devoted themselves to their secular duties as sovereigns. Moreover, because these great bishoprics and archbishoprics were principalities, the great nobles coveted them for their sons, and got the kings to give them to their sons when they got ordained, just for the sake of taking them, without the slightest regard for their fitness for a sacred office.

Now at this time the Archbishop of Cologne was a man called Anno. He was not a great nobleman. Henry III. had elevated him to the archbishopric in the hope of attaching him to himself and his house, but by birth he was a member of a small and needy family of gentlemen. When he became archbishop he was ravenous for power and wealth to bestow on his relations He was not a bad man, but he was a greedy man, greedy of power. He and the Archbishop of Mainz thought that if they could only get hold of the young king they would be able to squeeze what they liked out of him. So they made a plan to seize him.

One Whitsuntide the Empress Agnes was spending the pleasant spring weather on the island of Kaiserswerth in the Rhine. The trees were in their first leaf, and the buds were bursting. The two archbishops came to pay her a visit in a beautiful new ship with painted and gilded bows. After they had dined they asked Henry if he would like to see the boat. He was only too delighted, so they took him to where it was moored, got him on board, and then, at a signal, the rope was cut, the sail was spread, the rowers dipped their oars, and away darted the ship into the middle of the stream. Henry thought that he was going to be killed or put in prison, and jumped overboard, but the Margrave of Meissen, who was in the plot, jumped after him, and brought him back into the vessel. In the mean time, the empress ran along the beach wringing her hands and crying, and others shouted and stormed at the treachery; but the archbishops did not care; they pushed up the river to Cologne, and arranged that the king should spend half his time with Archbishop Anno and half with Archbishop Siegfried, of Mainz.

The news spread like wildfire, and the whole of Germany was in agitation. The Archbishop of Cologne, who had charge of the king first, was obliged to bribe the great vassals right and left to stop their mouths, and this he did by making the young king give them estates which belonged to the crown, and to the bishops who rebuked him he gave other bishoprics, to keep them quiet.

Anno was a hard, stern man, and he kept Henry under very severe discipline. He gave him no amusements, held him hard at lessons, and separated him from young lads of his own age who might have made agreeable companions. He was always cross, and scolding, and Henry acquired a perfect hatred

of him. It was much the same with the Archbishop of Mainz. So the archbishop saw that he
must put him with some one else, who was a

IMPERIAL HOUSE AT GOSLAR.   (HENRY III.)

friend, and would not act against him. He
therefore handed him over to Adalbert, Archbishop of Bremen. Now Adalbert was just the
opposite sort of man to Anno. He was very fond of
splendour, kept a grand court, ate and drank of the
best, and was a thriftless, good-natured person. He

allowed Henry to do what he liked, spoiled him, let him make friends with worthless young noble-men, and throw about his money on any folly, as he pleased.

The consequence of this sort of bringing up—at one time treated with harshness, at another with in-dulgence ; at one time refused rational pleasures, then allowed every indulgence unreproved—was that Henry's natural good disposition was com-pletely spoiled.

After he had been some years with Adalbert, Anno wanted to get him back again, as Adalbert was wasting, or allowing Henry to waste, all the rev-enues of the crown. So another plot was formed. A diet—that is, a parliament—met at Tribur, which was attended by the king, and the arch-bishop, and many of the great nobles. All at once the young king was surrounded, and ordered to dismiss Adalbert from his court or abdicate the throne. Henry was obliged to throw Archbishop Adalbert over. Anno was guilty now of a very stupid act. He forced the young king, when he was only sixteen, to marry Bertha, daughter of the Margrave of Susa, a plain-faced, uninteresting girl, whom he could not abide, and whom he treated in consequence with positive unkindness at one time and neglect at another. Moreover, it increased his detestation of Anno, so that Anno behaved in this matter imprudently for his own interests. On the king the effect was very bad, because, as he disliked his wife, he became more disorderly and subject to the leading of all sorts of persons, whereas, if he had had a wife whom he loved and who was sensible, he might gradually have been brought into better ways. But this was not all; his sons grew up to see their father rude and unkind to their mother, and they lost all respect and regard for him. What that led to, you shall hear presently.

No sooner was Henry his own master than he turned on those who had leagued with Anno against him—and these were the Saxon nobles —and treated them with contumely and severity ; indeed, he drove them into insurrection. At last, unable to endure his treatment, they appealed to the Pope. The Pope at this time was Gregory VII., a carpenter's son, whose head had been turned by his ele-

HENRY IV. WITH SCEPTRE AND
IMPERIAL GLOBE.
(From an Illuminated Manuscript.)

vation to the Papacy, and who was puffed up with pride and love of power. He summoned the emperor to come to Rome, that he might decide between him and the Saxon princes. Henry laughed at the summons. Charles the Great had gone to

Rome and called the Pope before him, and tried the case between him and those who had thrown him off his horse and tried to cut out his tongue; and should he, the emperor, go and be tried by the Bishop of Rome? He was then aged twenty-five, full of pride and in the plenitude of his power. He at once called some of the bishops together at Worms, and, urged by him, they deposed the Pope. This was a very thoughtless act on his part. He had to do with a much cleverer man than himself, and Gregory was delighted that he had thus given him a handle wherewith to humble him. Gregory at once pronounced excommunication against him, that is, he cut him off from the Church as completely as if he were a heathen, and bade all Christians hold aloof from him. He released all his subjects from their allegiance and declared him unworthy to reign. Henry only laughed at the sentence when he heard it, but the laugh died away on his lips when he saw the effect it wrought. He had behaved so badly in Germany, had been so despotic, had offended so many—the powerful princes by his insolence, the good people by his disorderly life, and the general mass of the people by his neglect of good government—that they were glad to seize the excuse to fall away from him and give themselves a better emperor.

Henry found himself deserted by every one but his despised wife Bertha. The great vassals proceeded to elect Rudolf, Duke of Swabia, who had married his sister, to be emperor in his place.

There was nothing for it, Henry thought, but for

RUDOLPH OF SWABIA.
(From his Tomb.)

him to hasten to Italy and make his peace with the
Pope. The winter of this year (1076) happened to
be colder than any within the memory of man,
and the Rhine remained frozen over from the
middle of November to April, 1077. It was in
this dreadful weather, about Christmas time, that
Henry set off secretly, attended only by Bertha,
his infant son, and a solitary knight. They crossed
the Alps to the Lake of Geneva; then they travelled over the St. Bernard pass, and Bertha, whom
neither danger nor distress could separate from
her husband, was drawn over the ice seated on an
ox-hide, whilst the emperor scrambled among the
rocks like a chamois-hunter.

The Pope was then in the castle of Canossa, situated on a rocky spur of the Apennines. With the
insolence of a beggar exalted to unlimited power,
Gregory treated the humbled emperor ignomin-
iously. He refused to see and absolve him till he
had undergone a degrading penance. On a dreary
winter morning, with the ground deep in snow, the
king, the heir of a line of emperors, was forced to
lay aside every mark of royalty, was clad in the
thin white linen dress of the penitent, and there,
fasting, he awaited the pleasure of the Pope in the
castle yard. But the gates did not unclose. A
second day he stood, cold, hungry, and mocked by
vain hope. At the close only of the third day did
Gregory receive and pardon him.

But Gregory had now, for his part, done more
than was judicious from his own point of view. His
severity, and the humiliation of their king, roused the

indignation and excited the disgust of the Germans and the Italians alike, and Henry found himself now surrounded by those who had forsaken him. At the head of an army he marched against his brother-in-law, Rudolf of Swabia, who had assumed the crown, and defeated him in a battle near Gera, on the Elster. When the duke was dying, some one showed him his right hand, which had been cut off by an axe. "It is well," said the duke, "I raised this right hand to heaven in token of fidelity when I took the oath of allegiance to Henry. God has punished me aright by suffering it to be smitten off."

Now it was Henry's turn to chastise the Pope. He crossed the Alps at the head of an army, took Rome, deposed Gregory, who fled to Salerno, and appointed another Pope in his room, who crowned him in S. Peter's Church, Emperor of the Romans, A.D. 1084.

Henry had now crushed his worst enemies, but the remainder of his life was not to be spent in quiet. He had sown the wind and must reap the whirlwind.

CONRAD, SON OF
HENRY IV.
(From an Illuminated MS.)

His reign was very long, fifty years ; his old age was embittered by the revolt of his own sons. Conrad rebelled against his father in Italy, and Henry in Germany. Conrad died before his father.

It was in 1104 that Henry, the best loved son of the old emperor, raised his hand against his father. The touching appeals of the emperor to his son having been disregarded, Henry IV. put himself at the head of his troops and marched against him, but discovering that he was betrayed by his followers, he fled in sorrow of heart. Then occurred an incident which has been versified by a German poetess. If ever you go up the Rhine, look at the ruins of the Castle of Hammerstein. In it, at the time of which I am telling you, lived a knight who had been true to Henry in all his troubles, but he was now very old and unable to take the field for his king. The knight was bitterly dissatisfied because he had no son, only two gentle daughters, and he could not abide to see them, as they were useless, he thought, whereas a son could have borne arms for the king. One night there came a knock at the castle door, and the old man was told that a stranger begged admission. He was shown in, and, lo ! the knight saw his white-haired sovereign, come to him for refuge from his enemies, begging for shelter, if only for a night.

" Ah ! well is thee ! " said Henry, looking at the two daughters of his host, " well is thee that thou hast gentle daughters to cling to thee, to love thee, and cherish thee in thy old age. I—I have had two sons, and both have risen against me."

The emperor was taken by his unnatural son and shut up in the castle of Bingen, and was required by delegates from him to surrender the crown jewels. The aged emperor placed the crown of Charlemagne on his head, threw the imperial mantle over his shoulders, and holding the sceptre and orb, appeared before the messengers, and defied them to touch the ornaments worn by the ruler of the world. But to these men nothing was sacred : the crown and mantle of Charlemagne were plucked off him, and carried to Mainz to adorn his rebellious son.

The fallen emperor was given into the hands of Gebhard, Bishop of Spires, who took a fiendish pleasure in humbling and tormenting him. He kept him without sufficient food, so that the old emperor was obliged to sell his boots in order to procure bread. He was forbidden the use of a bath, and of a barber to shave him. At length he found ways of escaping to Liege, where the bishop received him and treated him with great kindness till he died of a broken heart. From his death-bed Henry sent his ring and sword to his son in token of pardon for his rebellion.

XVII.

A BAD SON MAKES A STRONG KING.

(1099–1125.)

HENRY V. married Matilda, daughter of Henry I. of England, but he never had any children. He saw clearly enough that there was no hope for Germany to become united and great so long as the dukes, and margraves, and archbishops were so powerful and independent, and his father's long minority, and the incessant contests that followed, had made them so strong that the emperor could do little unsupported by them. Accordingly, he directed his efforts to reducing their power. But now again appeared one of the fatal consequences of the gift of the imperial crown to Charlemagne by Leo II. The popes were afraid of the emperors. The kings of Germany, who were also kings of Italy and Lombardy, were tremendously strong, and the popes were afraid of being completely at their mercy and being forced to do just what the emperors ordered. So it became a part of the settled policy of the popes to stir up strife at home to keep the empire weak and occupy the emperor in Germany. In order to help the vassals to weaken Henry, the Pope excommunicated him, and his reign was spent

HENRY V. RECEIVES INSIGNIA FROM POPE PASCHAL.
(From the Ekkehard Manuscript.)

in fighting first one vassal, then another. He was sometimes victorious, sometimes defeated, and a fugitive, just as he had made his father a fugitive. In the end he died a disappointed man, having utterly failed to do what he designed.

A TEMPLAR.

XVIII.

HOW THEY FOUGHT THE SARACENS.

(1096–1291.)

IT was customary in the Middle Ages for pious men to visit Jerusalem and Bethlehem, to see and pray at the spots where Christ was born, and died, and rose again. The Arabs, who ruled in Syria after the Romans had lost that province, did not disturb the pilgrims. But when the Seldjucs, a savage Turkish race, conquered Palestine, the Christians were oppressed and persecuted; pilgrims were maltreated, churches desecrated, and Simon, Patriarch of Jerusalem, was thrown down at the foot of the altar, and his hair plucked out.

A pious hermit, Peter of Amiens, saw these sufferings, when on a visit to Jerusalem; he returned to Europe with an appeal from the patriarch to Pope Urban II. The Pope sent Peter into France and through Italy to stir up the people to fight for the recovery of the Holy City. In 1095 the Pope held a council at Clermont, in France, and besought the faithful to take up arms to wrest Jerusalem from the hands of the unbelievers. "It is the will of God!" shouted the crowd, and they hasted to fasten little crosses of red cloth to their shoulders, in token that

they enlisted in the enterprise. Thence these expeditions took the name of crusades. The first
army started in August, 1096, under the generalship
of Godfrey de Bouillon. When the host crossed
over from Constantinople into Asia Minor it numbered 300,000 fighting men. On its way through
Asia Minor and Syria, privations, incessant fighting,
and disease had thinned it so that when it arrived
in the Promised Land only a tenth remained. This
remnant, however, inspired to enthusiasm by the
sight of Jerusalem, stormed and took the city.
Godfrey de Bouillon was the first to leap from the
walls into the town. The gates were thrown open
and the Crusaders poured in, to massacre all they
encountered. Godfrey de Bouillon was proclaimed
King of Jerusalem ; but he refused to wear a crown,
where the Saviour had been invested with a wreath
of thorns, and for his title chose " Guardian of the
Holy Grave." Next year, 1100, Godfrey died, and
his brother Baldwin took the government and the
title of king.

The new Christian realm was not, however, secured by the capture of Jerusalem. The city was
repeatedly threatened; and for its protection six
great armies went out of Europe. Jerusalem fell
back into the hands of the Saracens. With
Ptolemais, or Acre, the Christians lost, in 1291, the
last of their possessions in Asia. Thenceforth, the
Holy Land remained in the power of the Turks.
The conflict for the Holy Sepulchre lasted two hundred years, and cost Europe six millions of her best
fighting men. Nevertheless, the Crusades were an

advantage to the West. Minds were roused by contact with strange sights, interest quickened in geography, history, and natural science. A multitude of hitherto unknown products, as silk, sugar, spices, dyes, found their way into the West. Moreover, some of the most turbulent spirits went out

AN ASTROLOGER. (HOLBEIN.)

of Europe, as by a voluntary banishment, to exhaust their powers of doing mischief in the East, and the nobility were so weakened that the cities were able to develop commerce and manufacture unimpeded.

During the period of the Crusades, chivalry became more and more a flourishing and organized institution. Knighthood was not inherited like titles ; it was granted to a man for his worth, after hard trials and proof that the aspirant deserved the honour.

XIX.

HOW A NEW DYNASTY WAS BEGUN.

(1138–1152.)

IMPERIAL
GLOBE.

IF you look on the map you will see that at Stuttgart the River Neckar comes from the east and turns abruptly north, where it receives another river from the east called the Rems. Now between the Rems and the Neckar rises a tableland of dry limestone, and here and there this plateau is capped with the queerest hills, for all the world like thimbles put down by giants on the table. These conical hills with stumpy tops are not of limestone; they are volcanic, and have been driven up through the lime by the fires in the heart of the earth. One of these is called Hohenstaufen. You will remember that when Henry IV. went over the Alps in winter to Pope Gregory VII. one faithful knight attended him. This knight is said to have been Frederick of Büren. In consideration of his fidelity, immediately that affairs seemed prosperous, Henry created him Duke of Swabia, and gave him Agnes, his daughter, to wife. He thereupon built himself a castle on the hill I mention, and thenceforth called himself "Of Hohenstaufen."

There had been Frank and Saxon emperors; now there was to be a Swabian dynasty.

A HOHENSTAUFEN KNIGHT.
(From an Almanac of the 12th Century.)

In 1138, at Mainz, Conrad, the son of this Frederick of Hohenstaufen, was elected to be king of the Germans.

Besides Hohenstaufen, the family had a town, Waiblingen on the Rems, and as people then took their names from their estates, they were called variously "of Büren," "of Hohenstaufen," and "of Waiblingen"; but as Waiblingen was a town,

CONRAD HUNTING WITH FALCONS.
(From a Minnesinger Manuscript of the 14th Century.)

whereas the other places were only castles, they were commonly called the Waiblingers.

There was a strong opposition party in Germany to the Swabians, and that was headed by the Duke of Bavaria. The Bavarian dukes were called Welfs, from an ancestor of the name. This was a very powerful family, which held both the duchies of Bavaria and Saxony. As the policy of the Pope was to weaken the power of the emperor, he supported the Welfs. The Lombard cities also took the same side. In Italian mouths (unable to pronounce the W) Welf became Guelf, and Waiblinger became Ghibelline, and in Italy the Papal faction was called Guelf and the emperor's party was called Ghibelline.

The Waiblinger family has long ago died out, but the Welf remains. It is represented by Queen Victoria of England and the Duke of Brunswick. It is one of the most ancient reigning houses that exists. It dates back in unbroken pedigree to that old Welf, Count of Swabia and Bavaria, the father of Jutta, the wife of Louis the Pious, who sulked and hid himself in the Black Forest because his son took a feudal holding under the emperor. This Welf died about the year 824.

Conrad, the Waiblinger, did not succeed to the throne immediately after the death of Henry V. Lothair, the Saxon, was the next emperor, but Conrad came to the throne on his death, and at once the contest with the Welfs broke out. During this contest the little town of Weinsberg held out gallantly for the Welfs against the emperor. Exas-

HENRY THE LION, AND SPOUSE.
(From their Tomb.)

perated at the persistency of their defence Conrad threatened to kill all the men when he took the place. When at length Weinsberg was forced to yield, the provisions therein being exhausted, the emperor consented that all the women should be allowed, unmolested, to leave the place and to carry with them their choicest valuables. Then the gate was thrown open, and out through it, and down the hill to where Conrad sat before his tent, came the Countess Ida,* carrying her husband, Welf, on her back, followed by all the women of Weinsberg, carrying their husbands, and fathers, and brothers, and lovers on their backs.

Some of the army of Conrad were angry, and wanted to stop this strange procession and kill the men, but the emperor was touched at the devotion of the women, and he answered, " Not so ; I gave my word, and an emperor's word must never be broken."

The Welf whom the Countess Ida carried was Welf VI., of Bavaria, uncle of the Duke Henry, surnamed the Lion, who was then only twelve years old. After that, Welf VI. was made Duke of Spoleto and Margrave of Tuscany.

Conrad was forced by public opinion, against his good sense, to head a crusade. He started at the head of a large army in 1147 for the Holy Land, but his whole march was one of disaster and loss. As the Crusaders were crossing a river near Constantinople, agents of the Greek emperor tried to count

---

* She was a daughter of the Count Palatine of the Rhine.

them, but after reckoning 900,000, desisted. Not one tithe of this vast horde ever reached their destination. They died either of disease, starvation, or by the swords of the Moslems, in Asia Minor. Conrad returned home, in confusion and despondency, to find that Welf and Henry the Lion were stirring up a new revolt against him in Germany and Lombardy.

When he was at Constantinople he saw that the Byzantine emperor bore on his imperial standards a two-headed eagle, to represent the double empire, East and West, which had for a while been united under Constantine and his successors. Conrad was struck with the idea, and when he came home he assumed the double-headed eagle as the arms of his empires, and you will see it on the coins of both the Emperor of Germany and the Emperor of Austria at the present day. There is a story told, —but it is, of course, only a story,—that one of the grand dukes of Austria was out shooting in the Tyrol some years ago, and the huntsman with him brought down an eagle. When the grand duke picked it up, "Why," said he, "what a queer eagle! It has only one head!" He had seen the imperial eagle all his life on banners and coins, and thought all eagles had two necks and heads.

XX.

FREDERICK OF THE RED BEARD.

(1152–1190.)

FREDERICK I., or Barbarossa, was certainly the
greatest and strongest of the German emperors after
Charles the Great. He pacified the Welfs by giving Henry the Lion back the Duchies of Bavaria
and Saxony, which Conrad had taken from him.
But the great Welf duke was not grateful for this
act ; he repaid it with treachery.

If Frederick had only contented himself with the
government and discipline of Germany all would
have been well, but he could not forget that he was
King of all Italy and Emperor of Rome, so that he
continually crossed the Alps with armies to quell
the revolts that broke out there ; and when he was
in Italy disturbances burst forth in Germany, which
forced him back to subdue them. Duke Welf VI.,
the uncle of Henry the Lion, in his old age became
blind. He lived at Memingen, on the Lech, and
was very extravagant. He invited all the noblemen
of Swabia and Bavaria to come and eat, and drink,
and dance for weeks at a time at Memingen. He
got deep in debt, and the emperor helped him ; but
his nephew, Henry the Lion, never sent him any

STATUE OF FREDERICK BARBAROSSA.
(In the Cloister of St. Reno, Reichenhall.)

money. When he died he left all his estates to the emperor. This made Henry the Lion furious, and he resolved to be revenged. Frederick called on Henry as his vassal to assist him in a campaign in Italy. Henry obeyed. At the Lake of Como Frederick fell ill. Then Henry went to him and told him he would desert him unless the emperor yielded to his extortionate demands. The Lombards in insurrection were drawing near. The time was critical. Frederick entreated the duke to be true to him and his country. He even went down on his knees to entreat him, but Henry turned scornfully away. Then the Empress Beatrice raised her husband, saying, " God will help you, and remember the Welf's insolence some future day." A battle was fought with the Lombards, who far outnumbered the faithful Germans. Henry withdrew with his men, and left Frederick's army to be almost cut to pieces. The emperor escaped with difficulty and returned to Germany, where the indignation against the treachery of Henry was so general that Frederick put him under the ban of the Empire— that is, outlawed him—and gave the duchy of Bavaria to his faithful friend, Count Otto of Wittlesbach, who is the ancestor of the present King of Bavaria. The duchy of Saxony was divided, and to the Welfs nothing was left, after Henry the Lion had come on his knees and implored pardon of the emperor, but the territory of Brunswick, and it is thus, through the House of Brunswick, that the Queen of England descends from the ancient Welfs.

BARBAROSSA'S PALACE AT GELNHAUSEN. (RECONSTRUCTED PLAN.)

So that act of treachery at Como was the ruin of the greatness of the Welfs for many generations.

In his old age Frederick made a crusade against Saladin, Sultan of Egypt, who had retaken Jerusalem. As he was crossing a river Seleph he was carried off his horse by the current and drowned. When the news of his death reached Germany no one would believe it. There sprang up a story among the people that the red-bearded king is not dead, but sleeps in the Kyffhäuser Mountain, sitting at a stone table, and that his beard has grown through the table. They say also, that in the hour of peril to Germany Frederick will start to life and come forth to be the deliverer of Fatherland.

XXI.

A CRUEL KING PUT UNDER THE BAN.

(1196–1250.)

FREDERICK the Red-Bearded was followed by
his son, Henry VI., a cruel, hard man, who succeeded
in making the rule of the Hohenstaufen more hated
in Italy than that of the earlier emperors. At
Christmas, 1194, the season of peace and good-will,
this cruel tyrant deluged Palermo with blood, on the
pretence that he had discovered a plot against his
supremacy. Bishops, nobles, members of the royal
family of Sicily, none were spared; some were
hanged, some burned, others buried alive.* Richard, Count of Palermo, was tied to a horse's tail,
dragged through the streets of Capua, then hung up
by one leg to a gallows, till the emperor's fool,
after two days of misery, put an end to his pain by
tying a great stone to his neck. In the midst of
these scenes of horror the Empress Constantia became mother of a son, Frederick Roger, afterwards
the Emperor Frederick II., and the last emperor of
the race. It would almost seem as if the judgment
of Heaven, outraged by the crime of the father, was

---

* A Count Jordan was placed on a red-hot iron throne, and a red-
hot crown was nailed to his head.

BARBAROSSA'S PALACE AT KAISERSWERTH. (RECONSTRUCTED PLAN.)

to follow the son. Two years later Henry was dead, and the little child succeeded to the crown, under the regency of his gentle and pious mother. It would have been well for him had she lived, but she died shortly after her husband, when Frederick was scarce four years old. The poor little king was brought up among rough and ambitious nobles, in

SEAL OF OTTO IV.

the midst of intrigue, violence, and conflict, at Palermo. He grew to be a very handsome, graceful youth, with a face full of intelligence, benevolence, and nobility. At the age of fifteen he was married to Constantia, daughter of Peter, King of Arragon. The wedding was performed with great magnificence, but in the midst of the festivities, whilst bells were ringing, and soldiers parading, the plague broke out. People fell dead in the streets. Alphonso, the bride's brother, rose from table,

MONUMENTAL LION TO HENRY THE LION (IN BRUNSWICK).

staggered from the hall, and died. Others of the banqueters fell ill also, and before many hours had elapsed were corpses. Frederick and his young bride were obliged to fly.

During his minority there had been sad disturbance in Germany. Two opposition emperors had started up, Philip of Swabia and Otto IV., of Brunswick, the son of Henry the Lion, and for ten years they had devastated Germany by their rivalries. At last, in 1215, Frederick got the upper hand, and was crowed at Aix. This grandson of the Red Beard was an unfortunate man, beset with difficulties, with a strong will, but he never did great things, because his energies were exhausted in incessant contest with the popes. It was the old story over again.

SILVER PIECE OF OTTO IV.

You must consider that in France, in England, in Germany, the crown was not all-powerful. The nobles were very strong and much inclined to have their own way, and their own way meant fighting each other and disturbing the whole land. In France, the kings, by a compromise with the people, got the upper hand and crushed the nobility. In England, the nobles, by a compromise with the people, formed a check on the power of the crown, and founded a constitutional monarchy; but in Germany the greatest emperors squandered their talents and exhausted

HENRY VI.

(From a Minnesinger MS. of the 14th Century.)

the best strength of their country in pursuit of a fancy, and never learned by the experience of their predecessors to desist from the dangerous pursuit. Instead of turning their attention to the development of their country, to the curtailment of the powers of the nobility, to the establishment of their throne on enduring foundations, they were bewitched with the dream of a Roman-imperial world-monarchy, which was impossible to be realized when every nation was asserting more and more its characteristic peculiarities, and arriving at consciousness of national and independent life. The emperors were always divided between distinct callings, as kings of Germany and emperors of Rome. The Italians hated them, the popes undermined their powers and involved them in countless difficulties at home and in Italy, so that they could not establish their authority as emperors, and neglected to make good, or were impeded in attempting to make good, their position as kings in Germany. The bat in the fable was rejected by the birds because he was a beast, and by the beasts because he had wings as a bird.

This, that I have insisted on so strongly, must be borne well in mind by all who would master German history. The imperial eagle has two heads, turned in opposite directions, and the heads of the emperors shared this division and opposition.

Frederick was now King of Lombardy, of Naples and Sicily, as well as King of Germany. The popes were very uneasy, feeling as though placed in a vice, and they naturally sought to diminish the power of Frederick. One of the simplest expedients was to send him off crusading to the East, so they urged him to this, and got him to vow a crusade.   Pope Gregory IX. had the satisfaction of seeing him start at the head of a great host, but fever broke out in it ; the pilgrims perished by thousands.   Frederick himself fell ill, and his ship was obliged to put back to Italy, that he might recruit his health on the mainland.   The Pope was furious in his disappointment, and excommunicated the emperor.   Frederick sent three bishops to the Pope to assure him of his illness.   Gregory refused to receive them.   That was in September, 1227.

Next year, when Frederick was well, he started on his crusade.   One would have supposed that this would have contented the Pope : but no ; he cared for the crusade only as a means to weaken the emperor, and he picked a fresh excuse for continuing the excommunication of Frederick.   He ordered the Templars and Hospitallers to hold aloof from him ; he forbade the paying of taxes to help him, and he did everything in his power to bring the crusade of Frederick to an ignominious break-down.   Yet Frederick succeeded by this expedition in effecting more than any other that had had the advantage of the blessing of popes.   By a treaty with the Sultan of Egypt he recovered all the holy places.   He entered Jerusalem in triumph, took the crown of the Christian kings of Jerusalem from the altar of the Church of the Holy Sepulchre, and placed it on his head.

After his return, the strife with the Pope began again.   The Lombard cities were in revolt.   The

Pope had raised an army of mercenaries against him, who bore as insignia St. Peter's keys, and were nicknamed accordingly the key-soldiers.

The emperor was nearly always victorious, but a series of unhappy circumstances combined to embitter his life. His opponents in Germany had stirred up his son Henry to revolt against him. Frederick was forced to cross the Alps into Germany and quell the rebellion. Henry was deposed

PEASANTS BUILDING A VILLAGE (13TH CENTURY).
(Heidelberg Manuscript.)

and condemned to seven years' imprisonment in Italy. He died in prison before his father.

Pope Innocent IV., who succeeded Gregory IX., continued to resist the emperor, and for precisely the same reason. The claims of the German kings to be emperors did as much harm to the popes as to the kings themselves, for it diverted the attention of the popes from their spiritual cares to plotting how they might upset the emperors, or, at all events, curtail their authority. Innocent, afraid of the immense power of Frederick, fled to France, and excommunicated him again, and deposed him from all his offices. When Frederick heard this he laughed, and exclaimed, "Has the Pope deposed me? Bring me my crowns that I may see of what I am deprived." Then seven crowns were brought him, the royal crown of Germany, the imperial diadem of Rome, the iron circlet of Lombardy, the crowns of Sicily, Burgundy, Sardinia, and Jerusalem. He put them on his head, one after the other, and said, "I have them still, and none shall rob me of them without hard battle."

But the deposition and excommunication had its effect in Germany. It served as an excuse for the proud and ambitious to rise and set up an opposition emperor. An old historian says of that time: "After the Emperor Frederick was put under the ban, the robbers rejoiced over their spoils. Then were the ploughshares beaten into swords, and the reaping hooks into lances. No one went anywhere without steel and stone, to set in blaze whatever he could fire."

Italy also was in insurrection. The emperor's son Enzio, was captured by the Bolognese and imprisoned. The old emperor, crushed by his troubles, died in the arms of his son Manfred, and was succeeded by his son Conrad, who reigned only four years, and was never crowned emperor. Conrad left an only son, Conradin, not three years old, the one legitimate heir of the Red-beard and of Frederick II.

As soon as Frederick was dead, the Pope gave

away the kingdom of Naples to Charles, Count of Anjou.* He had no right whatever to do this, but he did it out of self-preservation, so as to have some one on one side of him to assist him against the Germans. Conradin, when aged sixteen, marched against the French holding Naples, to attempt to recover his kingdom, but was taken, and his head struck off, by order of the cruel Charles of Anjou.

Enzio was still in prison in Bologna; he was now the last of the Hohenstaufen, and heir to all the seven crowns. He contrived to be hidden in an empty wine cask, and thus to be carried out of the prison. But as he was being taken, one of his long golden locks fell out of the bung-hole, which had been left open that he might have air to breathe. This attracted the attention of the

A BISHOP IN ROBES.
(Codex of 12th Century.)

guards; the cask was stopped, broken open. Enzio was enclosed in an iron cage, and there died in 1272, the last of the noble Hohenstaufen race, after a miserable confinement of twenty-three years.

---

* Brother of King Louis IX. of France.

XXII.

THE ROBBER KNIGHTS.

IF you have travelled in Germany you will have noticed the abundance of ruined castles scattered over the country; not a rocky hill, not a spur of mountain, but is crowned by one, not always large, some consisting of little more than one tower and a few outer walls, others possessing several towers. Most of these castles belong to the period of which we shall have need to treat, a time when there was no strong emperor, when the firmament was without a sun, and every little star set up to be independent.

When the Hohenstaufen race died out, the glory of the empire was gone from Germany. No German prince would take the crown; all were afraid of it. Then the great bishops thought of electing a foreigner. Some chose Richard, Earl of Cornwall, brother of Henry III. of England, and son of King John; others chose Alphonso, King of Castile, in Spain. Richard came to Germany very rarely; Alphonso not at all. It was as though there were no king in the land. This was the saddest time that ever was in Germany. Every one did what he liked. The fist and the sword decided between right and

THE DRESS OF THE GERMAN LORDS, WORN BY CONRAD
OF THURINGIA, A.D. 1241,

wrong. The princes and the cities were in constant feud. The knights made themselves strong castles, and lived in them on plunder and murder. From their fortresses they swooped down on the merchants travelling from town to town and robbed them, or levied on them heavy tolls. They went plundering over the level land; they robbed the farmers of their cattle, devastated their fields, and burnt their houses.

Moreover, the neighboring nobles and knights quarrelled with each other and fought, so that the country was one battle-field. How Germany could have got through this terrible time but for two things it is hard to say. In the first place, the towns had become very strong. They had taken advantage of the crusades, which had drawn away a number of the knights, to buy their lands, and to become wealthy, and organize large bodies of fighting men. If, therefore, any knights proved troublesome, and meddled with the caravans passing from town to town, they attacked their fortresses and burned them, and hanged the robber knights from their own towers. Then, again, the church interfered, and ordered that a truce should be kept from all fighting for four days in the week, that is, from Wednesday evening to Monday morning. This was called the "Truce of God," and whoever broke it became an outlaw.

It is, however, a mistake into which travellers in Germany often and very generally fall, to suppose that all the castles were nests of robber barons, and that they always subsisted by robbery. The owners had certain duties which they fulfilled: those on the Rhine, and other rivers that are navigable, maintained the towing paths, and kept relays of horses or oxen to drag the boats against the

KNIGHT AND ATTENDANTS.
(From a Drawing of 1190.)

stream through their lands. For this a toll was paid. Those not on rivers kept up the roads, and entertained travellers, and furnished them with horses, and, if necessary, an escort, till they left the lands over which these barons exercised sway, and for this they were paid something.

The barons, in peaceful times, did not receive the

travellers in their castles perched on high rocks, for
indeed they did not care to live in them themselves
except in times of danger.   They had other houses
below, in the little towns or villages, and over the
doors of their houses they hung their shields; so the
travellers knew the houses where they might lodge,
and where they could get a change of horses, by
the shields, with the arms of the baron or knight.
This it is which originated the signs hung above inn
doors, signs of the red lion, the white hart, the brown
bear, etc.   The inn-keepers were the lords of the
place.   Now, if you happen to travel in the Tyrol,
where old customs linger on, you may find that in a
good many places the inn-keepers are still noble-
men, and that the signs of their inns are still their
coats-of-arms.   If you go into the church-yards you
will see the tombstones of the family of your host,
with the arms, and with coronets over them, showing him to be a baron, or a count.   I know a good
many such inns.   Elsewhere it is not so; the houses
have been sold, and though they still keep their
signs, the signs have no connection with the new
owners.

XXIII.

HOW THE GERMANS WROTE ROMANCES.

THE Germans of the 13th and 14th centuries were not only active soldiers, dealing and taking hard blows, but their minds were as active as their hands ; and so it comes about that we have a series of really grand poems that belong to this period, in the German language ; and not great poems only, but also short and beautiful pieces. The poetic art was cultivated first in Provence by the knights and gentlemen, and those who composed poems and sang them were called troubadours, which means "discoverers," from *trouver*, to find. They found out tunes as well as invented poems. The Germans were not slow to follow the example ; their poets were called "minnesingers," or "love-singers" ; because their lays were mostly love songs. Some of their songs are beautiful. But they did not content themselves with short lays, they composed also long poems. At first they took their subjects from abroad, from the stories of King Arthur and his knights, and so some of the finest and longest of the metrical romances of this time have their scenes laid in Britain. But, fortunately, they were not satisfied with borrowing from abroad, and they composed heroic poems on old German legends.

Charles the Great had made a collection of the national poems, but this was destroyed by Louis the Pious.   Though he destroyed the collection he had not destroyed the remembrance from men's minds, and the old stories lingered on and were passed from mouth to ear, from one generation to another, till at length the poets of Germany, about the time of which we are speaking, were induced to take them up, and invest them in new poetic garb, and give them a fresh spell of life.

Of these old heroic legends there are several distinct cycles, or groups, belonging to different branches of the German family.

The first of these is the Burgundian cycle, of Gunther the king, his wife Brunhild, his henchman Hagen, his sister Kriemhild, and his brother-in-law Siegfried. This forms the topic of the grand Niebelungen-Lied.

The second of these is the Frisian cycle, to which belong King Hettel and his daughter Gudrun ; and on their adventures turns the noble Gudrun-Lied.

The third of these is the Anglo-Saxon cycle, concerning Beowulf, the Jute king, and Wayland the Smith.   This was never recast after the 8th century.

The fourth of these is the Lombard cycle, concerning kings and heroes of South Tyrol, and the Rose Garden of Laurin the Dwarf, above Botzen. This was put into form in twelve poems, which com-

pose the Helden-Buch much later, in the 15th century.

The most famous of all these poems is the
Niebelungen-Lied, a grand epic in two parts, which
may take rank beside the Iliad. It is the greatest monument of German national poetry in the
Middle Ages.

Gunther was King of the Burgundians. He lived
at Worms. He had a beautiful sister called Kriemhild. Away in the North, at Xanten, on the Rhine,
lived a Netherland king, Siegmund, who had a
brave son called Siegfried. Siegfried had been
into the Niebelungen land, where he had slain a
dragon and carried off a vast treasure the dragon
guarded. He had, moreover, bathed in the dragon's
blood, which made him invulnerable, except at one
point between the shoulder-blades, where a linden
leaf rested whilst he bathed in the blood. He
heard of the beauty of Kriemhild and came to
Worms to see her. Now Gunther had heard that
in Iceland was a princess called Brunhild, who was
beautiful, and wealthy, and strong, and would not
marry any one who could not throw a spear, and
heave a stone, and jump farther than herself.
Gunther thought he would like to make her his
queen, so he persuaded Siegfried to accompany him
to Iceland, and help him to win her. Now, in the
treasure of the Niebelungen was a cap which made
the wearer invisible. So Siegfried put on this cap,
and stood behind Gunther and helped him to throw
the stone and hurl the spear and leap. Thus Brunhild was surpassed, and she consented to marry

Gunther, and she did not know how he had been assisted.

When Siegfried returned to Worms he was given Kriemhild to wife, and Gunther brought home his queen. One day when Brunhild and Kriemhild were going to church Brunhild wished, as queen, to enter the door first, but Kriemhild thrust her aside, and mockingly said that she should enter first, as her husband had helped Gunther to win Brunhild, and without his aid she never would have become queen. Brunhild was furious and meditated revenge.

Now, not long after this, a great hunt was to take place. Kriemhild was anxious about her dear husband ; she was afraid lest he should be wounded in the only vulnerable place. So she called Hagen, the henchman of Gunther, to her, and confided to him the secret, and made him promise in battle and in the chase to put his shield over Siegfried's back. She also marked a little red cross in his dress to show the place where alone he could be hurt.

Now Queen Brunhild egged on her husband to have Siegfried killed, and they took counsel with Hagen. So, when they were out hunting, and Siegfried, who was thirsty, stooped to drink at a fountain, Hagen ran him through with a spear where Kriemhild had marked his garment.

Then they took his body and laid it on the doorstep of Kriemhild's house, so that, next morning, when she came forth early, the first thing she saw was her dead husband, stark and cold.

After that she brooded on revenge. Hagen

feared what she might do, so he persuaded King
Gunther to let him carry away the Niebelungen
treasure and throw it into the Rhine, lest she
should use the wealth to stir up enemies against
the king.

After some years, Attila, or Etzel, King of the
Huns, asked for her hand, and she consented to
marry him. When she was Queen of the Huns she
got her husband to invite Gunther and Hagen to
visit him at Buda, on the Danube; and Gunther
accepted the invitation against the advice of
Hagen. When they arrived at Buda, and were
feasting in the palace, some armed men, at the instigation of Kriemhild, rushed upon the Burgundians and began to slay them. A furious contest
ensued, and when the Burgundians seemed to be
gaining the upper hand Kriemhild had fire put to
the banqueting hall and set it in a blaze. The
Burgundians fought their way out through the fire
and smoke, but were taken. Then Kriemhild sent
an executioner to Gunther and had his head struck
off, and she carried her brother's head to show it to
Hagen; then with Siegfried's sword she cut down
Hagen himself, whose hands were bound.

An old warrior, Hildebrand, enraged at her per-
fidy and cruelty, then smote her with his blade.
And so the story ends, amidst general massacre and
in volumes of flame.

XXIV.

HOW THE CITIES GAINED POWER.

As you have already heard, the cities had begun
to flourish during the crusades; they became busy
nurseries of art and learning, as well as of trade and
manufacture. By degrees they acquired great
privileges and power, and some were made by the
emperors "free cities," that is, they were under
no princes, but under the emperor only.

You will remember now that when Henry I. built
the castles for defence against the Hungarians the
noble families about were required to maintain
some of their men in the fortresses throughout the
year. In time these families became very domineer-
ing. The towns grew in size and importance, but
the families originally charged with the defence of
the *burg* remained the holders of power in it, and
managed the affairs of the town. When trades increased, each trade managed its own affairs by a
zünft, or guild, and the guilds combined against
the noble burgers to obtain some share in the management of affairs. After much rioting and fighting
they carried their point, and so the council was
formed of an Upper House of hereditary burgers,
who in the 15th century were called patricians,
and of a Lower House, to which members were

elected. If you go to Germany and walk through the aisles and cloisters of the great town churches you will see them crowded with splendid monuments, emblazoned with heraldic achievements. These are the tombs of the hereditary patricians, men who held themselves as proudly as the country aristocracy did in their castles.

The troubles occasioned by the interregnum, the interference with trade, the way in which the travellers were plundered, became insupportable, and in 1241 Hamburg and Lubeck agreed together to keep order in their neighborhoods. Then Brunswick and Bremen joined, and at last a hundred towns were leagued together, and formed so strong a body that the disturbers of the public peace were cowed into order. This league was called the Hansa. It maintained armies and fleets, and even carried on wars with the kings of Norway and Denmark, in which the Hansa was victorious. Its fleets swept the sea of pirates, and its troops taught the robber knights to cultivate peace.

PEASANT AND PLOUGH (13TH CENTURY).

XXV.

A GOOD KING FROM A SWISS CASTLE.

(1273–1292.)

AT last the condition of affairs became so intolerable that the German princes assembled to elect a new emperor, who might bring order out of the universal confusion. Their choice fell on Rudolph, Count of Hapsburg, a simple, courageous, and shrewd man. Hapsburg, or Habsburg, is a little castle near Königsfelden, in Switzerland. It was built in 1020 by Count Radbod of Altenburg, an ancestor of the family. The ruins still stand of this cradle of the Austrian imperial family, of which they were deprived by papal law one hundred and fifty years after Rudolph's elevation, and it has quite recently been restored to them, as a wedding gift, by the Canton of Aarau, on the marriage of Rudolph, the prince imperial, with a Belgian princess. From the broken tower the eye takes in at a single glance the whole original patrimony of the Hapsburgs,—an estate far more limited than that of many a British peer,—from which Rudolph was called to wield the sceptre of Charlemagne.

The first act of Rudolph was to march against Ottocar, King of Bohemia, who had gained posses-

RUDOLPH OF HAPSBURG.

sion of Austria, Styria, Carinthia, and Carniola. A great battle was fought in 1278 on the Marchfeld, near Vienna, in which Ottocar was defeated and killed. Rudolph then appropriated to himself the duchy of Austria, together with Styria and Carinthia, and they have remained ever since the patrimony of the Hapsburgs.

XXVI.

DID WILLIAM TELL SHOOT?

RUDOLPH'S son Albert was not acknowledged emperor till he had defeated his rival, Adolph of Nassau. Albert was the second son. The eldest had died early, leaving an infant son, John. Albert laid his grasp on the Hapsburg county in Switzerland, and refused to give it up to his nephew John.

Albert was a stern, cruel man, who had been embittered by his disappointment at not being recognized as emperor immediately on the death of his father. Albert was not content with depriving his nephew of his inheritance, he tried to unite Schwyz, Uri, and Unterwalden with his Swiss family possessions; but the simple Alpine shepherds claimed to be free under the imperial crown. Then Albert despatched governors to crush them into subjection. Among them was Gessler, appointed to rule Uri. He treated the people with great cruelty. At last the Swiss rose in revolt, and expelled the governors; Gessler was shot by William Tell. The story of Tell having been ordered to shoot an apple off his son's head is fabulous, but there really was such a man, and he got his name of Tell (Toll, Tölpel) from being half-witted. When Albert heard of the revolt he was filled with fury, and resolved on administering to the rebels a terrible chastisement. His revenge, however, was prevented by his own death.   He was journeying one day within sight of his castle of Hapsburg with his nephew John, whom he had deprived of it, and some Swabian knights, when he crossed the river Reuss, and was separated from his retinue.   John of Swabia, his nephew, and three others, all in the plot, were with him.   No sooner had he stepped out of the ferry-boat, than, at a word from John, one of the knights clove the emperor's skull with an axe.   The retainers on the further bank, terrified, took to flight, leaving their dying master to breathe his last in the arms of a poor peasant girl who happened to pass.

" A peasant girl that royal head upon her bosom laid,
  And, shrinking not for woman's dread, the face of death surveyed.
  Alone she sate.   From hill and wood, low sank the mournful sun;
  Fast gushed the fount of noble blood.   Treason his worst had done.
  With her long hair she vainly pressed the wounds, to staunch the tide,
  Unknown, on that meek humble breast, imperial Albert died."

A direful vengeance was wreaked by the children of the murdered monarch ; not, however, upon the murderers, for, with one exception, they had escaped, but upon their families, relations, and friends; and one thousand victims are believed to have expiated, with their lives, a crime of which they were totally innocent.   Agnes, Queen of Hungary, daughter of Albert, and heir to his gloomy, cruel spirit, is said to have presided at the executions.   When sixty-three unfortunate men were butchered before her, " Hah ! " she exclaimed, " now I bathe in May-dew ! "   Although this is asserted by most historians, yet we.

are glad to say that recent investigations by Swiss historians have completely disproved the part of Agnes in the tragedy, and we are rejoiced to think that such a stain does not rest on the character of the queen.

The Swiss remained resolute in their determination not to become serfs of the House of Hapsburg. Leopold of Austria, six years after his father's death, marched an army against them, but was completely defeated at Morgarten. Still more disastrous was the defeat of Leopold's grandson, Leopold III., at Sempach, in 1386. But it took another battle, nearly a hundred years later—that of Morat, in 1476—to prove to the world that the time of fighting in armour on horseback was over; that men on foot, lightly armed, were more than a match for knights clothed in steel. The weight of a charge of armoured men was great, but a knight, once dismounted and thrown down, lay like a log on the ground, unable to raise himself. Although the Swiss had proved their power to maintain their independence, it was not till the peace of Westphalia, in 1648, that Switzerland was finally and fully separated from the German Empire.

XXVII.

THE GOLDEN BULL.

(1347–1437.)

ON the death of Albert, the princes of Germany resolved again to commit the same blunder that they had made in electing Rudolph of Hapsburg, that is, to choose a petty noble and exalt him to be emperor. The little counts of Hapsburg had managed pretty well to enrich themselves, and make themselves very powerful. The choice fell now on Henry, Count of Luxemburg, a gallant knight, but that was all. He at once married his son John to Elizabeth, daughter and heiress of Wenceslas, King of Bohemia. The usual fatal attraction of Italy drew Henry VII. over the Alps. Brescia stood out against him, and his brother fell under the walls. Then Henry vowed he would cut off the noses of all the men in Brescia when he took the town; but plague broke out among his troops, whilst famine ravaged the besieged. Then a compromise was agreed to. Brescia would open her gates, and Henry would content himself with knocking off the noses of all the male statues in the city. Shortly after he was poisoned, whilst unsuccessfully besieging Siena. On his death, in 1313, discord broke out in Germany. One party elected Louis the Bavarian, the other chose Frederick of Austria, son of Albert I. Louis belonged to the Wittelsbach family, which had got the duchy of Bavaria after the expulsion of the Welfs. As neither would withdraw his claims, a long and tedious contest ensued, that

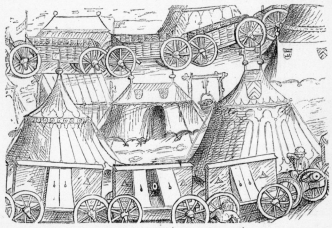

FORTIFIED CAMP (15TH CENTURY).
(From a contemporary Chronicle.)

lasted eight years, till at Mühldorf Frederick was defeated and taken and imprisoned. His imprisonment, however, did not bring peace, for his brothers continued the contest. Then Louis went to him in his prison, and Frederick promised that he would resign his pretensions, and, if he were unable to bring his brothers to agree to this, that he would return to prison. On these terms Louis set him free. At the instigation of the Pope, who dreaded the power of the Bavarian, Leopold, brother of

Frederick, refused submission to the compact. Thereupon Frederick honorably returned to captivity. Louis was touched by his integrity. He received him with affection and agreed to divide the realm with him. Thenceforth they reigned together, united with such cordial affection that they ate at the same table and slept in the same bed. Frederick died in 1330, and Louis in 1347. Then Charles IV., of Luxemburg, King of Bohemia, grandson of Henry VII., was elected. From him comes the socalled Golden Bull (1356). This takes its name from a golden seal (bulla) appended to the deed.

The Golden Bull was issued to determine who were to elect the emperors, and reduced the number of electors to seven—the archbishops of Mainz, Cologne, Trèves, and the temporal princes of Bohemia, Brandenburg, Saxony, and the Palatine of the Rhine—the King of Bohemia as butler, the Palatine as sewer, the Duke of Saxony as marshall, and the Margrave of Brandenburg as chamberlain. Frankfort was appointed as the place where elections were to take place, and Aix as the place where the emperors were to be crowned. Sometimes you may see in museums, sometimes in old curiosity-shops, metal plates of ancient German casting, with a circle in the middle, in which is seated a figure of the emperor, and round the rim seven medallions, in each of which is a figure representing an elector. The idea was, that as the sun was the centre of a system of seven planets, so should the German emperor, the sun of the earthly system, be the centre of a political planetary world, of which these seven electors were to be the

Septé electores eligüt henri cóite lutzilb i rege ro? fhlk. rcvij.

SEVEN ELECTORS CHOOSE FOR EMPEROR HENRY OF LUXEMBURG.

(From an illuminated Manuscript of Baldwin of Luxemburg.)

great luminaries. Charles hoped by this means to secure the imperial crown to his own family. He had already got the crown of Bohemia, and he was aiming to get hold of Brandenburg. He considered the Palatine of the Rhine easily managed. He was a shrewd man, and was the first to see the danger Italy was to the emperor, so he made no attempts to recover it for the empire, and he kept on good terms with the popes, who, thus relieved of anxiety for themselves, favored him. Charles did all in his power to aggrandize his family. He bribed the electors to choose his eldest son, Wenceslas, as his successor ; he married his second son, Sigismund, to Mary, daughter of the King of Hungary and Poland, in the expectation of succeeding to those countries. Wenceslas, who followed his father, was, if not a madman, as little suited as one to be emperor. He was addicted to drunkenness and sports. At one moment he jested, at another burst into insane fits of rage. The Germans thought him a fool ; the Bohemians regarded him as a maniac. As he coveted the possessions of the Bohemian nobles he invited them to meet him at Willamow, where he received them under a black tent that opened into two others, one white, the other red. The nobles were introduced one by one, and were required to cede their lands, and receive them back as fiefs of the crown. Those who consented were sent into the white tent, where they were well feasted ; those who refused were dragged into the red tent and put to death. He was surrounded by savage hounds, which accompanied him to the chase, and constantly attended him. Of these the two largest shared his bedroom. One night his wife, Queen Joanna, a Bavarian princess, rose from her bed, when one of

THE MARTYRDOM OF HUSS.
(From a wood-cut at Prague.)

the hounds sprang on her and so tore her that she died of the wounds.

At last his uncles and brother Sigismund, conscious of the ruin into which his crimes and folly were hurrying the family, seized him and imprisoned him in a castle in Austria.

His brother Sigismund succeeded him, a vain, arrogant, and deceitful man. Under him the great council of Constance was held, and the Hussite wars began.

Not only in the German Empire but throughout the whole Western Church the general disorder had affected religion; discipline was relaxed, and abuses had crept in. Moreover, there were at the same time three opposition popes, and some countries recognized one pope, some another, and others again the third. Accordingly, a council of the Church was summoned to assemble at Constance to put an end to these scandals. To restore unity to the Church the Council deposed all three popes and elected a new one, who took the title of Martin V. At this council appeared John Huss, a professor of the University of Prague, who had denounced the corruptions of the Church, and was bitterly opposed to the Church being endowed with temporal goods. This last ground embittered the bishops against him especially, and without a proper hearing, on the most frivolous charges—such as that he had maintained the existence of four gods—he was condemned and burnt. The flames of his pyre set Bohemia in conflagration. Huss had strongly opposed the withdrawal of the cup from the laity in communion. The cup was made the badge of the party of Huss, which was called after it Calixtine. The Bohemians armed, embroidered banners with a golden cup, met in tents, where they celebrated the communion and distributed it in both kinds. Ziska " with the 'Flail," a man with one eye, put himself at their head, entered Prague, and flung the burgomaster and the councillors out of the windows of the town-hall, on the pikes and pitchforks of his followers. Frightful confusion followed. A party,

JOHN, COUNT ZISKA, OF TROCZNOW.
(From an engraving.)

more extreme, separated from Ziska, and settled in an island of the Moldau. The one-eyed leader of the Hussites fell on them and cut them to pieces, with the exception of two. The strife which had begun about communion in two kinds soon became one of Bohemian against German, and the country ran with blood. The imperial army was defeated. Ziska, at the head of his Hussites, burst into Ger-

many, besieged towns, stormed castles, and butchered and burned without compunction. At Brod
he burned two hundred people in the church, and

SCENE FROM HUSSITE WARS.
(From a contemporary Chronicle.)

an unfortunate man, who was secretary to the chap-
ter at Prague, had his flesh torn off, and he was
then roasted in a tar barrel. Saxony was wasted by
the Hussites to the gates of Dresden.

The free imperial city of Altenburg fell into their hands. The citizens who were taken with arms were tortured to death. Men, women, and children were drawn into the blazing cathedral and burnt by hundreds. The sick and infirm were thrown into fires made in the streets. "This is John Huss's wake," said the Bohemians. "Oh!" exclaimed one of the sufferers, "the Catholics burnt one goose (Huss, in Bohemian, means a goose) and you are giving us the same."

The fairest regions of Germany, Bavaria, Franconia, as well as Saxony and Bohemia, were devastated, and the terror of the Calixtines surpassed that with which the Germans of old had regarded the Hungarian marauders. A splinter struck Ziska's remaining eye. Though blind, he still led his Hussites. On one occasion, having compelled his men to march day and night, they murmured, and said to him, "Although night and day be one to you, they are not so to us."

"How! you cannot see!" exclaimed Ziska, "set fire to the villages and walk by the blaze they give."

At last, in 1433, another council met at Basle, and at it communion in both kinds was granted to the Bohemians. Ziska was then dead. The country was worn out with war, and peace was proclaimed.

XXVIII.

A SLEEPY KING.

(1440–1493.)

THE Hapsburg or Austrian house succeeded that
of Luxemburg, having recovered the imperial crown
on the death of Sigismund, and thenceforth it remained in their family, almost exclusively, till the
dissolution of the German empire in 1806. Albert
II. reigned but one year. He was succeeded by
Frederick III. No emperor wore the crown so long
as he, and none cared less for its duties than he.
He often fell asleep whilst the most important
affairs of the state were being discussed, which
acquired for him the nick-name of "Emperor Nightcap." The robber-knights began again their dep-
redations, quarrelled with and fought each other,
as if there were no emperor above them to keep
order in Germany. Huge bands of robbers swept
the country, and Frederick bought them off. His
discontented citizens of Vienna besieged him in his
own palace. He had an adviser, Caspar Schlick,
whose only idea of policy was to patch up a compromise and put off settling difficult matters to a
future day. Indeed, one may say that Schlick's
doctrine was composed of two maxims, " Never do

ARTILLERY OF THE FIFTEENTH CENTURY.
(From Froissart's Chronicle.)

to-day what can be done to-morrow," and "Never do yourself what can be left to be done by another." This was just what suited Emperor Nightcap.

The peasants of the Rhœtian Alps asserted their independence, and formed a confederacy denominated the Grey-Band, from the grey frocks worn by the peasants, and this has given name to the canton of Grisons, or Graubünden. Their example was followed by Zurich and Schwyz. As the emperor was too lazy to take the field himself he invited a body of French mercenaries, called the Armagnacs, to invade Switzerland ; but though they killed fifteen thousand brave Swiss they lost so many of their own men that they retired dispirited.

On the south-east the Turks threatened Germany. They created havock in Hungary, and entered and devastated Austria ; but Frederick did nothing to repel them. He amused himself in his garden, picking caterpillars out of his roses and catching slugs with buttered cabbage leaves, and let the Turks destroy the villages and harvests of his people.

At last an Italian friar, S. John Capistran, put himself at the head of three thousand peasants, armed with flails and pitchforks, and fell on the Turkish host which was besieging Belgrade, when the town was hardly able to hold out another day. At the head of the peasants he routed the Turks and relieved the city.

The Hungarians gave themselves a valiant king, John Hunyadi, and his son Matthias ; and the

Bohemians placed themselves under the gallant George of Podjebrad. But this did not trouble Frederick ; the loss of two kingdoms was nothing to him.

His indolence so exasperated his wife Eleanor, that she said to her son, Maximilian, one day in a fit of impatience, "On my word, if I thought you would be like your father, I should be ashamed of being the mother of such a king!"

Fritz the Palatine also rebelled against the emperor, and built a tower to his castle at Heidelberg, which he named Flout Kaiser (Trutz Kaiser), as a mark of insolence to Frederick. The Margrave of Baden and the Duke of Wittemberg, however, marched against him, and, to devastate the harvests of the Palatinate more completely, tied branches of trees to their horses' tails as they rode among the wheat. The enraged peasants rose to a man and helped Fritz ; he beat the imperial army and took the duke and margrave prisoners. He gave them a sumptuous entertainment, but placed no bread on the table. The prisoner-guests asked to have a little bread with their meat. "Very sorry there is none," answered Fritz, " but you have spoiled all the corn, and so must do without."

Frederick was too lazy to put his hands to the doors, turn the handles, and open them. He went up to them with his hands in his pockets and kicked at the doors till some one came to open them, or he burst them in. He hurt his foot one day by so doing, and as mortification threatened, the surgeons cut off his foot. " Ah, me," said Frederick, "a healthy boor is better than a sick emperor."

Fortunately for Germany, his son Maximilian was the reverse of his father in everything. He was full of energy, intelligence, and with a noble heart.

For once a good idea came into the dull head of Frederick ; but perhaps it was not his idea, his wife may have thought of it. This was the idea, to get the sweet young princess, Mary of Burgundy, the only child of the duke, as wife for the gallant young prince. Maximilian was the handsomest man of his time ; he had bright, honest eyes, full of life, and long, fair, silky hair that fell over his shoulders. His nose was aquiline. If his face had a fault it was in the long lower lip, which he inherited from his father, and which is called the Hapsburg lip. You see it in the pictures of most of the princes and emperors of that house. Perhaps you have been so fortunate as to see Albert Dürer's engraved portrait of the Emperor Maximilian, or to have seen his figure in bronze on the great tomb he erected for himself at Innsbruck. These likenesses were taken when he was much older, but we can see from them what a royal and noble face he had. Also, Mary of Burgundy was very lovely. She was as good as she was beautiful. She was, moreover, heiress to all Burgundy and the Netherlands. The young Max went to Ghent to meet her. He rode into the town with a wreath of flowers over his long fair hair, with pearls twisted with the flowers, dressed in a suit of silver armour richly enamelled with gold, mounted on a fine bay horse. Mary

MAXIMILIAN AND BRIDE, MARY OF BURGUNDY
(From a Drawing in the Nuremberg Museum.)

came to meet him, on a white horse with silver trappings. When they met in the street of Ghent both dismounted, and whilst the bells of the town hall and the churches rang, and the people cheered and waved their caps, the beautiful young prince and princess met and kissed each other. They were married in 1477, when Max was only eighteen. Unfortunately, a very few years later, in 1482, poor Mary was hurt by a fall from her horse when hunting, and died of her injuries, in the bloom of life, but not till she had borne him a son, Philip, afterwards Philip I. of Spain.

The death of Mary was the signal for a revolt in the Netherlands. The Flemings refused submission to the Hapsburgs, and seized the person of the little Philip, whom they alone recognized as Mary's successor. A revolt broke out at Bruges, where Maximilian was taken prisoner by the citizens and shut up in the castle. His jester formed a scheme for his liberation; he provided horses for flight, and a rope-ladder, by which Max might descend from the window of his prison. Then the jester plunged into the canal which encircled the castle, to swim across. But the town kept swans in the moat, and when these swans saw the man swimming, they rushed at him with their great flapping wings and beaks, and so beat and pinched and frightened the poor fellow that he made the best of his retreat.

Max was kept a prisoner for four months, and was only set at liberty when he took a solemn oath not to chastise the citizens for having held him in bonds.

FREDERICK III.
(From the statue on his tomb at Vienna.)

XXIX.

BETWEEN THE OLD AND THE NEW.

(1493–1518.)

IF ever you get a chance of seeing Hans Burgkmair's "Triumph of Maximilian," look well and
patiently at the series of 135 wood-cuts. It represents the procession of the emperor after the
fashion of an old Roman imperial triumph, with
groups of figures depicting the different events of
his reign. This was the idea of Max himself, who
was filled with the old craze that he was the representative of the Cæsars, the head of the earthly
power, as the Pope was the head of the spiritual
power. Before you hear the history of the reign of
Maximilian you must be told something about
the set of pictures illustrative of his reign. Hans
Burgkmair was ordered to make a series of draw-
ings personifying the life, endeavours, and fame of
the emperor; glorifying his wars, conquests, and
alliances, and giving testimony to the splendours of
the Holy Roman empire, and the far extended
possessions of the House of Hapsburg. Burgkmair
began his work by making a series of miniature
paintings on parchment, to the number of 109.
Each of these was to be reproduced in two wood-

cuts, so that the work, when completed, would have made 218 plates. However, when the wood engraving was begun, the artist touched up and improved his designs, so that the engravings are not exactly like the miniatures. The latter are all preserved in Vienna. The work was begun in 1516, and was stopped forever by the death of the emperor in 1519. Only a few proof copies had been struck off when the wood blocks were dispersed, no one knows how or why. The few copies of the engravings were become very rare and fetched large prices, when some forty of the wood blocks were discovered in the castle of Ambras, near Innsbruck, and then ninety-six more were found in the Jesuit College at Gratz, in Styria. Thus 135 of the blocks have been recovered, but all search for the remainder has been in vain. In the year 1796 a few copies were printed from the original wood blocks, and may still be had, but at a high cost. One or two of the plates have, however, been reproduced of late years. Perhaps the most beautiful of the groups is that of the three standard-bearers, three knights in armour, bearing the banners of the Archduchy of Austria, a white fesse on a red field, of the Margraves with eagles, and of Styria with a panther. The faces of the knights are noble and beautiful, and we can get an idea from them of what good and generous knights were in those days. Another plate represents a princess on horseback, attended by ladies, and the bridle held by gentlemen with laurel wreaths round their heads. It is supposed that the princess is Mary of Burgundy, and, if so, we can understand how Max loved her, and all his life long thought of her. The figure is graceful, and the face simple and sweet. Her hair is done up in a silk net, or cap, over which is a golden crown, but little, light ringlets curl down from her brow on either side of her lovely face. She wears three gorgeous necklaces, very wide, made of plates of gold set with jewels, and so fitted as to set, one round the throat, the next over the bosom, and the third over the shoulders. She wears white linen sleeves gathered in twice between the shoulder and elbow. Her skirt is of the most superb silk and gold brocade, representing pomegranates in the leaf, and bursting fruit and flower. The caparison of the horse is of red velvet, embroidered with gold pomegranates, and over the saddle is cast a mantle of ermine. The gentlemen leading her white horse have magnificent chains round their necks, and ermine tippets, short cloaks, and tunics richly embroidered. They are both shown turning their heads and looking back and up at the lovely girlish face, as if that was the thing best worth seeing in the whole procession.

Maximilian married a second time Bianca Sforza, daughter of the Duke of Milan, but not till twelve years after the death of his dear Mary of Burgundy. He never really loved Bianca, who was a cold, hard woman, very proud, and without grace of mind or of disposition.

Maximilian stands as a boundary stone between the old and the new, between the mediæval and the modern times. He was brave and noble as a perfect knight, the pattern of chivalry, and he had an eager and active mind, a love of what is beautiful and what is good. He tried to improve what was bad and decaying, and he would have done more had the power been his to do so, but the empire was a magnificent sham. His father's weakness, the growing power of the vassals, the hostility of the popes had broken its strength, and he was hampered throughout his reign by his want of means to carry out those schemes which he planned for the good of the country. Even his enemies acknowledged his virtues and ability. Once when a courtier in the presence of Louis XI. of France sneered at the emperor, and called him "the Burgomaster of Augsburg," Louis, who was the bitter foe of Maximilian, answered, "You fool, to scoff at Max! Do you not know that when this burgomaster pulls the bell all Germany springs to arms, and France trembles?" In order to put an end to the incessant quarrels which went on between the little princes and nobles, in 1495, at a diet or parliament at Worms, the emperor made a law that no man should be suffered to redress his wrongs, real or imaginary, by violence; if he had a complaint against another, he must bring it before the imperial courts. In order to improve the administration of justice the empire was divided into ten districts, or circles,—Swabia, Bavaria, Franconia, the Upper Rhine, Westphalia, Lower Saxony, Austria, Burgundy, the Rhenish Electorate, and Upper Saxony. Maximilian wanted to organize and govern the empire through these divisions, but was so opposed that he was unable to carry out his idea.

Under him the post was first arranged. An Italian, Count de la Torre, was at his court, and he was entrusted with the organization of a postal system. This was gradually perfected, and was left under the control of the family which originated it, and which became princely, and was entitled Turn und Taxis. If you look through a collection of postal stamps you will see that the early German stamps bear the "Turn u. Taxis" and the arms of that family on them; and the family only lost the post-office in late times, bit by bit; the last control was taken from them in 1866.

To manage the post-office in the empire was no easy task, as all the little princes and petty states and free towns had to be brought to agreement. The roads had to be put in order, post-horses provided in relays along them, and the post-messengers had to be protected from robbers. As the empire comprised two thousand independent territories the Turn and Taxis family had enough to do. A great debt of gratitude is owed them by Germany, but the postal monopoly enriched them. They now possess large estates and several palaces from the profit of the post-office, which they held for three hundred years.

The great enemies of Germany at this time were the Turks, the French, and the Pope. The Turks were a constant menace, and the emperor was obliged to call the princes together separately, and entreat for men and money wherewith to oppose them. But they did not care ; they thought that it was a long way from Constantinople to West Germany, and there was all Hungary and Austria between. The French king was jealous of the emperor because he had got hold of Burgundy, so that Maximilian had foes on his east and west. Moreover, Italy was disturbed, and he had to enter that with a small army—he was unable to scrape together a large one. The French had overrun the North of Italy, and had carried off Ferdinand, King of Naples, in chains; but Maximilian could do nothing to oppose France.

The popes, moreover, were draining Germany of money, and they kept the empire weak by embroiling it with other kingdoms, and by stirring up discord within it.

Maximilian had the happiness to unite his son Philip to Joanna, the daughter of Ferdinand and Isabella of Spain, heiress of all Spain, and of the newly-discovered continent of America. Moreover, by agreement, the kingdoms of Hungary and Bohemia were re-united under the House of Hapsburg. Thus it did seem likely that the empire would fulfil its dream and become a world-wide sovereignty, embracing all Germany, the Netherlands, Burgundy, Italy, Spain, and America. This was flattering to the ambition of the emperor, who did not see that it was really sowing the seeds of ruin for the empire and for his own house. When a man has a small capital he can manage a small farm, but, if he is ambitious, and tries to secure three and even four farms in the hopes of prospering on

them, when he has not the means of properly culti-
vating them, it is pretty certain that he will soon be
bankrupt. Now this is precisely what the Hapsburgs were doing. Instead of contracting their
ambition within their means, and trying to farm
Germany well, they took on all these other farms,
which they could not supervise, and which drained
their money away, exhausted their energies, and
distracted their attention.

KING JOHN OF BOHEMIA.
(From his seal.)

XXX.

MEN BEGIN TO PRINT BOOKS.

BOOKS had hitherto been written with the hand,
and this made them very costly. They were written on parchment, on waxed tables, or on papyrus.
At last a German, at the beginning of the 14th century, discovered how to make paper out of linen
rags. If you hold paper sheets to the light you will
see that there are peculiar marks on them, called
water-marks; these were originally the badges of
the makers. The very earliest of these marks is a
circle with a cross on it, and was adopted by the
first inventor in 1301. Many of the water-marks
are the badges of noble families, whose tenants
made the paper. Thus the letters P and Y, sometimes separate and sometimes conjoined, are the
initials of Philip the Good, Duke of Burgundy, and
his wife, Isabella of Portugal. Other symbols are
the fleur-de-lys, the unicorn and the anchor.
Fools' cap paper is so called because paper of that
size was originally marked with a joker's cap and
bells, and *post* paper takes its name from a bugle
which was in use as a water-mark on paper of
this size by the manufacturers from 1370. It sometimes appears on a shield, and in the 17th century

is surmounted by a ducal coronet, in which form it is still used on ordinary writing paper.

The first paper factories in Germany were between Cologne and Mainz, about the year 1320. In Nuremberg a factory worked by water-power was established in 1390 which was quite a novelty.

Printing was discovered by John Gutenberg in 1436. Already wood-cut pictures, and even written sentences, had been printed, but no one had thought of making movable letters. At first the paper was pressed down on the engraved block, and printed on one side. The outlines only of figures were printed, and then they were painted in by hand. At last John Gensfleisch, of Sulgeloch, known as Gutenberg, which was the maiden name of his mother, saw how much better it would be to have movable types. As he was a poor man he went to a rich goldsmith, John Fust, of Mainz, and to Peter Schöffer, a professional copyist, of Gernsheim to get help. Schöffer drew and wrote beautifully, and he was to design the letters, and Fust was to find the money for casting them. They also invented printers' ink, and in 1457 issued the first printed book, the Latin psalter, and five years later the first printed Bible. Fust behaved very badly to the inventor. As soon as he had the secret, and saw that the experiments were likely to be successful, he asked Gutenberg to pay him back the money he had advanced him, and when he was unable to do this brought an action against him, and seized his printing-press and blocks. Poor Gutenberg was forced to leave Mainz, and then Fust and Schöffer finished printing the Bible without him. The rapidity with which copies were turned out of the press, the exact resemblance one bore to another, created astonishment and suspicion, so that it was reported that Fust was in league with the Devil, who helped him to multiply copies of the Bible. Thus came about the story of John Faust, who sold himself to the Devil for wealth, a story which was afterwards used by the greatest of German poets as the foundation of the greatest of German poems.

XXXI.

A GREAT STIR IN THE CHURCH.

ABOUT this time began that first crack or schism in the Church, which, after a little while, spread and separated a large part of Christendom from the Catholic Church. This large part that separated itself was called Protestant, whilst that part which remained was called Catholic. This schism arose because there was great cause of discontent with the conduct of the popes, and this discontent was well founded.

At last the Germans had come to see that the Pope was the enemy to their national unity. But the popes were only so because they dreaded the power of the emperors, who claimed to be kings of Naples and Sicily,—and so had a claw cutting into the popes from the South,—and also to be kings of Lombardy and Rome, and so drove a long sharp claw into their hearts over the Alps from the North. They did not want to be made the domestic chaplains of the emperors, so they worked against them with might and main; and as Germany was a very loosely compacted state, where every prince set up to be independent, and many of the bishops and some abbots were sovereign princes also, the popes were able to stir up confusion in Germany with the greatest ease. The archbishops and bishops had been made sovereigns by Charles the Great, in the hope that they would help the emperor against the other princes; but instead of that they were always ready at the call of the Pope to head opposition against the emperor. The archbishops of Cologne and Mainz, of Trèves and Salzburg, the bishops of Würzburg, Eichstädt, Münster, Paderborn, Bamberg, etc., the abbots of Fulda, Berchtesgaden, etc., were all independent sovereigns, owing very slight obedience to the emperor, and the empire was reduced to little more than a high-sounding name, without cohesion. The emperor was head of the state, but the members moved independently of the head. The condition had become intolerable. Law, order, everything was in confusion, and suddenly Germany woke to see its misery and resolve to bring it to an end, and, to begin, it determined to have done with the interference of the Pope, and to get rid of the archbishops and bishops and abbots who acted as his henchmen.

It happened at this time that the Pope was in want of money wherewith to build St. Peter's Church at Rome, which he desired to make the most magnificent cathedral in the world, as became the Mother Church of Christendom. He set about it by the sale of indulgences. These were farmed out to certain men, who went through Christendom disposing of them. In Germany appeared a Dominican friar, Tetzel by name, who sold them in great quantities, and was unscrupulous in the way in which he did it, trading on the ignorance and

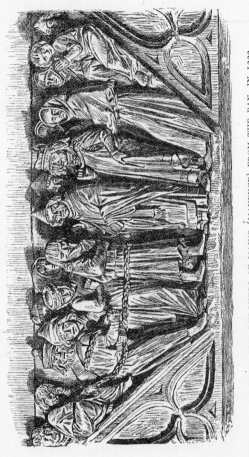

FREEING THE BURGHERS OF MAINZ (MAYENCE) FROM THE BAN, IN 1332.
(From a Bas-relief in the Mainz Cathedral.)

credulity of the people, to the great scandal of right-feeling men. You must understand what indulgences really were, because a great deal has been said about them which is not true. According to Catholic teaching, when a man does that which is wrong two results follow: he becomes guilty in the sight of God, and he incurs consequences to himself that are painful. For instance, if you were to become drunk, you would incur sin and suffering, the suffering being a headache. Now the Catholic Church taught that all sin entailed suffering, and that however much the guilt might be put away, the suffering remained to be gone through in this life or in the next. The Church taught that the *guilt* was expiated by true repentance, which is made up of three parts, contrition, confession, and amendment. But though a man might be restored to God's favor by repentance he was not let off the chastisement. The popes claimed the power of remitting the suffering consequent on sin, and indulgences were releases from these consequences; but they were only granted conditionally on true repentance, and this condition was always printed or written on them. Now it is easy to see what use unscrupulous men would make of these, and it was a startling thing to see the popes claiming to grant them.

A Wittenberg monk, named Martin Luther, wrote to the Archbishop of Mainz to complain of the harm done to ignorant people by the sale of indulgences, and then he fastened up to the door of the castle church at Wittenberg ninety-five theses, or reasons against indulgences, which he declared he was ready to maintain in disputation.

This was the beginning of the great strife which speedily involved all Western Christendom.

LUTHER.
(From a Miniature by Lucas von Cranach.)

But this was not all. Luther propounded a new doctrine, which was like a little packet of dynamite: wherever it was dropped it blew to pieces the whole structure of Catholicism. You will never really understand what the Reformation was unless you get hold of this.

Hitherto, the Catholic Church had taught that no

man could be *certain* of pardon for his sins, of being justified before God, and of eternal salvation. Everything was conditional. A man was pardoned his sins *if* he was truly sorry, *if* he confessed them, and *if* he did his utmost to make amends for the wrong done. Justification was the becoming perfectly good and pleasing to God, and man was to aim at this all through life, with hard struggle, helped by divine grace, and the sacraments were the means whereby divine help was given him to push on to perfection. So this, also, was conditional. Lastly, salvation was certain to none without final perseverance. Now, Martin Luther was a very eager, anxious-minded man, and he could not be happy unless he were quite certain of pardon, justification, and salvation. He suffered great distress of mind, through fear of falling short and losing heaven, knowing himself to be a man of violent passions. All at once a new idea struck him, which made all easy and secure. If a man *felt* that he was pardoned, justified, and saved, then the certainty was his. To this feeling of assurance that all was right he gave the name of faith, and called the change from a state of uncertainty to one of confidence,—justification by faith. No more conditions were required, no more chance of fall remained. This doctrine made immense way; it was seized with eagerness. Of course it did away, inevitably, with sacraments and with the priesthood, for help is no more needed by those who are secure; but Luther did not follow this to its legitimate conclusion. If sacraments and priests were no more needed then bishops were also unnecessary; and here the very thing was found which would enable the Germans to get rid of the bishops. That the bishops were of any good might well be doubted in Germany, where they lived in royal state, and neglected their spiritual duties or devolved them on others. If ever you go up the Rhine, look into the Cathedral of Mainz. There, along the red sandstone pillars, you will see the monuments of the dead archbishops. They are represented on them clothed in armour, with spurs on their heels, holding a sword in one hand and a shepherd's crook in the other. On their heads they wear mitres surrounded by crowns. These tombstones give you an idea of what the archbishops were, in reality: secular princes, at home on horseback, clad in mail, and with only so much of the religious character about them that they bore the title and wore the insignia of spiritual princes. Now the Germans, knowing bishops such as these, only said with reason, What a farce this is! These men are not pastors over their flocks, they are kings masquerading as bishops. Away with them! We have too many sovereigns already in Germany!

XXXII.

WALLED CITIES AND THEIR IMPORTANCE.

It was only about the beginning of the 15th century that the cities of Germany rose to great importance, and became remarkable for their stately
buildings, for their wealth and influence.

They were all enclosed within walls, with a moat
surrounding the walls. At intervals in the ring
were towers of various shapes. Indeed, the fancy
was indulged of making all different, so as to add to
the beauty of the appearance of the town. Very
few of the great German towns remain walled in
with their towers, but some have these ornaments
intact. Ratisbon had fifteen towers, variously
capped, making the distant view of the city a vision
of beauty. All have been pulled down but one.

At the beginning of the 13th century the houses
were all built of wood and plaster, and thatched
with straw. But such fires ensued, consuming large
parts of the towns, that the inhabitants were driven
to build of better material, and to use tile or slate
instead of thatch. Nevertheless, a good many old
timber and plaster houses remain. Indeed, even the
castles were only partly built of stone; they were to
a large extent composed of buildings of more per-
ishable material. A little way up a tributary of the

Moselle is an old castle, Schloss Elz. It is one of the few castles that has escaped being destroyed. It has its tower of stone and walls of stone, but the principal buildings for the inmates, hall of banquet

A GERMAN CITY IN 15TH CENTURY.
(From a Pencil Sketch in the Library at Erlangen).

and bedrooms, are of black timber with plaster fill-ings.

At first, in the towns, only the churches and town-halls and other public buildings were of stone, but in the beginning of the 15th century the patricians—

that is, the ruling families and merchants, who were very wealthy—began to build themselves handsome stone houses. Even in such an important place as Frankfort-on-the-Main nearly all the houses, down to the end of the 14th century, were of combustible materials, and were without chimneys, the smoke escaping through a hole in the roof. The streets of Paris were paved in 1185, but though some attempts at paving were made in Germany in the 13th and 14th centuries, it was not till later that they were systematically paved. Passengers picked their way in the mud as best they might. In the life of S. Elizabeth, the Landgravine of Hungary, we read of how, as she was thus trying to get along a street in Eisenach, a rude woman pushed her off the stepping-stone on which she had lighted, and she fell down into the black slough and was splashed from head to foot.

There were not many windows filled with glass before the 15th century. Even at Zurich, where the town-hall was built in 1402, the windows were filled with oiled linen strained to frames. In Zurich the first fountain was erected in 1430, and this is about the date of most of the fountains that decorate so many of the German towns. The houses in the towns were very different in plan from old English houses. Let me tell you what I saw one summer's day at Villingen, in the Black Forest. This is a walled town, the walls nearly perfect, with all the towers standing, but with the water let out of the moat, which is turned into gardens. When I visited the place it was at the time of hay harvest, and wains laden with hay were coming into the town. The old houses have very steep roofs, and the gables are towards the street, with a large door in the attic, and a crane over it. The chain from this contrivance was run down and the bundles of hay were raised and piled up in the garret of the house, which served as a great hay store. Later, the corn would be brought in, and the flax, and stored away in the same place. The roof of the house formed the barn. Then the cows and horses were driven into the ground floor rooms—they were really stables, vaulted with stone, and to enter the house where the people lived one had to ascend steps. As the citizens of a small town were landowners and farmers they thus made their houses compact farm dwellings. That was how they managed in small towns. In large cities they used the roof for stores of merchandise and the basement for shops. When you ascend the stairs you find in these old houses that there is a great deal of room given up to passage, and that this passage is paved, and sometimes vaulted. It served as a place for the children to play in wet weather, and meals were also taken in it when the company was large. These corridors are called *Lauben*. The rooms open out of these corridors and are comparatively small. In old times, before fire-engines were invented, the only way by which fires could be extinguished was with pails. The first fire brigade was established at Frankfort in 1439, and the first fire-engine used at Augsburg in 1518.

We have many accounts from the 15th century

of the social and architectural condition of the
German towns. Nuremberg especially was regarded
as the ideal of a beautiful mediæval town, and to the
present day, with its stepped gables, solar windows,
corner turrets, and rich sculpture, it retains more
of its mediæval character than any other town.
Italians, however, declared that a more beautiful
city than Cologne could not be found, a verdict we
in the present day would be far from endorsing. It
is now a collection of hideous and vulgar houses
surrounding many preciously beautiful churches.
The illustrious Frenchman, Montaigne, declared
that Augsburg was more lovely than Paris. Æneas
Silvius Piccolomini (afterwards Pope Pius II.) could
not find terms in which to praise the wealth and
splendour of the German cities. There is some exag-
geration when he says, "Where is a German inn at
which silver plate is not used? What citizen woman
—not necessarily noble—does not adorn herself with
gold ornaments?" Of Vienna he says: "The town
lies in a crescent on the Danube; the city wall is
5000 paces long and has double fortifications. The
town proper lies like a palace in the centre of the
suburbs, several of which rival it in beauty and size.
Nearly every house has something to show, something remarkable in or about it. Each dwelling
has its back court and front court, large halls and
smaller, good winter apartments. The guest-rooms
are beautifully panelled, richly furnished, and
warmed with stoves. All windows are glazed;
some have painted glass, and have iron-work guards
against thieves. On the basement are large cellars

and vaults, which are devoted to apothecaries, ware-houses, shops, and lodgings for strangers. In the halls many tame birds are kept, so that in passing through the streets one hears the sounds of a green pleasant forest. The market places and streets teem with life. Without reckoning the children and those under age there are 50,000 inhabitants and 7000 students. Enormous is the commerce of traders, and enormous the sums of money here earned and spent. The whole district round Vienna is like one vast and beautiful garden covered with grapes and apples, and studded with the most charming country houses."

There is, however, another side to the picture. Æneas Silvius says : " By night and by day there is fighting in the streets. Sometimes the artisans are assailing the students, sometimes the court people are quarrelling with the citizens, and sometimes it is citizen who has sword drawn against citizen. A festival rarely concludes without bloodshed."

You have heard how poetry and romance flourished with the nobles. The citizens did not cultivate these arts, they were too practical; but they produced chronicles, and some of them were in verse. For instance, Gottfried Hagen, of Cologne, wrote a rhymed history of his city between 1250–1270. Many of the large towns of Germany produced their chroniclers, and it is needless to say of what importance their writings are to the historian.

But if the cities did not cultivate poetry they nursed music. They all had their master-singer guilds, and on Sunday afternoons the performers sang in the town-hall or the churches. Prizes were given for the best compositions. The highest prize was a representation of King David playing on the harp, stamped on a gold slate. The others consisted of wreaths of filigree wire of gold or silver. This performance was called "school singing." The last performance at Nuremberg was in 1770, and the very last of all at Ulm in 1839.

XXXIII.

HIGH GERMAN AND LOW.

GERMANY is not divided by great rivers. It has, indeed, two main arteries, the Rhine and the Danube, the former flowing north, then west into the German Ocean, the latter flowing east into the Black Sea. The Rhine is a great main artery of trade, and always has been since Germany was civilized, from Mannheim to the mouth. Above Mannheim the river is too rapid and too full of shifting rubble-beds to be safely navigated. The Danube is only navigable below Linz. Above, it rushes at a pace so headlong that boats can be drawn against the stream only with infinite labour. If you travel up or down the Rhine you pass numerous villages and towns; but the Danube, between Passau and Linz, runs between great wooded hills, where scarce a village spire, hardly a castle is to be seen. The Danube and the Rhine, though their sources are not so very far apart, and though the violence of their streams is considerable, were not connecting links of trade. Trade passed along roads rather than rivers, and the difficulty of navigation in the higher courses of the two great rivers did not tend to bring the peoples seated about them into commercial, social, and political unity.

Germany is physically divided into two great sections, *determined by elevation.* If you had a raised map of Germany, marking the hills and plains, you would see that all the North of the country is one vast flat, and that the South is elevated. To the south are numerous chains of mountains, or rather hills, and between these chains are elevated plateaus. The hill country of Germany is richer than the plain country. The latter is mostly sandy, pebbly, boggy land. Moreover, the South is more blessed with a bright sky. All over the flat North land fogs from the cold Baltic Sea roll and form a grey canopy. The dreary plain, the dull sky, the ungrateful soil have combined to make the North German less cheerful than the German of the South. Moreover, the conquering Saxons of the Northern plains found them peopled by plodding, sad, Sclavonic races. There is a certain difference in characteristic, therefore, between the German of the high land and the German of the low land. Moreover, there is a difference in dialect. The low land German is called Platt-Deutsch,—that is, flat or Low-Dutch,—and the high land German is called Hoch-Deutsch, or High-Dutch. Dutch is Deutsch, that is, German. We call the inhabitants of Holland *Dutch*, but they belong only to the Low German race, and have no proper exclusive claim to that designation.

In mediæval times the literature was both high and low, according as the author of a book was a High German or a Low German ; but now-a-days the literary and spoken language of the nation is

High German. This came about, to a great extent,
through Luther's having been a High German, and
having translated the Bible into High German.
There were earlier translations of the Bible than
that of Luther. For instance, there was one by a
monk of Halle, Martin Von Beheim, a very good
translation, which no doubt formed the ground-work
of Luther's more modern version. But the Reformation caused the Bible to be much more read
than previously, and its language became familiar in
every household in Protestant Germany; and this
gave an immense advantage to High German.
Moreover, at the period when German literature
was taking its definite and final cast, the greatest
writers issued from South Germany, so that now
High German is alone recognized as the literary
language.

In England there are many dialects, but no single dialect has, in like manner, imposed on the rest
and become the literary tongue. The court and
aristocracy in England have, ever since the court
was Norman, had their own peculiar dialect. The
dialect of English culture, and the literary language
of the English people, is the language of the upper
class of society; whereas, in Germany, it is the language of the upper elevation of the soil which has
mastered all classes, and made court and aristocracy submit to speak and read in it as the sole dialect which is allowed to be regarded as literary.

XXXIV.

A MIGHTY EMPEROR.

(1519–1555.)

CHARLES V., the grandson of Maximilian I., was the mightiest of the emperors since Charles the Great. He reigned over more lands than any other prince in Christendom. He was King of Spain, Naples, Sicily, Austria, Hungary, Bohemia, and the Netherlands. In the New World the colonies there established looked to him as their sovereign, so that it may be said that his empire was one on which the sun never set. Yet his career was not a happy one. His life was spent in fighting the King of France, and the Pope, and the Protestant princes of Germany. He was not fond of splendour; he had not the beauty of Maximilian, but he was a fine man, with dignity in his bearing. He had the long lower lip and underhung jaw of the Hapsburgs. His character was cold, and his demeanour grave. He had a ready insight into men's characters, and, as Prescott says, "to the end of his reign he employed no general in the field, no minister in the cabinet, no ambassador to a foreign court, no governor of a province whose abilities were inadequate to the trust which he imposed on them. He placed un-

PROXIMVS·A·SVMMO·FERDNANDVS·CAESARE·CARLO
REX·ROMANORVM·SIC·TVLIT·ORA·GENAS
AET·SVAE·XXIX
ANN·M·D·XXXI

FERDINAND I.
(From an Engraving by Beham.)

bounded confidence in his generals; he rewarded their services with munificence; he never envied their fame, nor discovered any jealousy of their power. There were, nevertheless, defects in his political character which must considerably abate the admiration due to his extraordinary talents. Charles' ambition was insatiable, and his desire of being distinguished as a conqueror involved him in continual wars, which not only exhausted and oppressed his subjects, but left him little leisure for giving attention to the interior government and improvement of his kingdoms, the great objects of every prince who makes the happiness of his people the end of his government." On the death of Maximilian the Austrian territories fell to Charles and his brother Ferdinand conjointly; but as Charles was occupied in Spain, in 1521 he ceded to his brother Austria, Styria, Carinthia, Carniola, and in the ensuing year Tyrol. By this cession the House of Austria was divided into two separate branches —the Spanish branch, under Charles; and the German, under Ferdinand.

In the mean time the split in the Church was widening. Pope Leo X., in 1520, issued a bull—that is, a deed—whereby he excommunicated Luther, or cut him off from communion with the Catholic Church as a heretic; and all Christian princes and states were warned against his doctrine, and exhorted to arrest him and put a stop to his teaching.

One December morning, in the same year, Luther made a pile of wood outside the eastern gate of Wittenberg and burnt on it publicly the Pope's bull.

MELANCTHON.
(From a painting by Durer.)

Next day he mounted the pulpit and said, "The burning of yesterday was a matter of little importance; better were it had the fire consumed the Pope, or rather the See of Rome."

To put a term to the agitation of spirits Charles V. called together a diet, or assembly of the states, at Worms. It met on January 6, 1521. Luther was cited to appear at it, and the states prepared a long list of grievances against the Papacy, which they required the emperor to redress.

Luther's journey to Worms was like a triumphal procession. Crowds assembled to see and cheer him; on his arrival at Worms his apartments were thronged by persons of the highest rank.

When he appeared before the diet he absolutely refused to recant his opinions. Charles found that many of the princes, notably the electors of Saxony and of the Rhenish Palatinate, favored him. He was compelled to wait till the latter had withdrawn from the diet before he could pass an edict against Luther, placing him under the ban of the empire. As Charles had given him a promise of safe-conduct he was dismissed unmolested, with an imperial guard to protect him. As soon as Luther had sent back the officer, he was taken charge of by some masked horsemen, sent by his friend and supporter, the Elector of Saxony, who carried him to the castle of Wartburg, where he remained nine months in concealment.

Whilst there, a disciple of his, called Carlstadt, headed a mob of people and broke into the churches of Wittenberg, where they tore down the altars and destroyed the crucifixes and statues. This was going much further than Luther approved, so he left his place of hiding and suddenly appeared at Wittenberg to stop the disorder.

The princes now began to lay their hands on the church property. They turned out the monks and nuns and seized on their lands. They carried off the gold and silver vessels from the churches and melted them into coin to relieve their own necessities. The Margrave of Brandenburg was Grand Master of the Teutonic Knights. This was an order of warrior-churchmen, which had been instituted to hold the frontier against the heathen Sclavs. They had conquered Prussia, and ruled it like princes. The margrave took advantage of his position to make himself sovereign over Prussia, and annex the possessions of the order to his family.

After the holding of the diet of Worms Charles had gone back to Spain, and in his absence there was no one to enforce the edict against Luther. Indeed, Luther had far too many protectors for the emperor to have enforced it, had he been in Germany in person.

XXXV.

HOW THE PEASANTS WAKED UP.

(1524–1526.)

THE peasants were influenced by the new ideas, and as they suffered under grievous wrongs they rose in revolt over the whole of Germany. The entire burden of taxation fell on them. You may see in farmhouses in Germany a curious picture, which represents a triangle of steps, resting on the back of a farmer who ploughs. At the top of the pyramid sits the emperor, and from his mouth proceeds the sentence, "All there sustain me." On a step below is a soldier, saying, "I am paid to fight"; on another, a lawyer, saying, "I plunder all alike"; on another, a parson, with the legend, "I live on the tithe"; on another, the noble, saying, "I pay no taxes"; and below, the peasant groans, "All these are sustained by me." So it was. The gentleman paid no taxes. All the burden was on the farmer, or peasant—the German term is *bauer*. When the Reformation began to make way in Germany the peasants came out in swarms, armed with pitchforks, scythes, and flails, with the double intention of abolishing Catholicism and the feudal system. This latter was turned into a system of cruel oppression. The bauers were mulcted of their time, their produce, and their money, and were treated little better than slaves.* Their wrongs were very real and very grievous.

The first outbreak of the peasants arose out of a very small matter. The Countess of Lupfen ordered the peasants on her estates to spend the Sundays in summer in gathering strawberries for her table, and snail-shells for making ornamental pin-cushions. They refused to do so, and in a few days the country round was in arms. In a short time the insurrection extended through the South and East of Germany; it spread along the Main, the Rhine, the Danube. The peasants of the Odenwald rose to a man. Franconia was in a blaze, the Grand Master of the Teutonic Order was driven from his domains. Towns were threatened, and threw open their gates. The Palatinate was in insurrection ; so were Hesse and Thuringia. The mountaineers of Styria, of the Tyrol, of Salzburg were in arms. Austria was in commotion. The peasants of Bavaria alone remained unstirred. The insurgent farmers called themselves "the Christian Army," or "the Gospel Brotherhood." They burned the castles and monasteries, and plundered the churches. You will see everywhere in Germany, especially in the South, ruined castles, and if you ask when they were ruined, you will receive

---

* Instead of paying rents in money for their farms, they mostly paid by supplying farm produce, and giving free labor to their landlords.

the almost invariable answer, "In the Peasants' War."

You shall hear of the taking of one little town by the peasants, the town of Weinsberg, as an example of the scenes which were enacted through the land. Weinsberg was under the command of the Count of Helfenstein, who had married a daughter of the Emperor Maximilian.

On Easter morning, 1525, a black wave of peasants appeared rolling down the hill sides upon the town, and speedily surrounded it. They were under the command of two men, Florian Geyer and Little Jack (Jäcklein Rohsbacker). As their standard, they carried a pole with a shoe on top of it. Before the host hovered a black-draped hag, screaming her incantations, to make the rebels invulnerable. This was the "Black Hoffmann," a witch possessing great influence over the minds of the peasants. When they surrounded the walls they summoned the place to surrender. "Open your gates," they shouted, "or you shall all be put to the edge of the sword. Every person and thing will be burnt or killed." A shower of bullets was the reply. Soon, however, the peasants swarmed over the walls, and the count and the soldiers retired to the castle, whilst the citizens fled to the church. They were unable to hold out. The garrison offered to surrender if their lives were spared, and promised to pay a ransom. "A ton of gold would not suffice," was the answer, "we want your flesh." The soldiers were butchered. One was ordered to jump from the top of

the tower on the lances and pitchforks below.
"I would rather jump up than jump down," he
answered.   This elicited a roar of laughter and his

THREE PEASANTS, 16TH CENTURY.   (DURER.)

life was spared.   The insurgents stood in two rows,
armed with scythes, swords, and pitchforks, forming
a lane, and the prisoners were ordered to run down
this lane, to be hacked to pieces by the weapons.
"Count Louis of Helfenstein," said Little Jack,

"you shall open the dance." At that moment the countess, with her babe in her arms, burst through the crowd and flung herself at the feet of the captain, imploring pardon for her husband. "Friends," shouted Little Jack, "look at me, how I treat the daughter of an emperor." He threw her down and knelt on her breast. Then a peasant, standing by, threw his sword at her, and wounded the babe, whose blood spirted over its mother's face. Then Little Jack ordered the men to raise and hold up the countess, and force her to see the murder of her husband. He also commanded a fiddler to strike up a dance tune and go before the count, capering down the lane. Count Helfenstein had not gone far before he fell; then the Black Hoffmann, the witch, rushed after him, and literally tore him to pieces with her hands. Then a cart was heaped with dung, and the poor countess, hugging her bleeding babe, was mounted on it, and so driven away, among the jeers and yells of the insurgents.

The peasants, finding that the princes were arming against them, gave the command of their host to a notorious robber-knight, Goetz with the Iron Hand; but the host was quite undisciplined, and when they had plundered a castle or a town, or an abbey, hastened home with their booty. The Truchsess (steward) of Waldburg marched at the head of an army against the rebels and succeeded in defeating them. Other princes also met them and routed them, and at last the insurrection was put down; but it was subdued with great and unnecessary severity. The poor peasants had been driven to rebellion by their wrongs, and the only idea their victors had was to re-rivet the chains they had struggled to cast off. Even Luther wrote a pamphlet against them, calling on the princes "to strangle and stab them, as a man would treat a mad dog."

LUTHER AND MELANCTHON.
(From a painting by Cranach.)

XXXVI.

THE SAD FATE OF BERNARD KNIPPERDOLLING.

(1524–1536.)

I MUST now tell you of an extraordinary event that took place in Westphalia. There is a grand opera by Meyerbeer, "The Prophet," founded upon it, the overture and the grand march in which you are sure to know, as they are favorite instrumental concerted pieces. Meyerbeer has not stuck to historical truth in his opera; what the real facts were you shall now be told.

Münster is a town in Westphalia, the seat of a bishop, walled round, with a noble cathedral and many churches; but there is one peculiarity about Münster that distinguishes it from all other old German towns; it has not one old church spire in it. Once it had a great many. How comes it that it now has none?

In Münster lived a draper, Knipperdolling by name, who was much excited over the doctrines of Luther, and he gathered many people in his house, and spoke to them bitter words against the Pope, the bishops, and the clergy. The bishop at this time was Francis of Waldeck, a man much inclined himself to Lutheranism: indeed, later, he proposed

to suppress Catholicism in the diocese, as he wanted
to seize on it and appropriate it as a possession to
his family. Moreover, in 1544, he joined the Protestant princes in a league against the Catholics; but
he did not want things to move too fast, lest he

SCHOOL-ROOM IN 16TH CENTURY.
(From a wood-cut by Hans Leonard Schauffelin.)

should not be able to secure the wealthy See as
personal property.

Knipperdolling got a young priest, named Rottmann, to preach in one of the churches against the
errors of Catholicism, and he was a man of such
fiery eloquence that he stirred up a mob, which
rushed through the town, wrecking the churches.
The mob became daily more daring and threatening.
They drove the priests out of the town, and some of
the wealthy citizens fled, not knowing what would
follow. The bishop would have yielded to all the

religious innovations if the rioters had not threatened his temporal position and revenue. In 1532 the pastor, Rottmann, began to preach against the baptism of infants. Luther wrote to him remonstrating, but in vain. The bishop was not in the town; he was at Minden, of which See he was bishop as well.

Finding that the town was in the hands of Knipperdolling and Rottmann, who were confiscating the goods of the churches, and excluding those who would not agree with their opinions, the bishop advanced to the place at the head of some soldiers. Münster closed its gates against him. Negotiations were entered into; the Landgrave of Hesse was called in as pacificator, and articles of agreement were drawn up and signed. Some of the churches were given up to the Lutherans, but the cathedral was reserved for the Catholics, and the Lutherans were forbidden to molest the latter, and disturb their religious services.

The news of the conversion of the city of Münster to the Gospel spread, and strangers came to it from all parts. Among these was a tailor of Leyden, called John Bockelson. Rottmann now threw up his Lutheranism and proclaimed himself opposed to many of the doctrines which Luther still retained. Amongst other things he rejected was infant baptism. This created a split among the reformed in Münster, and the disorders broke out afresh. The mob now fell on the cathedral and drove the Catholics from it, and would not permit them to worship in it. They also invaded the Lutheran churches,

and filled them with uproar. On the evening of
January 28, 1534, the Anabaptists stretched chains
across the streets, assembled in armed bands, closed
the gates and placed sentinels in all directions.
When day dawned there appeared suddenly two
men dressed like Prophets, with long, ragged beards
and flowing mantles, staff in hand, who paced
through the streets solemnly in the midst of the
crowd, who bowed before them and saluted them as
Enoch and Elias. These men were John Bockelson,
the tailor, and one John Mattheson, head of the Anabaptists of Holland. Knipperdolling at once asso-
ciated himself with them, and shortly the place
was a scene of the wildest ecstacies. Men and
women ran about the streets screaming and leap-
ing, and crying out that they saw visions of angels
with swords drawn urging them on to the extermi-
nation of Lutherans and Catholics alike. Many
Lutherans and Catholics, frightened, fearing a general massacre, fled the town. Mattheson mounted a
pulpit, and cried out that Heaven demanded the
purification of Zion, and that all who did not hold
the right faith should be put to the sword. This
would have been carried into effect but for the in-
tervention of Knipperdolling, who persuaded the
rabble not to kill, but to expel those who refused
to be re-baptized. Accordingly, a great number of
citizens were driven out, on a bitter day, when the
land was covered with snow. Those who lagged
were beaten; those who were sick were carried to
the market-place and re-baptized by Rottmann.
"Never," says a witness, "did I see anything

more afflicting. The women carried their naked babes in their arms, and in vain sought rags wherewith to cover them; miserable children ran barefooted, hanging to their father's coats, uttering piercing cries; old people, bent with age, and sick women, tottered and fell in the snow."

This was too much to be borne. The bishop raised an army and marched against the city. Thus began a siege which was to last sixteen months, during which a multitude of untrained fanatics, commanded by a Dutch tailor, held out against a numerous and well-armed force.

Thenceforth the city was ruled by divine revelations, or rather, by the crazes of the diseased brains of the prophets. One day they declared that all the officers and magistrates were to be turned out of their offices, and men nominated by themselves were to take their places; another day Mattheson said it was revealed to him that every book in the town except the Bible was to be destroyed; accordingly all the archives and libraries were collected in the market-place and burnt. Then it was revealed to him that all the spires were to be pulled down; so the church towers were reduced to stumps, from which the enemy could be watched and whence cannon could play on them. One day he declared he had been ordered by Heaven to go forth, with promise of victory, against the besiegers. He dashed forth at the head of a large band, but was surrounded and he and his band slain.

The death of Mattheson struck dismay into the hearts of the Anabaptists, but John Bockelson took

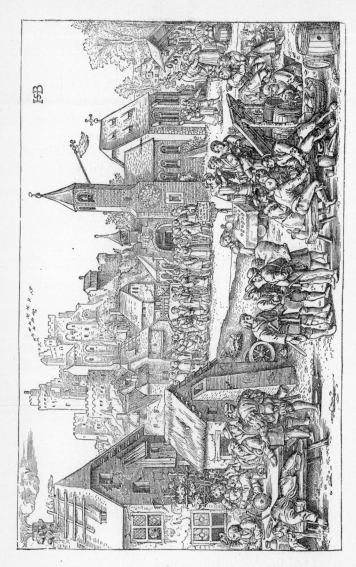

CONSECRATION OF A CHURCH, 1530.

(From a wood-cut by Beham.)

advantage of the moment to establish himself as head. He declared that it was revealed to him that Mattheson had been killed because he had disobeyed the heavenly command, which was to go forth with few. Instead of that he had gone with many. Bockelson said he had been ordered in vision to marry Mattheson's widow and assume his place. It was further revealed to him that Münster was to be the heavenly Zion, the capital of the earth, and he was to be king over it. Then he ordered all the people in the place to bring him every article of value they possessed, gold and silver and jewelry; also all provisions they had, and he arranged that all meals should be taken in common. Then he had another revelation that every man was to have as many wives as he liked, and he gave himself sixteen wives. This was too outrageous for some to endure, and a plot was formed against him by a blacksmith and about two hundred of the more respectable citizens, but it was frustrated, and led to the seizure of the conspirators and the execution of a number of them. Twenty-five were shot and sixty-six were decapitated by Knipperdolling, whom John Bockelson had constituted his executioner. With the death of these men disappeared every attempt at resistance. It may be asked how it was that there were still so many people in the place. The reason was that before it was invested Anabaptists had swarmed into it from Holland and the North of Germany, thinking it was a favoured city of Heaven.

Next, Bockelson created twelve dukes, to whom

WOMAN'S COSTUME. 16TH CENTURY.
(From a painting by Holbein.)

he gave titles to as many parts of Germany. They were all tailors, shoemakers, coopers, and bakers. He also appointed twenty-seven apostles to go through Europe, converting people and calling on them to come to Zion.

In the market-place a pulpit and a throne were erected, and thrice in the week Bockelson administered justice from the throne, clad in royal apparel, surrounded by his dukes and pages gorgeously dressed. When the court was over a sermon was preached from the pulpit, and when that was concluded, the king, his sixteen queens, the preacher, and the court danced to the strains of the royal band.

One of his wives, disgusted with the profanity and her degradation, entreated leave to depart from the town. King John cut off her head with his own sword before all the people. One of the bishop's soldiers, having been taken prisoner, was urged to embrace the doctrines of the Anabaptists. He had the audacity to reply that whatever their doctrines might be their practice was devilish; whereupon King John, foaming with rage, hacked off his head with his own hand.

At last, on midsummer eve, 1536, after a siege of sixteen months, the city was taken. Several of the citizens, unable longer to endure the tyranny, cruelty, and abominations committed by the king, helped the soldiers of the prince-bishop to climb the walls, open the gates, and surprise the city. A desperate hand-to-hand fight ensued; the streets ran with blood. John Bockelson, instead of leading his people, hid himself, but was caught.   So was Knipperdolling.

When the place was in his hands the prince-bishop entered.   John of Leyden and Knipperdol-ling were cruelly tortured, their flesh plucked off with red-hot pincers, and then a dagger was thrust into their hearts.   Finally, their bodies were hung in iron cages to the tower of a church in Münster.

Thus ended this hideous drama, which produced an indescribable effect throughout Germany.   Mün-ster, after this, in spite of the desire of the prince-bishop to establish Lutheranism, reverted to Ca-tholicism, and remains Catholic to this day.

XXXVII.

HOW THE PROTESTANTS PROTESTED.

(1530–1547.)

THE Reformation, which had been successful in Germany, spread with equal rapidity in the neighboring countries. At Zurich was Zwingli, a man of more daring mind than Luther; his equal in intrepidity, and his superior in learning. He went much further than Luther, and completely overturned the whole fabric of established worship. As early as 1524 the canton of Zurich renounced the supremacy of the Pope; and in 1528 Bern, Basle, and Schaffhausen, and part of the Grisons, Glarus, and Appenzel, followed the example. In Geneva Calvin took another line from Luther. He did not accept his doctrine of free justification, but he taught that some men were predestined to eternal life and others to eternal damnation; that the former could not fall away, and that nothing that the latter did could gain them heaven. Luther and Calvin looked on each other with great hostility. In some parts of Germany Calvinism spread, in other parts Lutheranism. The Lutherans were called Protestants, and the Calvinists were called Reformed. The name of Protestant was thus acquired:

Charles V. summoned a diet (that is, a parliament of the states) to meet at Spires in 1529, to discuss the means of resisting and driving back the Turks, who had overrun Hungary, and threatened the Austrian dominions; and also to settle something relative to the religious contests. By a majority of voices a decree was passed which forbade further innovation in religion, and ordered that the Catholic subjects of Protestant princes should be allowed to exercise their religion in freedom; that no hostilities were to be committed under pretence of religion, and that the ministers of the Gospel were to preach the word of God according to the interpretation of the Church, and to abstain from ridiculing and abusing the doctrines hitherto held as sacred. The Lutherans, upon this, drew up a *protest*, which they delivered to the diet. They argued that Protestant princes could not tolerate the exercise of a religion in their lands which they held to be against God's word, and that the ministers could not follow the interpretation of the Church, which they regarded as antichristian.

This protest was signed by the Elector of Saxony, the Margrave of Brandenburg—Anspach, the duke of Brunswick, the Landgrave of Hesse-Cassel, the Prince of Anhalt, and fourteen free imperial cities. It is from this protest that the Lutherans acquired the name of Protestants, which has since been applied to all who separated from the Church of Rome.

Charles V. made many efforts to pacify the strife without coming to severe measures. He called together another diet, to meet at Augsburg in 1530.

At the very opening of the diet, evidence appeared of the uncompromising character of the Protestants. The parliament began with a mass, attended by the emperor and his high functionaries. The Elector of Saxony was grand marshall and bore the sword of state. At first he refused to attend, and was only persuaded by one of the Lutheran pastors, who reminded him that the prophet Elisha permitted Naaman to bow himself in the house of Rimmon. However, though he and the Landgrave of Hesse attended, they refused to kneel, and remained standing upright whilst the whole congregation was bowed.

When the diet began proceedings the Lutherans presented to it a formulary of their belief as far as they had settled it at the time. This was drawn up by Philip Melancthon, and goes by the name of the "Augsburg Confession."

On November 16th Charles published a decree, insisting that all things should remain on their ancient footing till a council of the Church assembled, which was to be in six months' time; and also ordering the restoration of all the lands and buildings seized by the nobles and princes which had belonged to the Church. Charles gave the Protestants till April to consider, and if they then refused submission he threatened them with the ban of the empire.

Thereupon the Protestant princes assembled in the little Hessian town of Smalkald (December, 1530) and made a league with one another for mutual support against the emperor. They also entered into a secret treaty with Francis I., King of France, and they received promises of help from the kings of

JOHN FREDERICK THE BOLD, ELECTOR OF SAXONY.
(From portrait by Cranach.)

England, Sweden, and Denmark. Both parties prepared for war, and the imperial chamber commenced proceedings against the Protestant princes for the restitution of the ecclesiastical states they had confiscated. The heads of the league were the Elector, John Frederick of Saxony, a hearty supporter of Luther and a sincere man, and the Landgrave, Philip of Hesse, a man with two wives, and of bad character, whose reforming zeal sprang chiefly from greed after the spoils of the Church.

In the year 1545 a council of the Church assembled at Trent, to correct the abuses in religion, but the Protestants would take no part in it. This opposition angered the emperor, and he prepared for hostilities.

When the army of the Smalkald league marched against him he pronounced the ban of the empire against the leaders, that is, declared them outlaws, deprived of imperial protection and of their principalities. The confederates replied by a letter renouncing their allegiance, and refusing him the imperial title. The Protestant princes were weakened by internal dissention and jealousies, and Charles found himself deserted by the Pope, who was, as usual, jealous of his power in Italy. Francis I., of France, moreover, sent money to the Smalkald union. Fortunately for Charles, Francis died, and when the league were least expecting his attack he hastened to assail their forces on the Elbe. He threw a bridge of boats over the river at Mühlberg, though the enemy occupied the highest bank, and the river was three hundred paces wide. Whilst his bridge was being constructed he suddenly crossed the river by a ford, at the head of his cavalry, in a fog which concealed his movements, and burst on the Protestant army at the same moment that a light wind dispersed the vapors and the sun blazed out. The battle that ensued ended in the success of the Imperialists. John Frederick, Elector of Saxony, was wounded in the face and taken prisoner. When brought before Charles he bowed to kiss his hand, saying, "Most powerful and gracious emperor, the fortunes of war have rendered me your prisoner—" "Hah!" exclaimed Charles, "*now* you entitle me emperor, the other day you styled me Charles of Ghent."

Charles then made his triumphal entry into Wittenberg, and conducted himself with great magnanimity. The elector was deprived of all his dominions except Gotha, and they were given to Maurice of Saxony.

There were then two Saxon ducal houses, called the Ernestine and the Albertine, descended from two brothers, Ernest, who died in 1486, and Albert, who died in 1500. These brothers had divided the paternal inheritance between them. The Ernestine dukes retained the title of electors of Saxony, the Albertine dukes were called dukes of Saxony. John Frederick, who was deposed after the battle of Mühlberg, was the grandson of Ernest, and Maurice of Saxony was grandson of Albert.

Maurice was a very crafty man. He had quarrelled a good deal with John Frederick, as his dominions were intermixed with those of the elector, and as he possessed a joint share in some rich mines. When the Smalkald union was formed he refused to join it, though he was a Protestant, and he courted the favour of the emperor without vigorously fighting for him. In return for his loyalty Charles now gave him the electorate of Saxony, with the lands from which John Frederick had been ousted. This was what Maurice had been aiming after. No sooner had he got all he wanted from the emperor than he turned against him, and became his most bitter and dangerous opponent.

Charles gave him occasion. The Landgrave of Hesse had given himself up and been imprisoned, when he found himself deserted and powerless. Charles, it is said, had sent him private assurance that he would be set free if he made his submission, but Charles still kept him in confinement, and this angered Maurice, who had married the landgrave's daughter.

When, as he supposed, the war was at an end, Charles retired to Innsbruck, and dismissed the army he had collected. Maurice now secretly made a league with Henry II., King of France, by which it was arranged that the French were to attack Lorraine, and find Maurice a large monthly sum of money as long as he continued in arms against the emperor. At the same time he did all he could to throw dust in the eyes of Charles. He hired a house at Trent for his reception, and had it magnificently furnished, and declared his intention of going to the council. Then, when all was ripe, and Charles lulled into unsuspicion, Maurice suddenly

threw off the mask, uttered a proclamation, in
which he declared that he took up arms in defence
of Protestantism, to oppose the emperor becoming
absolute monarch, and to release the landgrave.

GERMAN PATRICIANS IN 1550.
(From a wood-cut by Ammann.)

He swept at once through Bavaria, without suffering the emperor time to collect an army against
him. No words can express Charles' astonishment
and consternation at the revolt of Maurice. He saw

a great number of German princes in arms against him at a moment when he had despatched a large body of his troops into Hungary to resist the Turks. At the same time Henry II. invaded Lorraine, captured Toul, Verdun, and Metz, and threatened Strasburg. Augsburg surrendered to Maurice. Nuremberg joined the confederacy.

Charles threw a few soldiers into Fuessen to guard the Scharnitz pass, but Maurice, advancing with rapid marches, dislodged them, advanced up the Lech valley, crossed into the Inn valley, and would have surprised and taken the emperor had he not made his escape in a litter—for he was ill at the time with gout—across the mountains, by roads almost impassable, in a dark and stormy night, only a few hours before Maurice entered Innsbruck.

Maurice gave up the palace and property of the emperor at Innsbruck to pillage.

Dismayed by this disaster, unable to gather together an army to fight at once the Turks in Hungary, the French in Lorraine, and the Protestants in the midst of the empire, Charles was forced to come to an agreement with Maurice and the Protestant princes, which was concluded on the 2d of August, 1552, and this is called the "Pacification of Passau." By it he agreed to release the landgrave, and to allow liberty to the Protestants in Catholic lands ; and the Protestants on their side agreed to allow Catholic worship to be performed for Catholics in their territories. When the agreement had been signed Maurice marched against the Turks, and

Charles, anxious to wipe away his recent disgrace, collected an army and entered Lorraine. But fortune had deserted him. He was unable to retake Metz, and in the Low Countries also his troops met with reverse. In Italy, moreover, his inveterate enemy, Pope Paul IV., joined with France in a league for the conquest of Naples. Paul was like the German prelates, a great prince as well as a prelate, and he cared more for his temporal power than for the welfare of the Church. Consequently, though Charles strove hard, and exhausted himself for the good of the Catholic religion in Germany, he was hampered and countermined by the Pope, who was jealous of his power. But for the Pope it is by no means improbable that Charles would have re-established Catholic supremacy through Germany.

At last, sick at heart and failing in health, the great emperor resolved to lay down the crown that had been to him a burden through life. In 1555 he gave up to his son, Philip II., the Netherlands, Naples, Spain, and the rich colonies of America. To his brother, Ferdinand I., who was already King of Bohemia and Hungary, he gave over the German-Austrian lands and the imperial title. Then he withdrew into the monastery of S. Just, in Spain, where he died, three years later.

His death was brought about in a very strange way. He took it into his head that he would like to have his funeral service performed over him before he was dead. He was dressed in a winding sheet and laid in a coffin, whilst his attendants, in deep mourning, holding tapers of unbleached wax, stood around him. The funeral service was said, and the hollow voice of the monarch was heard joining in the prayers from the coffin. But the grave-clothes were damp; he caught a chill which produced fever, and hurried him to his grave on the 21st of September, 1558, in the fifty-ninth year of his age.

XXXVIII.

THIRTY YEARS OF WAR ABOUT RELIGION.

(1618–1648.)

NOTWITHSTANDING the Pacification of Passau and its subsequent ratification at a diet held at Augsburg in 1555, quarrels continued between the Catholics and Protestants, and between the Lutherans and Calvinists, and even between discordant factions among the Lutherans themselves. In Saxony the Lutheran elector, Augustus, cruelly persecuted the Calvinists, and in the Palatinate the Calvinist prince expelled all the Lutherans, and cut off the head of a pastor who denied the doctrine of the Trinity. On his death his son, who was a vehement Lutheran, called back the Evangelicals and ordered all the Calvinist ministers who refused to recant to be driven out of the country.

In the mean time Alva, the Spanish governor of the Netherlands, was subjugating the Low Countries for Philip II. with great cruelty, and driving out the Calvinists.

Gebhard of Waldburg had been elected Archbishop of Cologne. He fell desperately in love with a beautiful maiden, Agnes of Mansfeld, and turned Calvinist, and wanted to make the archbishopric the property of himself, to descend to his children by the beautiful Agnes, whom he married. But the people of Cologne were against him; the Lutheran princes would not help him because he had turned Calvinist; however, he got promise of help from the Palatine, and from the Dutch and French, and carried on a desultory war to obtain possession of Cologne. At last he was completely defeated, and retired to Strasburg.

All the bishoprics in North Germany had been seized and annexed to their dominions by the princes of Brandenburg, Brunswick, Mecklenburg, and Saxony. In the hereditary possessions of the House of Hapsburg the Reformation was suppressed. The maxim had been formulated that as was the prince so should be the people, and so the princes everywhere insisted on making their people believe, or disbelieve, or change about like themselves.

Ferdinand I. and his son, Maximilian II., were gentle and good emperors, so that the general antagonism did not break out into violent hostilities under them; but it was otherwise when the gloomy Rudolph II. came to the throne. He was the son of Maximilian II. He was an apathetic man, utterly unsuited to govern, fond of horses, of which he kept a great many, though he never mounted their backs, and very fond of chemistry, and alchemy, which was then allied to chemistry. He had been educated in Spain, and the Protestants were alarmed at his appointment, fearing that he would use his power without moderation, and with intolerance. They accordingly formed an union, and placed the Elector Palatine Frederick at the head. Thereupon the Catholic princes also united, and bound themselves to assist each other and defend the Catholic religion. At the head of their League was Maximilian of Bavaria. And now, with the Protestant Union on one side, and the Catholic League on the other, armed and watching each other suspiciously, only a signal was wanted to make them draw swords.

That signal was given on May 23, 1618.

On the death of Rudolph II. (1612) his brother, Matthias, succeeded, but he was an old man, and unable to cope with the forces gathering to explosion in the empire. Accordingly, he committed the government to his nephew, Ferdinand, whom he caused to be proclaimed King of Bohemia. Ferdinand went at once to Prague, and nominated seven Bohemian Catholic nobles and three Protestants to form a council to govern the country. The most influential of these were Slawata and Martinitz, the former of whom was especially disliked by the Protestants because he had become a Catholic after having been brought up as a Lutheran.

Rudolph II. had issued an imperial manifesto, granting freedom of worship in Bohemia to Lutherans, Calvinists, Calixtens, and Catholics alike.

The Protestants began to erect two new churches for themselves. Impediments were thrown in their way. They appealed to the emperor, Matthias, and received a curt reply. It came to their ears that this was not dictated by the emperor himself, but proceeded from his council in Prague. They rose tumultuously, took arms, and, led by Count Matthias of Thurn, attacked the imperial castle at Prague, burst in, and flung Slawata and Martinitz, with their secretary, out of the window of the council chamber, and fired at them as they fell. The height was ninety feet, yet, marvellous to relate, they were not killed. Under the window was a heap of litter, and old papers, and the mud of the ditch. Slawata was indeed dreadfully shattered, but recovered. The poor secretary tumbled upon Martinitz, and is said to have apologized for his apparent rudeness. He was afterwards ennobled and given the name of Hohenfall, or "High Fall," This act of violence brought on the terrible Thirty Years' War, which lasted through three reigns, those of Matthias, Ferdinand II., and Ferdinand III., and caused almost unparalleled misery in Germany.

Ferdinand at once raised two bodies of troops, placed them under foreign generals, Dampierre and Bouquoi, and prepared to chastise the insurgents. But Count Thurn felt that the die was cast, and open war was inevitable. He gathered a large army, was assisted by the Silesians and Lusatians, defeated Dampierre and Bouquoi, and laid siege to the cities of Bohemia that remained faithful to the emperor. The elector palatine and the Protestant Union sent a body of mercenaries into Bohemia, under the command of the able general Mansfeld. At this juncture of affairs Matthias died, and his nephew, Ferdinand, succeeded.

Count Thurn left Mansfeld in Bohemia to hold Bouquoi in check and marched swiftly through

Moravia, increasing his army, and entered Upper Austria. Ferdinand was in Vienna with a small garrison, and no prospect of help. He knew that the loss of Vienna would be the loss of his crown and the ruin of his house. The Bohemians surrounded the city ; the cannon battered the walls of his palace; many of the citizens were in secret correspondence with the besiegers. Sixteen members of the states burst into his apartment, and with threats and reproaches insisted on the gates being opened to the insurgents, but Ferdinand never wavered for a moment. He had been kneeling in prayer in his cabinet when all seemed lost, when suddenly the conviction came over him that his delivery was at hand. At the very moment when all hope seemed gone, and the mutinous citizens were preparing to open the gates, a peal of trumpets announced the arrival of succour. It was only five hundred horsemen sent by Dampierre, who had effected an entry into the city unperceived by the besiegers. Their arrival operated like magic. The students, the burghers flew to arms ; additional succour arrived. The news speedily followed that Bouquoi had defeated Mansfeld, dispersed his army, and was marching upon Prague. Count Thurn hastily broke up the siege and hastened back into Bohemia. Ferdinand now went to Frankfort, where he was elected emperor, the Protestant electors being too divided in interest to oppose him. The Bohemians, however, refused to acknowledge him as their king. They elected the Count Palatine Frederick, who

WIEN.

VIENNA, EARLY IN THE 17TH CENTURY.

had married Elizabeth, daughter of James I., of England.

The Hungarians also revolted, under Bethlen Gabor, prince of Transylvania. Gabor obtained possession of Presburg by treachery, where was preserved the crown of Hungary, and marched upon Vienna, which was again besieged. Dampierre and Buquoi menaced the Hungarian rear, and Gabor was obliged to fall back; but he caused himself to be crowned King of Hungary.

Ferdinand found himself excluded from nearly every town in Bohemia and the greater part of Hungary. Frederick, elector palatine, was a vain and ambitious man, void of genius, and fond of display. He was inflated with pride at his election to the throne of Bohemia. He went to Prague, where he gave offence to the Lutherans by destroying the sacred representations which they admitted into their churches, and by his levity and folly.

The Catholic League was not idle. It had gathered an army under Maximilian of Bavaria, which marched to Prague, and finding the troops of Frederick and the Union outside the city on the "White Mountain," attacked and completely routed them (Nov. 8, 1620). The battle lasted little more than an hour. With the loss of only three hundred men the army of the League took all the standards and cannon of the enemy, left 4000 of them dead on the field, and drove a thousand more into the river Moldau; and thus, at one blow, dissipated the hopes of Frederick, and decided the fate of Bohemia. Frederick mounted his horse and galloped away, leaving his crown and treasure to fall into the hands of the Imperialists. One winter had seen him flourish and fade, and thence he received the nick-name of the " Winter King."

Frederick escaped to the Netherlands. The emperor placed him under the ban, deprived him of his electorate, which he gave to Duke Maximilian of Bavaria, together with the Upper Palatinate, that remains to Bavaria to the present day.

The Bohemians were forced to return to the Catholic Church, and many thousand Protestant families left their native land rather than submit.

XXXIX.

A BOHEMIAN GENTLEMAN.

WITH the subjugation of Bohemia it seemed for
the moment that the war was at an end. The Protestant union was broken up, and the elector palatine, its head, a refugee in Holland. But now several other Protestant princes entered the field to
carry on the war for the restoration of the banished
palatine. These were the Margrave George Frederick of Baden-Durlach, Duke Christian of Brunswick, Count Ernest of Mansfeld, and finally, Christian IV., King of Denmark.

In the great battle of the White Mountain a
Netherland general called Tilly, a man of very remarkable military genius, had distinguished himself on the side of the Imperialists. He was now
given command of an army. The Protestants, on
their side, had a leader of hardly inferior ability, the
adventurer Mansfeld.

Tilly was defeated by Mansfeld in the spring of
1622, and was reduced to the defensive, whilst he
saw a powerful combination rising on every side
against the House of Austria. He bided his time,
waiting till he could attack singly, these enemies
whom he could not resist when united. The oppor-

ILL.mus ET EXCELL.D.D.IOAT.SERCLAES S.R.I. COMES DE TILLY &c. S. CAES. MA. SER. ELECTORIS BAVARIAE ET VN. CATH. GENERAL

Aüling sculpsit. 1677.

JEAN TZERCLAES, COUNT TILLY.

tunity presented itself by the Margrave of Baden leaving Mansfeld to enter Bavaria. Tilly suddenly gathered some Spanish troops together, and thus reinforced swept down on the margrave at Wimpfen, where he utterly routed him, with the loss of half his army, and took his whole train of artillery and military chest. Without a pause he hastened after the Duke of Brunswick, caught him at Höchst, as he was crossing the Main, drove him back upon Mansfeld, who was besieging Ladenburg, and sent their united forces flying across the Rhine, to seek a refuge in Elsass. Hitherto the war had been carried on by the Catholic League for the emperor. Now the emperor resolved on sending an army of his own into the field, but he was without money. Then a Bohemian gentleman, Albert of Wallenstein, volunteered to raise an army of 50,000 fighting men, which would maintain itself, and put the emperor to a comparatively trifling expense. Wallenstein had been born at Prague in 1583. For his attachment to the royal cause in the troubles of Bohemia he had been banished and deprived of his estates by the Protestant party. On the triumph of the Imperialists his property was restored to him. When he made his offer to the emperor, Ferdinand was at first inclined to treat it as the craze of a heated imagination. But he soon found that the scheme had been well thought out and weighed. He therefore gave his consent. In a very short while Wallenstein had collected an army of 30,000 men, adventurers, flushed with hope of advancement and a

ALBERT VON WALLENSTEIN.

thirst for pillage. Before long the host had swelled
far beyond the stipulated number. The old Protestant Union had gone to pieces, but now a Protestant League was formed, supported by Christian
IV., King of Denmark, Gustavus Adolphus, King of
Sweden, and James I., of England. Christian of
Denmark took the field and entered Thuringia.
Tilly at once flew to meet him, and defeated him.
The king left 5000 men dead on the field, 2000
prisoners; and lost half his officers and all his artillery and baggage.

At the same time Wallenstein went in search of
Mansfeld, who had invaded Hungary, where he had
effected a junction with Bethlen Gabor. The
news of the defeat of Christian, however, came to
the Protestant host, and as disease had broken out
among them they were discouraged. Bethlen
Gabor concluded a hasty treaty with the emperor,
and disbanded his troops. Those of Mansfeld melted
away with disease and desertion, and the count
tried to escape with twelve officers to Venice, but
fell ill on his way and died. Wallenstein, having
delivered Hungary, hastened to unite with Tilly to
drive King Christian out of Germany. They pursued him into his own territories. He was driven
from place to place, and from post to post. The
troops which he ventured to bring into the field
were scattered in all directions, and before the
close of 1628 only one fortress remained in his
possession of the whole country between the Elbe
and the extremity of Jutland.

Now, once more, peace might have been restored

to distracted and miserable Germany but for the pride and elation of Ferdinand, who refused the overtures made by the King of Denmark.

By the Pacification of Passau, in 1552, it will be remembered that the Protestant princes undertook not to confiscate any more of the estates of the Church, bishoprics and abbeys. They had not, however, acted scrupulously in this matter. By a subterfuge more ingenious than justifiable they had managed to get hold of all the ecclesiastical principalities. At this time the Margrave of Brandenburg had got possession of the archbishopric of Magdeburg and the bishopric of Halberstadt. The Duke of Holstein had the bishoprics of Lübeck and the archbishopric of Hamburg and Bremen, and Frederick II., Prince of Denmark, had the bishopric of Werden. They abolished Catholicism, and did away with Episcopacy, yet retained for themselves the titles and the possessions and principalities of the bishops.* The Protestant princes would not yield up such rich and important possessions, and the war was prosecuted. Wallenstein drove the two dukes of Mecklenburg from their duchies, and laid siege to Stralsund. The citizens of this town, however, held out with great determination. Although the King of Denmark was defeated on land, his fleet, with that of the King of Sweden, came to the aid of Stralsund, and baffled all the efforts of Wallenstein. He is said to have declared that " he would reduce Stralsund, even if

---

* They had taken two archbishoprics and twelve bishoprics.

bound to heaven with chains of adamant." His perseverance would have succeeded had not the citizens invoked the aid of Gustavus Adolphus, King of Sweden, who threw a Swedish garrison into the town, and Wallenstein, exhausted by fatigue, was forced to retire.

In the mean time Wallenstein's soldiers had become the dread of Germany. Wherever they went they pillaged Catholics and Protestants alike. They were mere mercenaries fighting for plunder, and quite indifferent on which side they fought. They burnt villages and towns, robbed and mur-dered and maltreated wherever they went. Some impoverished citizens killed themselves to escape the misery of a lingering death by hunger. Moved by the distress of the country, the Catholic League assembled at Heidelberg in 1629, and requested the emperor to restore peace and remedy the evils occasioned by Wallenstein's army.

Ferdinand was obliged to submit, and the com-mand of the United League and imperial army was taken from Wallenstein and given to Tilly. Wal-lenstein, whom the emperor had created Duke of Friedland, retired to his estates in Bohemia.

XL.

A SWEDISH KING IN GERMANY.

THE emperor now insisted on the restoration of
the two archbishoprics and twelve bishoprics seized
by the Protestant princes, and began forcibly to
wrest them away. He took the archbishopric of
Magdeburg and appointed his son Leopold to it,
and gave him also the archbishopric of Hamburg
and the bishopric of Halberstadt, and the abbey of
Hersfeld, on which the Landgrave of Hesse had laid
his hands. The Protestant princes appealed for
help to Gustavus Adolphus, a king of great military
skill, vast energy and resource. He landed with a
small but well-organized army on the coast of Pomerania. When the news reached the Emperor
Ferdinand, his courtiers said that this was only a
snow king menacing him, who would melt away as
he came South under the rays of the imperial sun.
But the army of Ferdinand soon saw the fallacy
of this. Gustavus Adolphus drove it out of Pomerania, and then hastened to the relief of Magdeburg, which was besieged by Tilly. His assistance,
however, came too late. Tilly took the city, and it
became a prey to his lawless soldiers, who plundered and fired it. For one whole day the place

was at their mercy.   The most dreadful scenes were enacted.   The wild Croatian mercenaries rushed up and down the streets massacring every man they met, and throwing burning brands into the houses. They even burst into a church and killed the women they found huddled there.   On the second day only did Tilly enter the city to stay the slaughter and ruin.   He was a tall, haggard-looking man, dressed in a short slashed green satin jacket, with a long red feather in his high-crowned hat, with large bright eyes peering from beneath his deeply furrowed brow, a stiff moustache under his pointed nose.   He sat on a bony charger, and looked round on the ruins.   Smoke and lambent flame rose on all sides.   The wood and plaster houses were destroyed; only the cathedral, the churches and stone-built houses stood intact.   In the streets lay the stark bodies of twenty thousand dead men.   The cathedral doors were opened, and four thousand men who had taken refuge in it were brought forth, pale, famished, and trembling, almost all that remained of the inhabitants.   Tilly wrote to Vienna, "Since the destruction of Troy and Jerusalem no such a siege has been seen."

With the capture and destruction of Magdeburg the luck of Tilly turned.   Hitherto he had been resistless; now the shadow of this crime weighed on him and paralysed him.   Gustavus Adolphus marched against him, and the two armies met at Breitenfeld, near Leipzig.   Tilly, who could boast of having won thirty-six battles, was here beaten for the first time, and had to seek safety in flight.

A VILLAGE FESTIVAL IN THE SIXTEENTH CENTURY.

(From a wood-cut by Beham.)

Gustavus Adolphus now swept through Germany, driving out the Catholics, as Tilly had expelled the Protestants. At Merseburg two thousand of the Imperialists were cut to pieces. Wurzburg was taken, and all the monks found in it given up to the soldiers to butcher. The Swedes were as unsparing as the Imperialists. Only within the last five years have the skulls been buried of all the male population of Kirchoven in the Breisgau who were slaughtered by the Swedes, after having induced them to surrender with promise of life.

The palatine and his wife Elizabeth returned, and the latter, in her delight at the successes of Gustavus, on meeting him threw her arms round his neck and exclaimed, "Not Tilly, but I, have taken Gustavus the Great a prisoner!" They accompanied him in his triumphant march through Bavaria, and with him entered Munich; and in mockery both of the religion of the people and of the arms of the city, which is a monk, she made a monkey ride on a horse at her side dressed in monastic habit, with a rosary in its paw, blinking and making faces at the people. Again Tilly gathered an army and met Gustavus, but in a battle on the Lech was defeated, and a cannon ball shattered his thigh. His dying warning to Maximilian, Elector of Bavaria, was to garrison Ratisbon, at any price, as the key to Austria and Bohemia.

The cruelties and outrages committed by the Swedes now exasperated the peasantry to the last degree, and they rose against them, and, hiding in the birch woods that cover so much of the rubbly plain of Bavaria, sallied forth and fell on all the stragglers of the Protestant army. Banner, an officer of Gustavus, took a fearful vengeance on the town of Friedstadt, where the citizens had murdered some of his soldiers, who had been plundering and outraging the people. He burnt the place to the ground, and put all the inhabitants to the sword.

Gustavus was a sturdily-built man, with a tall head, pale blue or gray eyes. He wore no armour, but a buff leather jerkin, and on his head a white hat with a green feather in it, and high top yellow leather boots. He had landed in Pomerania with only sixteen thousand men, but his army rapidly swelled as that of the Imperialists melted away. The snow king, instead of melting, like a snowball gathered size as he rolled on. He had now 70,000 men. In his dire distress, not knowing where else to turn for aid, the emperor appealed once more to Wallenstein. Wallenstein, fully aware of the emperor's helplessness, coldly refused unless his own terms were acceded to, that the whole of the imperial troops should be placed solely and unreservedly under his command, and that every conquest made by him should be entirely at his disposal, and that he should be allowed to confiscate whatever property he chose for the maintenance of his troops. These were hard terms, and placed the emperor and his dominions at the mercy of an unprincipled adventurer. But in his necessity Ferdinand had no resource but to yield. Wallenstein had been living in more than royal state in Bohemia

on the spoils of his first campaign. He had a magnificent palace at Prague, with six gates guarded by
sentinels. Fifty halbardiers, clothed in splendid
uniforms, waited in his ante-chamber; six barons and
as many knights attended his person; his table was
daily spread for sixty guests; his stables were furnished with marble mangers. When he travelled
his numerous suites were conveyed in twelve state
coaches and fifty carriages; as many waggons bore
his plate and equipage, and the cavalcade was accompanied by fifty grooms on horseback, with fifty
led horses richly caparisoned. Wallenstein was a
tall, thin man, with sallow complexion, red, short
cropped hair, with small twinkling eyes. He did
not talk much but he was very observant, and he
quickly took the measure of the abilities of a man
with whom he had to do. He was grand and noble
in his ideas, disdained dissimulation, hated flattery
and every vice that evinced meanness and timidity
of character. He was very generous to all who did
him a good turn, but implacable in his resentments.

No sooner was it rumoured that Wallenstein was to
be general again than mercenaries came to him
from all quarters, and he found himself at once at
the head of sixty thousand men. Gustavus was then
at Nuremberg at the head of only sixteen thousand.
Wallenstein marched against him, but would not
attack him. If ever you go to Nuremberg by rail
you will cross a long, level plain, very bare of trees,
but you will see some rising ground before reaching Nuremberg, crowned by a town. This is Fürth,
which name means a fort. It was a strongly forti-

fied place. Gustavus made it his headquarters. Wallenstein occupied a low wooded hill, about two miles south of Fürth, surmounted by a ruined castle, where he intrenched himself, and quietly waited his time. Some one asked him why he did not attack the Swedish king, as he had so many more men. "No," answered Wallenstein, "too much has been staked on battles. Wait; we will try other means." Now he was himself eager to measure his military skill against Gustavus, who was considered the greatest general of the day, but he restrained his ardour, and waited, watching him for three whole months. Gustavus could not get away. He was cramped in Fürth. He was short of provisions, but then he was gathering help from his allies, till his army swelled to the size of that of the Imperialists. The Duke of Bavaria became impatient, and remonstrated with Wallenstein. "Wait," answered the Bohemian general. His soldiers became clamorous. "Wait," he said. And he was right. At last Gustavus could bear inaction no more; pestilence had broken out in his army, and he determined to drive Wallenstein from his position. The attack was commenced by the German troops in the Swedish service, but a shower of balls, rained down from a hundred pieces of artillery, soon compelled them to retreat. Gustavus then, to shame them, led on his own sturdy warriors, the Finlanders; but their ranks were shattered by a cannonade, and bravery availed nothing against an enemy who was not to be reached. A third attack met no better success. A fourth, fifth, sixth, from fresh bodies of troops, proved equally hopeless, and at last, after a ten-hours' engagement, and a loss of 3000 men, Gustavus was compelled to draw off his forces. The difficult task of effecting a retreat in the face of the enemy was skilfully executed by Colonel Hepburn, a Scotch officer in the Swedish service.

Offended at the promotion of an inferior officer above his head, he had sworn not to draw his sword for Gustavus again; but now the king, in his emergency, begged of him this favour, the brave soldier forgot his resentment. "Sire, this is the only service I cannot refuse to perform, since it requires some daring," was his answer, and he executed his task most gallantly. But it was not Wallenstein's intention always to remain on the defensive. At length, on Nov. 6, 1632, just two months after the battle of Fürth, the imperial and Swedish armies were ranged against each other for a decisive engagement at Lützen, not far from Leipzig. A thick fog that hung about till eleven o'clock hid each army from the other. The Imperialists were drawn up in line with four squares of infantry in the centre, which were further protected by trenches lined with musketeers and flanked with cannon.

The king himself led the attack. Annoyed by the trenches he leaped from his horse, seized a pike and led on his men to pass them, and the imperial infantry were driven back. But at that moment Gustavus heard that his left was wavering, flew to its assistance, but, in the fog, missed his way, and was surrounded by a body of Imperialist horsemen, who fired. A ball struck and shattered his arm; a second pierced his breast. He fell from his saddle, and his masterless horse, dashing along the front of the lines, proclaimed to the troops the loss of their king. The Duke of Saxe-Weimar cried out that Gustavus was not dead, but a prisoner, and the Swedes rushed like an avalanche on the Imperialists, mad with rage, and eager to rescue their sovereign. The Imperialists gave way. Two of their powder waggons exploded, and the victory would have declared for the Swedes had not reinforcements arrived to arrest their victorious career. Then the fog came down with the approach of night, dense, raw, and blinding, and put an end to the battle. But for the death of Gustavus the rout of Wallenstein would have been complete. He had lost his cannon, and his men were disorganized. He withdrew to Bohemia to reconstruct his army, and there he remained for a long time inactive, whilst carrying on a secret correspondence with the enemy.

Ferdinand, in the mean time, was very uneasy at the tremendous power exercised by the general, and he desired to escape from the obligation wherewith he had bound himself when asking Wallenstein's help. The town of Ratisbon, which was the key to Bohemia, was besieged by the Duke of Weimar, and the emperor ordered Wallenstein to relieve it. But the Duke of Friedland (that was Wallenstein's title) refused to be ordered about by the emperor, as against the compact, and allowed Ratisbon and two other important towns to be taken by the enemy without attempting to stay them. This conduct irritated Ferdinand, and he resolved on dismissing him from the supreme command. Then Wallenstein, in his anger and disgust, sent offers to the Protestant princes to come over to their side. But they suspected that he was only deluding them and put him off. The imperial court was well aware of the meditated treachery, and in alarm at its result. Who could resist Wallenstein, combined with the Protestant princes and the Swedes? In indignation Ferdinand deprived him of the command and pronounced against him the ban of the empire. But Wallenstein was confident in his power over his men. He was mistaken.

There were two Scotchmen, Gordon and Leslie, and an Irishman, Butler, whom he specially trusted. They had, however, been gained by the imperial court. Another, Captain Devereux, was taken into the plot. At midnight of February 25, 1634, Gordon, at the head of thirty soldiers, burst into Wallenstein's bedroom after he had retired to rest. Alarmed by the tramp he sprang from his bed in his night-shirt, and forced open his window to call for assistance. Devereux shouted, " Are you the traitor who are going to deliver the imperial troops to the enemy, and tear the crown from the head of the emperor?" Wallenstein made no reply. He stretched out his arms. Gordon held aloft the flaming candle, and a halbert was run through the body of the great general.

Though the treachery of Wallenstein is undeniable, his murder must ever remain as a stain on the history of Austria.

XLI.

PEACE AFTER THE LONG WAR.

(1648.)

AFTER the death of Wallenstein the command over the imperial army was given to the son of the emperor, afterwards Ferdinand III., and in the place of Gustavus Adolphus, Duke Bernard of Weimar and the Swedish general, Horn, commanded the Protestant armies. At Nordlingen the latter were completely defeated. Horn was taken prisoner and Bernard fled, with the loss of all his treasure and twelve thousand men. The French, now jealous of the power of the emperor, came to the assistance of the Protestants, and formed an army, burning, butchering and plundering over the Rhine. Success swayed from side to side; neither obtained decisive victory. The country was become too exhausted to endure further war. Attempts at concluding peace were begun at Osnabrück and Münster, and finally concluded in 1648; and this is known in history as the PEACE OF WESTPHALIA.

This peace brought the terrible Thirty Years' War to an end, but by it Germany lost some of her fairest territories. France took Elsass, Sweden took Pomerania. Switzerland and Holland, which had hitherto been united to the German Empire, were separated, and recognized as independent states. The supreme power was invested in the *Reichstag*, or Imperial Diet, which was to sit permanently at Ratisbon. The several German princes were made almost wholly independent, so that the empire as an unity was reduced to a shadow. With regard to religion, Catholics, Lutherans, and Calvinists were put on the same footing of equality. All church lands seized by the Protestants were to remain in the hands of the Protestant princes. Pope Innocent X. protested and published a bull against this decision, but no one paid attention to him. Germany was sick to the heart of war.

Of the devastation wrought in those terrible thirty years it is hard to realize the extent. Two-thirds of the inhabitants had perished, not only by the sword, but by the miseries which followed in the train of war—famine and pestilence. Hundreds of villages had disappeared; others stood empty, unpopulated. The corn-fields were trampled down and untilled. Trade had failed in the towns. The streets were deserted and grass-grown, the doors of the houses broken in. The shattered windows of many dwellings showed that the inhabitants were dead or were wanderers. But to come to particulars. In the little duchy of Würtemberg, in the Thirty Years' War, 8 towns, 45 villages, 68 churches, and 36,000 houses were destroyed. In the seven years between 1634–1641, in Würtemberg alone, 345,000 persons perished. In Thuringia, before the war, in 19 villages were 1773 families; of these only 316 remained after it. Before the war there were half a million inhabitants in the Palatinate; at the Peace of Westphalia there were 48,000. In 1618 the population of Germany numbered between 16 and 17 millions; in 1649 there were not quite 4 millions. So terrible had been the famine during the war that cases of cannibalism were not rare. Bands of men were formed who lived like wild beasts, preying on those they caught. Near Worms such a band was attacked and dispersed, as they were cooking in a great cauldron human legs and arms. Starving creatures cut down criminals from the gallows to eat them. So great was the depopulation that in Franconia the state passed a law authorizing every man to marry two wives, and forbidding men and women from becoming monks and nuns.

XLII.

THREE STROKES BY A MAN IN YELLOW.

(1657–1705.)

TEN years after the Peace of Westphalia Leopold, the son of Ferdinand III., was elected emperor. His long reign of nearly fifty years was for the most part taken up with war against Louis XIV., of France. This crafty and powerful monarch had made up his mind that the Rhine should be the frontier of his realm. Leopold was an amiable but weak sovereign, reigning at a time when one of very strong character and iron will was necessary to bind together the loosely cohering empire, and to meet and frustrate the intrigues of Louis.

The princes of Germany were so selfish, so indifferent to the welfare of fatherland in their greed of personal advancement, that they were ready to lend an ear to the wily advice of th French king, and to act as his tools against their country's peace and prosperity. Accordingly, many of the German princes sided with the French king against their emperor. By the Treaty of Westphalia Charles Louis, son of the contemptible Frederick, the winter king, was reinstated in the Palatinate of the Rhine, of which Heidelberg was the capital, but he was not given back the Upper Palatinate, which remained to Bavaria. This irritated him, and he readily received bribes from Louis XIV. The Duke of Würtemberg also sided with the French, as well as the electors of Mainz and Cologne, and the dukes of Brunswick and Hesse-Cassel.

The result of this was that some of the fairest parts of Germany, especially the right bank of the Rhine and the Palatinate, were wasted by the French. Towns and villages just recovering from the Thirty Years' War were burnt again. Several important towns were lost to Germany, especially Strasburg, which was treacherously seized by Louis in time of peace (1681). Louis had for some time been in correspondence with some of the magistrates of Strasburg. One day M. de Louvois, the French minister of war, summoned a gentleman to him named Chamilly, and gave him the following instructions : " Start this evening for Basle. On the fourth day from this, punctually at 2 o'clock, station yourself on the Rhine bridge, note-book in hand, and write down everything you see going on for two hours. Then at four o'clock come back, travelling night and day without stopping."

Chamilly obeyed. He reached Basle, and on the day and at the hour appointed stationed himself, note-book in hand, on the bridge. Presently, a market-cart drives by. Then an old woman with a basket of fruit passes. Anon, a little urchin trundles his hoop by. Next, an old gentleman in blue top-coat jogs past on his grey mare. Three o'clock chimes from the cathedral tower. Just at the last stroke a tall fellow in yellow waistcoat and breeches saunters up, goes to the middle of the bridge, lounges over, looks at the water, then strikes three hearty blows with his stick on the parapet. Down goes every detail in Chamilly's book. At four o'clock he jumps into his carriage, and at midnight, after two days of incessant travelling, presents himself before the minister, feeling ashamed of having such trifles to record. M. de Louvois took the notebook, and when his eye caught the mention of the yellow-breeched man a gleam of joy flashed across his face. He rushed to the king, roused him from sleep, spoke in private with him for a few moments, and then couriers were sent off in haste with sealed orders. Eight days after, the city of Strasburg was surrounded by French troops and summoned to surrender. It capitulated, and threw open its gates on the 30th September, 1681. The three strokes of the stick given by the fellow in yellow were the signal that the magistrates were ready to receive the French.

Three pacifications were concluded with the French: that of Nimwegen, which concluded the Dutch war in 1678, that of Ryswick, at the end of the Orleans war, carried on because of the claim of the Duchess of Orleans to the estates of her brother Charles, the elector palatine, who died without children (this was concluded in 1697); and that of Utrecht, after the Spanish War of the Succession, in 1714. The people called these treaties the peaces of Nimweg, Reissweg, and Unrecht (take-away, tear-away, and unright), because Germany lost something by them all. In order to facilitate his schemes Louis XIV. stirred up the Turks to invade the empire. They poured through Hungary and laid siege to Vienna, which held out valiantly for two months. The Turks swept the neighborhood and sent eighty-seven thousand of the inhabitants into slavery. They blew up the walls, and the city was surrounded by ruins and piles of rubbish. Still the dauntless Viennese held out, animated by their gallant commander, Count Stahrenberg, who, though wounded, was carried in a litter, and by their bishop, Kolonitsch, who devoted himself zealously to ministering to the wounded. At last, in despair,

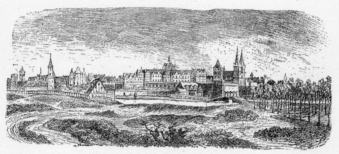

BERLIN IN 1660.

they sent up a flight of rockets from the top of the spire of S. Stephen's Church. It was answered by the discharge of fire-arms; John Sobieski, King of Poland, had come to the rescue. The Turks were defeated and driven back with a loss of twenty thousand men. When the tent of the visir who commanded the Turks was taken, the letters of Louis XIV. were found in it, inciting him against the Austrians.

During this sad time of hostility two men especially distinguished themselves by their high characters, genius, and courage, these were the " Great Elector " and Prince Eugene.

XLIII.

A NOBLE RULER.

(1640–1688.)

By the Peace of Westphalia Germany was divided into a great number of independent states. The princes of these states, as already said, cared little for the commonwealth, and were bent on their own selfish ends, and they set the emperor at defiance. The Elector of Brandenburg was a noble exception.

Henry I. had created the Margravate of Brandenburg as a bulwark against the heathen Wends, who lived on the Baltic. It was not then called Brandenburg but the Northmark. But Albert the Bear, who conquered the greater portion of the Wendland and annexed it to his state, called himself Margrave of Brandenburg. His race died out, and at the time of the Council of Constance, Frederick of Hohenzollern, Burgrave of Nuremberg, bought the margravate from the emperor Sigismund, in 1415. You may remember an account given of Hohenstaufen, the cradle of the great Swabian emperors. Hohenzollern, the cradle of the kings of Prussia and present emperors of Germany, is just such another conical hill, in the same Swabian table-land. It be-

longs now to the emperor, who has rebuilt the castle with great splendour. You may remember also
how you were told that Albert of Brandenburg,
Grand Master of the Teutonic Order, became a
Lutheran and seized on Prussia, which was the
possession of the Order, and made it his own as a

MEN OF WAR OF THE GREAT ELECTOR.
(From model in Berlin.)

hereditary state. Albert left granddaughters, and
Joachim Frederick, Elector of Brandenburg, married Eleanor, the younger, and his son, John Sigismund, married Anna, the elder, and secured the
Duchy of Prussia to their family. The relationship
was strange. Eleanor was thus stepmother to her
elder sister, and the stepmother was seven years
younger than her stepdaughter. Frederick William,
the Great Elector, was grandson of John Sigismund
and Anna. Under him a great deal of additional

territory was got, but he gained his name of "The
Great Elector" partly by his wise government of his
states, and partly by his brilliant military achievements.   He stood faithfully by the side of the emperor and resisted all the overtures of the King of
France.   Louis XIV., to keep his dangerous opponent engaged at a distance from the Rhine, made a
league with the Swedes, and induced them to attack
Brandenburg whilst the elector was on the Upper

THE GREAT ELECTOR AND WIFE.
(From a medal.)

Rhine.   But no sooner did he hear of their descent
than he hastened home with forced marches and
encountered them when they least expected his
presence.   A battle was fought at Fehrbellin.   During the fight his equerry, Frobenius, observed that
the enemy's fire was mainly directed against the
elector himself, who was distinguished by the white
horse he rode.   Frobenius induced the elector to
change mounts with him.   Scarce had he done so
and gone two paces from his master when a cannon-ball struck him dead.   Shortly after, Frederick

William saw himself surrounded by the enemy, but he had nine dragoons with him, and they hewed their way through. After a desperate struggle the Brandenburgers won the day, and the Swedes, who had been thought invincible, were obliged to take to flight. In the winter of 1678 the Swedes again invaded Prussia, but were repulsed by the elector, who pursued them in sledges over the frozen Gulf of Courland, caught them again at Riga, and again defeated them.

XLIV.

BITTERLY FIGHTING THE TURKS.

PRINCE EUGENE of Savoy was a small man of no presence, whose mission it was to check the advance of Louis XIV. in Germany on the West, and in the East to break the power of the Turks. On account of his feeble body he had been designed for the Church, and was nicknamed "the little Abbot." But Eugene felt no call for the religious life, and a very great desire to be a soldier. He first offered his services to Louis XIV., but that king dismissed him contemptuously, and then he left France and took part in the Austrian wars against the Turks. During the siege of Vienna, in 1683, he displayed such heroism that the emperor gave him the command of a regiment of dragoons. The great dragoons scoffed at their officer and said, "Hah! the Abbotikin in his grey cloak won't reach the chins of the Turks to pull their beards." But they were mistaken. He not only pulled their beards, but pulled them over and made them bite the dust. In 1697 he was given his first command over an army, and was sent to oppose the Turks, who had invaded Hungary under the lead of the sultan. Eugene came on them as they were crossing the river Teiss on a temporary bridge, and with the loss of only 500 men completely routed the Turks, who lost 30,000 men, and sent the sultan flying back to Constantinople.

Louis XIV. now did all in his power to gain the little man. He offered him the title of field-marshal, the governorship of a French province, and a large sum of money. But Eugene sent the messengers back with the answer, " Tell your king that I am field-marshal to an emperor, which is quite as honourable an office as that he offers me. As for money, I do not want it. As long as I faithfully serve my master, he will not suffer me to lack." Prince Eugene completely won the hearts of his soldiers. He looked carefully after their wants, and when their pay was in arrear he would pay them out of his own pocket. He was frank and kindly in address; and when the little man called to his soldiers to show their metal, it was like sending an electric shock through them; they would go anywhere, do anything he told them. He gained great renown through his success against the Turks, who were not only the enemies of Austria, but of Christendom. He defeated them in several battles, and at length forced them to conclude a peace greatly to the advantage of the emperor.

Eugene was soon to gain even greater renown by his victories over the French.

XLV.

ALL EUROPE AT WAR.

(1701–1714.)

AFTER the death of Charles II. of Spain, without children, Louis XIV. of France, the emperor, Leopold I., and Joseph Ferdinand, Elector of Bavaria, all put in a claim to the crown of Spain. This occasioned a war of thirteen years, in which the principal European states were involved. It began under Leopold I., was carried on by his son, Joseph I., and only came to an end under Charles VI., the brother of Joseph I.

On the side of the emperor were Holland, England, Portugal, the Elector of Hanover, and the Elector Frederick of Brandenburg, who, with the consent of the emperor, assumed the title of King of Prussia.

The command of the allies was given to Prince Eugene and the illustrious English general, the Duke of Marlborough. Against such able commanders the French could do nothing. They were beaten in Germany, beaten in the Netherlands, and beaten in Italy. Their allies were the Elector of Bavaria and the Pope. Moreover, an insurrection broke out in Hungary at the very time that they

FREDERICK I., KING OF PRUSSIA.
(From the painting by Wenzel.)

were invading Germany, so as greatly to distract
the imperial forces. Prince Eugene began the war
in Italy, but speedily Germany became the scene
of conflict, as Louis XIV. poured an army over the
Rhine, across the Black Forest to the Danube,
threatening Vienna. This great army, which was
joined by the Bavarians, numbered 56,000 men,
and Marlborough and Eugene were only able to
oppose 52,000 to them. The great and decisive
battle, upon which the fate of the House of Austria
hung, was fought at Blenheim, a village on the
Danube, between Ulm and Ingolstadt. The French
were drawn up behind the small stream, the Nebel-
bach, which forms swamps and marshes, before
it falls into the Danube. In addition to these
swamps ninety pieces of cannon protected the
centre. On the right the French had the village
of Blenheim; and the left rested on a thick wood.
Marlborough and Eugene drew up before the
swamp, in order of battle, Marlborough on the left
and centre, and Eugene on the right. The battle
began with an attack by the British infantry on
Blenheim, but they were repulsed, after repeated
encounters, with great slaughter. Then Marlborough suddenly gathered them together and drove
them like a wedge against the centre, scrambling,
floundering through the swamps, but going on
as Englishmen will go, although the 90 cannon
pounded them. A cannon-ball grazed his horse
and threw Marlborough to the ground; the troops
trembled for their leader; the fate of Austria
hung suspended on the life of the general. But

next moment he was seen mounted again. A ringing cheer burst from the British, and on they went,
flinging bundles and faggots before them into the
marsh, and stepping over on them. Marlborough
got the cavalry over first and charged up the slope
at the French and Bavarians. After the cavalry
came the infantry. The centre gave way, recoiled;
the enemy's force broke up, and nothing remained
but a disorganized multitude. Of the enemy 40,-
000 men were killed, wounded, or taken prisoners.
They lost 300 standards and 120 pieces of cannon.

The present post-road has been carried over the
battle-field, and, to make a foundation, heaps of
bones of horses and men have been shovelled in
that were found there when the road was constructed. Broken, dispersed, and ruined, the
wretched remains of that army which had threatened Germany with bondage, and spread terror to
the gates of Vienna, made the best of its way back
to the Rhine and Vosges, pursued by the allies.
The first result of this victory was the submission
of the Duke of Bavaria; the next was that the
emperor was able to send troops into Hungary to
quell the insurrection there. The battle of Blenheim was fought on Aug. 2, 1704. The scene of
warfare now passed to the Netherlands; but Marlborough remained inactive all 1705, watching the
French, who contemptuously invented and piped a
song, " Marlborough s'en va t'en guerre," which
was played before his lines to fire him into activity;
but Marlborough knew what he was about, and
on May 12, 1706, he went to war in good earnest,

JOSEPHVS ROMANOR. IMPERATOR.

JOSEPH I., EMPEROR OF GERMANY.

met the French at Ramillies and totally defeated
them. He beat them again in 1708 at Oudenarde,
and again with great loss at Malplaquet in 1709.
At the same time Eugene was defeating the French
in Italy. Overwhelmed by these disasters Louis
XIV. tried to make peace. He offered to give up
all claim to Spain, and even to supply money to
help the allies to expel his grandson, Philip of
Anjou, the new king, out of Spain. But the allies
were not satisfied with these offers. They insisted
on Louis himself driving his grandson out of Spain,
and binding himself to do it within two months.
This was asking for the impossible, and Louis XIV.
said, with reason, "Well, if I must fight, let it be
against my natural enemies, not against my own
children."

"Pride," says the proverb, "goes before a fall."
This proved true now. Fortune turned quite unexpectedly, and favoured the French king. The emper-
or Joseph I. died without children, and the Austrian
inheritance passed to his brother Charles, who
claimed the throne of Spain. But European sovereigns did not want to have an emperor with the
dominions of Charles V., so he was forced to give up
his claims to Spain, and the grandson of Louis XIV.
was acknowledged as king and took the title of
Philip V. This was the result of the agreement
come to by the powers at the Peace of Utrecht in
1713, and the emperor was obliged next year to consent to it at the Treaty of Rastadt.

XLVI.

POWDERED WIGS AND PATCHES.

WE are now at the period of powdered wigs and patched faces. It is called the period of rococco, from *roche* and *coquille*, rock and shell, as the ornamental work in architectural decoration affected a combination of rock and shell work. There was a general reaction against the stiffness of former times. All straight lines were avoided; gentlemen even studied to stand in curved attitudes. The ladies in the 16th century had worn rich and thick damask silks, embroidered till they were stiff. At the marriage of a princess of one of the Saxon families she found it impossible to kneel, and was obliged to be married standing, like an extinguisher, with her skirts hard as board. But now the ladies wore light silk and satin, with their skirts looped up in paniers, showing petticoats of another colour. Their heads of hair were, however, piled up and interwoven with ribbands and chains of pearls, and feathers and flowers were stuck into them, so that before going out in such array they could not lie down to sleep in their beds.

Gentlemen wore white powdered wigs, velvet coats richly frogged, and long satin embroidered waistcoats, satin breeches, and silk stockings. They had their faces closely shaved. The story is told of a duchess, Louise Maria Gonzaga, niece of Louis XIV., when she was shown the portrait of Ladislas, King of Poland, whom she was to marry, that she exclaimed:— "But—he is deformed! He has two great moles, like rats' tails, growing on his upper lip!"—These were his moustaches. She had never seen, or supposed it possible, that men's hair grew thus.

HEAD-DRESSES. (TIME OF FREDERICK WILLIAM II.)

A great deal of building went on in Germany at this time, and the churches in the Catholic parts, which had been half wrecked by the Swedes, were restored. Statues were sculptured in theatrical attitudes, and covered with tinfoil washed over with colour to represent satin. Everything that could be gilt was overlaid with gold leaf. It was a splendour-loving time. In the courts, luxury and extravagance were unbridled, and the peasantry were ground down with taxes to supply funds for this prodigality.

During the Thirty Years' War most of the old country nobility had died out or been impoverished. The only people who had gained by these wars were the princes, who were left alone, with no one to stand between them and the people, and they ruled by caprice, levying taxes as they wanted money.

The emperor took to issuing patents of nobility and selling titles to raise money, and the princes did the same. Any one who could find money was able to obtain what title he desired.

The poetry of the period is pompous and unnatural, but to this rococco age one art owes its birth, that of music.

XLVII.

THE TROUBLES OF A NOBLE QUEEN.

(1740–1745.)

GERMAN history enters on a new epoch in the year 1740. In this year Frederick II. became King of Prussia, and Maria Theresa became sovereign in Austria. But the insatiable greed of increasing their power, which seems to have been inherent in the Hohenzollerns, impelled Frederick into war with Maria Theresa at the very beginning of their reigns, costing many thousands of men their lives and wasting many fair provinces. The occasion was this :—

The emperor, Charles VI., died without male issue. His efforts had been directed during his reign chiefly to one point, to secure the Austrian dominions to his admirable daughter, Maria Theresa. To this end he contrived that an agreement should be signed both by the estates of the empire and the Austrian monarchy, and also by the reigning princes of Europe. This agreement was called " THE PRAG- MATIC SANCTION." When Charles VI. died, in 1740, Maria Theresa, who was married to Duke Francis of Lorraine, seized the reins of government of all the lands belonging to Austria, that is, Bohemia, Hungary, Austria proper, Tyrol, Styria, Carinthia, etc. But, in spite of the Pragmatic Sanction, various claims were made for several of these lands. The ambassador of Charles Albert, Elector of Ba-

FREDERICK THE GREAT.
(From a Drawing by Chodowiecki.)

varia, entered Vienna to announce that his sovereign could not acknowledge the young queen as heiress and successor to her father, because the House of Bavaria laid claims to the Austrian inheritance.

Frederick II. of Prussia, also, seeing that he had

to do with a young and feeble woman, bluster-
ingly demanded some of the Silesian principalities.
As Maria Theresa had sufficient spirit to refuse
these insolent demands war broke out, in which
France, Spain, and Poland took part with Bavaria
and Prussia against her. These wars go by the
name of the "War of the Austrian Succession,"
and the "Three Silesian Wars."

Maria Theresa is one of the noblest and best of
women who have made themselves a name in history. In the spring of her life, nobly built, her
dignity of majesty and charm of womanhood combined to turn the scale of her fortunes at the most
critical period in her career. The Elector of Cologne
acknowledged her only by the title of archduchess.
The Elector Palatine sent her a letter by the common post, superscribed, "To the Archduchess Maria
Theresa," and the King of Spain refused her any
other title than Duchess of Tuscany. Her husband was a poor creature, who treated her without
regard, and was no strength to her in her trials.
At first only the King of Prussia seemed to stand
by her ; he promised his support whilst collecting
his troops for a descent on Silesia. It was with
surprise, therefore, that the young queen received an insolent demand for Silesia from the
rude messenger of Frederick II. Even the ministers of the Prussian king blushed at their master's
conduct.

A battle was fought at Molwitz. The right wing
of the Prussians was broken ; whereupon King
Frederick galloped away as hard as his horse could

carry him, in spite of the entreaty of his officers to
stay, and never drew rein till he came to Oppeln,
where, to his dismay, he found a party of Austrian
hussars, who fired, but before they could gain their
horses the king galloped back to his troops, and
found to his astonishment that they had gained a
complete victory during his absence.

After this victory his insolence was unbounded.
The English sent an ambassador to mediate, and
spoke of magnanimity. " Magnanimity! Bah!"
he shouted, "I care only for my own interests."
Maria Theresa offered to yield three duchies in
Silesia. " Before the war they might have contented me. Now I want more," said Frederick.
" What do I care about peace? Let those who
want it give me what I want ; if not, let them fight
me, and be beaten again."

XLVIII.

THE QUEEN'S BABY BOY.

(1741–1748.)

WHEN things had come to this pass, the Elector of Bavaria, supported by the French, advanced his claims by force of arms. He marched upon Vienna. At Linz he had homage done to himself as Archduke of Austria. He was within three days' march of Vienna, and Maria Theresa was without an army, for that in Silesia was held in check by Frederick of Prussia. Her treasury was empty. She fled from her capital to Presburg in Hungary, convoked the magnates, and appeared among them attired in Hungarian costume, the crown of S. Stephen on her head and his sword at her side. Radiant with beauty and spirit she addressed the diet, and called on the nobles as cavaliers to stand by a woman in her jeopardy. Then she held up her baby boy in her hands before the assembly, and the tears came welling out of her beautiful eyes. Then came the answer. The whole diet rose and flashed their swords from their scabbards, and as a roll of thunder, " Moriamur pro rege nostro, Maria Theresa!" (" We will die for our sovereign, Maria Theresa.")

MARIA THERESA.
(From a painting by Kilian.)

In England the unprovoked aggression of the King of Prussia had excited general indignation, and Parliament granted 300,000 pounds to the queen.

In a short time a considerable army of Hungarians and Croats was assembled, which in a few weeks cleared Austria of the Bavarians and French, and pursued them into Bavaria, and took the capital, Munich. The French, who were in possession of Prague, were blockaded, but broke out in the depth of winter and escaped over the snowy fields, leaving their course strewn with frozen corpses. Out of forty thousand men who had entered Bohemia only 3000 survived the miseries of the retreat and returned to France.

But the Austrians opposed to Frederick II. had been less successful. The king defeated them again, and then, alarmed at the gathering power of Maria Theresa, concluded a peace with her, by which she made over to him a large portion of Silesia.

On the very day on which the Austrian army entered Munich the elector was crowned emperor at Frankfort, under the name of Charles VII., but the new emperor was unable to show himself in his own dominions. His reign was short, and full of trouble, which he had brought on himself. The war continued, with varying fortune. George II. of England himself took part in it at the head of an army of Hanoverians and Hessians, which, united to the imperial army, gained a signal victory over the French at Dettingen. The news of the victory reached Vienna before the queen heard it. She was far down the Danube, but on her return she found the banks for nine miles lined with people cheering, the cannon on the fortifications were booming, and the bells of the churches pealing. She entered her capital in a sort of triumph, and went at once to the Cathedral to return thanks to God. Shortly after, other good news came to her: Egna Neumarkt was taken, and all her hereditary possessions were secured to her.

Frederick II., "the Great," was uneasy at these successes, and feared that Maria Theresa would be demanding back the Silesian duchies. Accordingly, with great secrecy, he intrigued with the English, and drew them away from the Austrian alliance, and then suddenly and unexpectedly invaded Bohemia, and defeated the imperial generals in several battles. He was greatly helped by a very odd man, a relative, the Prince of Dessau, a rough soldier, gaunt in shape and long in limb. Prince Eugene was wont to call him the "Bull-dog." He would not let his sons have a tutor, as he said he wanted them to make themselves, and not to be manufactured by others. He had a French chamberlain, called Chalesac. One night the prince came in very drunk, and his chamberlain ventured to remonstrate with him. The "old Dessauer" seized a pair of pistols, and aiming at Chalesac's head, roared, "You dog! I will shoot you!" "Do so if you will," answered the chamberlain, "but it will look ugly in history." The prince thought a moment, laid down the pistols, and said, "Yes, it would not read respectably." One day, in church, the preacher gave out the first verse of a hymn :—

" Neither hunger nor thirst,
    Nor want nor pain,
  Nor wrath of the Great Prince
    Can me restrain."

The prince, thinking he was alluded to, grasped his walking-stick, and made a rush up the pulpit stairs to thrash the pastor for his insolence. The minister screamed, " Sire! I mean Beelzebub, Beelzebub, not your highness!" and scarce pacified the furious prince, and saved his own hide.

The first Silesian war was from 1740 to 1742. The second war was from 1744 to 1745, and was concluded by the treaty of Dresden, whereby Maria Theresa was once more compelled to cede Silesia to the victorious Prussian. In this year the emperor, Charles VII., whom Maria Theresa had refused to recognize, died, whereupon her husband was elected emperor, under the title of Francis I. Maximilian, the son of Charles VII., received back the duchy of Bavaria, and gave up his claims on the Austrian inheritance.

In 1748 peace was concluded at Aix, whereby Maria Theresa lost two provinces in Italy. Silesia was already lost, as you have heard.

You have not heard of the fighting that went on in Italy, but the war had raged there, as well as in Germany and the Netherlands, and the King of Sardinia had been the queen's great adversary in Italy.

XLIX.

THE HARDSHIPS OF A YOUNG PRINCE.

FREDERICK WILLIAM I.,* King of Prussia, the father of Frederick the Great, was a brutal, hard man, but not without some good points in his character. He hated ceremony, but not ceremony only,—the very decencies of life. His great amusement was to get foreign guests into his *Tabagie*, or smoking-room, and there ply them with beer till he made them sick. He despised and hated learning, and when Baron Gundling, a very learned man, was invited to dine with the king, Frederick William had an ape introduced, dressed exactly like the savant, and made the ape sit by him at table. To show his scorn for learning, he moreover insisted on having Gundling, when he died, buried in a cask, instead of a coffin. His daughter, in her memoirs, says, " My brother Frederick told me that one morning, when he went into the king's room, our father seized him by the hair, flung him down, and after he had exhausted the strength of his arm on the boy's poor body he dragged him to the window, took the curtain rope, and twisted it round his neck. The prince had

---

* Frederick William I. was grandson of Frederick William, "the Great Elector."

presence of mind and strength to grasp his father's hands and scream for help. A chamberlain came in and plucked the boy away from the king."

As Frederick William was riding round Berlin one day he saw a poor Jew slink out of his way. He stopped, seized him, and asked him his reason. "Sire! I was afraid of you!" said the scared Hebrew. The king caught him by the nape of the neck, and, laying on to him with his riding whip, with fury roared, "Love me! You shall love me! I'll teach you to love me!"

His great ambition was to make of Prussia a warlike state. His recruiting officers went everywhere, securing very big men for his grenadier guard, whom they obtained by the most underhand means.

He hated the French, their language, their culture, their manners, and to show his detestation of them he ordered the jailors to be dressed in the last Parisian fashions.

The young prince, Frederick, was hated by his father because the boy was timid, and shrank from him. He mistook this timidity for cowardice, and sought to make the poor child love him by beating him, after the way of his teaching the Jew. The young Frederick took eagerly to French, read French books, and played the flute. Unfortunately, the books that fell in his way were those of Voltaire, who held up religion and morality to ridicule, and scoffed at all that Christians hold sacred. Frederick was forced by his father to attend longwinded Calvinist sermons. He was denied innocent pleasures, such as his flute, and the result was that

he became, whilst quite young, dissipated and unbe-
lieving. The king went out of his way to insult
the prince in public, and
to show him and all the
court how he hated him.
But when the king tried
to force him to surrender
his claim to succession to
the throne, the prince replied, " I would rather
have my head cut off than
abandon my right."

At last the situation
became intolerable, and
when, finally, the king
was about to marry Fred-
erick against his will, the
prince resolved to fly to
his uncle, the King of
England. His sister,
Wilhelmina, and two
friends, Keith and Katte,
were in the plot. He
made his attempt to es-
cape when attending his
father on a journey to
the Rhine. But the plan
was divulged to the king,
and he was arrested.
When brought before his

ONE OF FREDERICK-WILLIAM'S
GRENADIERS.

father, Frederick William was in such a fury that
he drew his sword and would have run him through

the body with it had not one of his generals who was present sprung between, caught the king's arm, and cried out, "Sire! run me through if you will, but spare your own son." Then the prince was thrown into prison at Küstren. His friend Katte was condemned to death, and the king forced his son to see his friend hanged before the window of his prison. Keith had saved himself by flight. The king had sentence of death pronounced against the prince. Then an old general exclaimed, "Sire! if your Majesty will have blood, take mine, and welcome; but as long as I have a voice to raise in protest you shall not have that of the crown prince." The emperor, Charles VI., also interfered, and informed the king that the crown prince could only be condemned capitally at an imperial diet. "Very well," said the king, "then I will hold my own court on him at Königsberg, which is outside the confines of the empire, where no one can control me." A faithful servant boldly answered, "Only God, sire, will be over you there, to call you to task for shedding your son's blood." At these words the king became grave, and said no more about the execution of Frederick.

All this while the prince was in close confinement. He had a hard bench for his seat, the floor for his bed, and he was fed on prison fare. At last he wrote a penitential letter to his father, acknowledging that he had done wrong, and promising not to be disobedient for the future. In order thoroughly to crush his obstinacy the king did not give him his freedom at once, but kept him under watch at Küstren for two years. At last, on the marriage of his sister Wilhelmina to the Prince of Baireuth, his father allowed him to return to Berlin. Father and son were reconciled, and thenceforth Frederick William called him his "dear Fritz."

The king bought for him the castle of Rheinsberg, near Neu-Ruppin, for his residence. There Frederick spent the happiest days of his life. He collected the most famous men of letters about him, and devoted himself to science and music; and he carried on a correspondence with Voltaire and other celebrated French philosophers and poets. Both father and son learnt to regard each other with mutual esteem, and Frederick William exclaimed in his last illness, "I thank my God that I shall have so worthy a successor; I shall die content."

The treatment which Frederick had received left its fatal effects on his character; it made him hard, selfish, and unscrupulous; and so it came about that he behaved unworthily of a great man about the Silesian duchies.

L.

THE ARMY OF CUT-AND-RUN.

(1756–1763.)

MARIA THERESA could not forget Silesia snatched from her unjustly. Moreover, the growth of the power and influence of Prussia was a cause of envy to other princes. Maria Theresa was able by this means to unite a large confederation against Prussia. France, Russia, and Saxony took part against it; and it was proposed to deprive the king of his royal title, and reduce him to be merely Margrave of Brandenburg. Prussia succeeded in securing England as her ally. George II. himself disliked Frederick, and would willingly have continued the alliance with Austria, but the English parliament ranged itself on the side of Prussia. Following his usual tactics of making cat-like leaps before his enemies expected an attack, Frederick, without even declaring war, invaded Saxony, defeated the Austrians, and surrounded and captured a Saxon army. This was the opening of the Seven Years' War, or Third Silesian War.

In this war Frederick proved himself a general of the first order. Although he had half Europe opposed to him, yet he was almost always conqueror. He defeated the Austrians at Prague and Leuthen; an imperial and French army was routed by him at Rossbach; a Russian army was put to flight by him at Zorndorf. However, he met with reverses at Kollin and Hochkirch before the Austrians. Moreover, he lost the battle of Kunersdorf when opposed to Austrians and Russians united. But in spite of all his heroism and his many successes Frederick would certainly have been overwhelmed in the end if the allies had not gradually withdrawn their assistance from Austria, till at length Prussia and Austria were left alone, face to face. As both were exhausted by the long war, peace was concluded at the hunting lodge Hubertsburg, in Saxony, and Silesia was left in the hands of Frederick. It remains Prussian to this day.

Among all the great and remarkable battles fought in the Seven Years' War, that of Rossbach deserves special notice.

Late in the year of 1757 Frederick the Great had advanced at the head of 20,000 men to the River Saale, to drive the French and a division of the imperial army out of Saxony. The latter were thrice as numerous as the Prussians, and rejoiced at the prospect of a battle with such preponderance, thinking that now at last they would be able to surround and crush the king.

Frederick had encamped on rising ground. The French marched round the hill with their bands playing, thinking to enclose the Prussians. With the capture of the king they trusted to bring the war to an end. The Prussians remained motionless ; the smoke rose from their camp-fires, they were eating their breakfasts. Frederick was in the castle on the hill. He knocked a hole in the roof, climbed through, and sat there for an hour watching the movements of the enemy, then he came down and ate a hearty breakfast. When he saw the heads of the enemy's columns opposite his left flank he gave the signal. At once the tents were furled, the soldiers sprang to arms, the drums rattled, the lines formed, the concealed cannon began to spout flame, and roar; the cavalry general, Seidlitz, charged down the hill at the enemy, hurled himself at their ranks, and broke them before they had time to form into line of battle. The enemy, unprepared for such rapid movements, gave way in panic, and in less than half an hour the battle was won, with the loss on the Prussian side of not more than 300 men, whilst on the side of the allies 4000 were killed and wounded, 7000, with eleven generals, were taken prisoners, and sixty-three cannons and twenty-two standards fell into the hands of the conquerors. The French fled without reforming, a broken, disorganized, panic-stricken rabble, and did not stop till they had placed the Rhine between themselves and the formidable Prussians. The popular humour nicknamed the French host thus defeated the Army of Cut-and-Run (Reiss-aus-Armee).

LI.

OLD FRITZ REPAIRS RUINS.

AFTER the victorious conclusion of the Seven
Years' War the king devoted his attentions to the
repair of the ruin wrought by it. The war had
caused his subjects terrible sufferings. It is said that
14,500 houses lay in ashes, and so many men had
been consumed in his armies that there were not men
to till the fields, nor horses to draw the harvest
wanes. In Saxony 100,000 men had perished of
famine alone; in Bohemia 180,000 had died of
hunger; but Prussia and Silesia had suffered less
from this cause, because the king and his minister,
Schalaberndorf, had enforced the cultivation of
the potato. At first, great prejudice had existed
against this useful tuber, but Frederick saw its value
and insisted on its growth. As many as twenty
thousand persons emigrated from Bohemia, from
the trampled and burnt corn-fields, to eat the po-
tatoes in Prussia and live. The king had the
ruined villages rebuilt. He provided the impoverished farmers with grain to sow, and he imported
horses which he distributed among them. He
had drains and canals cut to dry swamps, and he
improved the roads. Every year he went the
round of his land, to see how it was prospering,

FREDERICK THE GREAT.
(From the Painting by Bause.)

and to remedy abuses. When he saw a tract under cultivation which had before been moor or marsh, he was wont to say, "I have gained a new province." He encouraged science and art, built schools, and improved the administration of justice. He was familiar with his subjects, always had an ear open to their grievances, and a hand ready to rectify them. He was specially fond of the agricultural population. He liked to go among them, talk to the farmers, and learn their wants and their opinions. Consequently, he was greatly beloved by them, and they spoke of him as "Father Fritz," or as "Old Fritz." His early acquaintance with the infidel writers of France had driven all belief in Christianity out of his heart, and, believing nothing, he was tolerant. When he heard of a dispute about some hymn-books, which was referred to him as head of the Evangelical Church in his lands, he said, "Bah! Let them sing what tom-foolery they like."

As he did not believe in religion, he had, unfortunately, no trustworthy standard of right and wrong. At his court was a Scotchman, named Keith, a man so honorable, truthful, and good that Frederick said of him, "That man almost makes me believe in virtue." Whether his care for the good of his people sprang from mere selfishness, a knowledge that their prosperity secured his own power, or whether his heart was better than his principles, one cannot tell. We will hope the best.

He had stooping shoulders, wore a three-cornered laced hat on his head, and a long pig-tail. His uniform was threadbare, blue with red facings. He wore short black breeches and long boots. Many droll stories are told of him. The people of Potsdam stuck up a caricature, representing him with a coffee-mill in his lap at a street corner. He saw it as he passed. "Put it lower, that it may be better seen," said the king, and passed on. One of his guards, too poor to buy a watch, attached a bullet to his chain and wore it in his pocket. The king once asked him the time of day. The officer pulled out the bullet and said, "My watch points but to one hour, that in which I am prepared to die for your Majesty." After that, of course, Frederick handed him his own gold watch.

The king was fond of snuff, with which he stained his clothes. Once when he met the Austrian emperor, he assumed, out of compliment, the Austrian uniform of white embroidered with silver. But the snuff got over the cloth and made a sad mess of the beautiful suit. He looked at the officers in splendid trim who surrounded the emperor, and said, "Gentlemen, I am not clean enough for your company; I do not deserve to wear your colours."

Here is one of his good sayings: "Nothing is nearer akin to death than idleness. It is not necessary that I should live, but it is necessary that whilst I live I be busy." As long as he lived he loved his flute, and when thinking over affairs of state he used to stride through the corridors and chambers of his palace at Potsdam playing on this instrument.

By his prudent government he raised the kingdom of Prussia to the level of Austria, France, and England, as one of the first-class powers in Europe. His army was certainly the best disciplined on the continent; but he allowed the soldiers to be flogged for small offences. Louis XV. supposed that the success of the Prussians was due to the cat-o'-nine-tails, so he introduced it into his army. But when one of the subalterns was ordered to flog a private he killed himself rather than do so.

When Frederick the Great died in 1786 the news of his death filled Germany with sorrow. He left to his successor a flourishing kingdom with six millions of inhabitants, a splendid army, and a full treasury.

Frederick well merited the appellation of "the Great," for he set a great example to the sovereigns of Germany. His unfortunate bringing up, which both hardened his heart and killed his faith, were the cause of his not being the greatest of modern kings, or of being really, as he was called in French, "Sans pareil."

LII.

THE DOINGS OF TWO HUNDRED PRINCES.

WHEN the Thirty Years' War came to an end there were something like two hundred independent states in Germany, and the fashion set in to regard France as the pattern by which all must live and rule. The Thirty Years' War had nearly extinguished culture in the land, and France was highly cultivated, consequently there was much excuse for the princes. Unfortunately, French culture was not sound at core; it was a glittering soap-bubble.

Louis XIV. was a great monarch, but in exactly the opposite way to Frederick II. Louis gained a splendid name, and ruined France, and sowed the seeds of the revolution which destroyed the throne. Frederick made Prussia prosperous, and planted the basis of his throne so deep that it has stood unshaken, and has become the centre of the new German empire. The princes of the 18th century did not see the mistake Louis XIV. was making; we can, because we have history to teach us. None of the princes could escape the fashion of copying France. Even Frederick the Great felt its influence as you have heard, and its influence was pernicious to him.

When Louis XIV. built his palace at Versailles

and created a city in the midst of a sandy waste, most of the princelings of Germany followed suit, and sought to create towns in the most unsuitable places.

George Samuel, of Nassau Idstein, unable to create a city in his diminutive county, resolved, at least, to call a village into being and give it his name; so he erected Georgenborn on the top of a bald mountain. The village was built, and roads to it were engineered; it was provided with a mayor and pastor, and then the wretched peasants were driven, by an edict of the count, from their old homes into the cold new houses. After a lingering life of thirty years, the successor of George Samuel issued an edict ordering the place to be destroyed, and its name to be blotted out of the map. But, queerly enough, just then a new industry had sprung up in Georgenborn, and the little village suddenly began to prosper. Georgenborn still exists, a monument to all the world that villages are not to be created or extinguished by the caprice of rulers.

More grotesque still was the attempt of Count William of Bückeburg, whose ambition it was not to have a palace and town like Versailles, but a fortress like Metz. His county was so small that a cannon-ball could cross it at a shot. At great expense he created a fortified place and mounted guns on the ramparts, but within were nothing to defend but a range of wooden huts, an observatory, and a potato field.

You know by pictures, if you have not seen it, the beautiful castle of Heidelberg, the finest ruin of a

palace in Germany. Heidelberg *was* the capital of
the Palatinate, but the elector, Charles Philip, in
1720, made Mannheim his capital. He built it
entirely, taking a chessboard as his plan. In it is a
hideous palace, and the town is placed on a dead flat
piece of ground. Baron Pöllnitz, who wrote his
memoirs at the time, says, " I have seen partridges
where are now palaces. The whole town is laid out
in a most regular and charming manner; and it is
without dispute one of the prettiest places in Europe." How taste alters! We should say it was,
with the exception of Darmstadt, the ugliest. Duke
Eberhard Louis of Würtemberg also transferred
his capital from Stuttgard to a new town he built
and called after his name, Ludwigsberg. The cost
was enormous, and, what was more grievous, it was
undertaken at a time of famine. When the foundations were laid bread was thrown among the starving peasants to still their murmurs. The palace
contains four hundred apartments. The city was
planned in square blocks, like Mannheim and
Darmstadt, with seven squares, eight gates, and
three parish churches. Now this town is only
kept from falling into ruin by being converted into
an arsenal; but grass grows in the streets, and the
palace is decaying.

Karlsruhe was built by the Margrave of Baden-
Durlach, Charles William, about his hunting lodge,
which was in the depths of a forest, but which he
converted into a palace.

Baron Pöllnitz says of this: " The present margrave, Charles, laid the plan and the foundation of

this city and its palace.   Imagine the palace at the
entrance of a great forest, in the centre of a star
formed by thirty-two walks.   Behind the palace is a
lofty octagonal tower commanding the walks.   On
the other side of the palace is the town.   Between
the houses run five streets.   The main street is in a
line with the centre of the palace.   At the end of
the three chief streets, opposite the palace, are three
churches, one for the Lutherans, another for the
Calvinists, and the third for the Catholics."

You will remember how that in the rococco period
straight lines and stiffness were avoided ; now the
fashion was run in the opposite extreme, everything
was formal and regular.

Darmstadt was rebuilt in the same detestable
taste, about the same time, by the electors Louis I.
and III., who laid out the town in the form it now
wears.   One street is just like another, one house the
counterpart of another.   At the head of the main
street is the unsightly palace ; at the two ends of the
cross street two unsightly churches, one for the
Calvinists, the other for the Catholics.

Those who did not build cities erected palaces.
The Baron de Reichenbach, a Belgian traveller of
the beginning of this century, says : " The princes
seem to have been actuated by a feverish rivalry
who should be best housed.   No little potentate
could pass muster who had not his Louvre and his
Versailles."

At Würzburg the bishop erected a splendid
palace, the foundations of which were laid in 1720,
although he had two others in the place, one the

castle of Marienberg, the second only finished the year before he began the third. This new palace contains two hundred and eighty-four apartments, one devoted to a merry-go-round for the amusement of the prelate, his chaplains, and court on rainy days. The prince-bishop occupied a little carriage in the whirligig, hung with episcopal purple velvet, embroidered with the mitre and arms of the See.

LIII.

GOOD KING JOSEPH.

(1780–1790.)

AMONG all the German princes who ascended the imperial throne Joseph II. takes one of the first places. He was the son of Maria Theresa and inherited from her the good qualities which made her the darling of her people. This noble emperor devoted his whole life to the service of the state, and at a time when gambling was the rage never played for money. On the occasion of a visit to Versailles he declined to take a hand at cards. "A prince who loses," he said, "loses the money of his subjects." He was not a drinker or a gourmand. He loved music, and played the violoncello. He was eager to redress wrongs, almost too eager, for he made sweeping changes before his people were prepared to accept them, and Frederick the Great was right when he said that Joseph always took the second step before he made the first.

From youth up he was a great admirer of Frederick, whom he took as his pattern in his attempts at amendment. When he met Frederick for the first time at Neisse, he exclaimed joyfully, "Now my wishes are fulfilled, as I have had the honor of embracing this great king and general." After a second meeting Frederick said to those who surrounded him, "I have seen the emperor, and am satisfied that he will play a great part in the affairs of Europe. He was born at a most bigoted court, and has shaken himself free from superstition. He was nurtured in pomp, and yet has simple habits. He has had the incense of flattery burnt under his nose, and yet is modest. He glows with love of fame, yet sacrifices his ambition to duty. He has had pedants for teachers, yet his taste for the best books is healthy."

You have been told how the princes built their new towns on plans of the strictest uniformity, making streets, houses, and churches all alike. Joseph II. tried to do the same thing in governing his territories, and so showed that want of common sense which Frederick II. possessed, and which saved him from committing gross blunders. In the Austrian dominions ten principal languages were spoken, and each nation had its own laws and administration. Joseph formed the scheme of uniting them all into one and ruling all by one simple system ; and of abolishing all distinctions of religion, language, law and manners. In the Austrian monarchy there were thirteen governments. He suppressed these, did away with the local parliaments, made the German tongue obligatory in all the public offices, and allowed the officers only two years for learning it, and abolished old customary forms, cancelled charters, and suppressed privileges. He meant well. It was very difficult to govern

Hungarians, Bohemians, Germans, Moravians, Italians, Flemings, Croatians, Tyrolese, Transylvanians, etc., by different laws, and it would facilitate government greatly if they were all ruled directly from Vienna, by one system of government. But Joseph did not consider that these several nations might be warmly attached to their own laws and traditional customs. So, instead of doing good, he threw the system of government into great confusion.

Then he drew up a catechism of government for the people to be taught in the schools, in which he reduced his laws to a sort of table of commandments, which was profane and absurd. Here are some of his commandments. " Thou shalt not send hare-skins out of the country. Thou shalt not keep useless dogs. Thou shalt not plant tobacco without permission."

But though Joseph made mistakes, he did a vast amount of real good. His heart was in the right place. He was conscientious and earnest in his desire to rectify abuses, but his head was not strong enough to show him where to stop.

The peasants had been kept under by feudal laws, and were almost bondsmen. He removed their bonds and cancelled all the intolerable restrictions which kept them from prospering. He encouraged the schools, and extended and improved the system of education. He also reduced the number of monasteries and convents from over two thousand to seven hundred, and he abolished all those which were of no practical utility. Monks, friars, and nuns must either teach, preach, or nurse the sick. He would not allow any orders to remain which were idle. The principal religious orders were the Benedictines, who cultivated learning and kept schools; the Jesuits, who taught in schools and preached; and the Franciscans or Capuchins, who lived on what they could beg.

The Jesuits made themselves particularly obnoxious by meddling with politics; the Capuchins, recruited from the lowest of the people, were ignorant, and great encouragers of superstition. The money and buildings acquired by the suppression of so many monasteries were devoted to useful purposes—schools, hospitals, libraries, etc. Joseph placed all the monasteries under the supervision of the bishops of the dioceses in which they were. This was an excellent rule, as hitherto they had been independent and gone their own way and did what they liked, without any control. The occasion of this was the discovery of great cruelties committed in a Capuchin convent in Vienna. One of the friars there, named Fressler, informed the emperor that there was a prison in it in which some of the friars had been kept locked up for many years. One had been there for fifty, another for forty, a third for fifteen, and a fourth for nine years. The emperor thereupon issued an inquisition and suppressed the begging orders. He lessened the revenues of the largest bishoprics, suppressed some, and created others, and granted the free exercise of their religion to all denominations. The Pope, Pius VI., alarmed at these high-handed proceedings, thinking he was going to emulate the course of

Henry VIII. of England, made a journey to Vienna
to remonstrate with the emperor in person. Joseph
received him with slight courtesy, and kept him almost as a prisoner. He had the doors of his lodging walled up, with the exception of the front door,
over which a guard was placed, to prevent the Pope
from receiving private visits and stirring up discontent. After spending four weeks without effecting
anything, Pius at length departed with a heavy heart.
The emperor accompanied him as far as the abbey
of Mariabrunn, and two hours after the Pope had
left its shelter he ordered the monastery to be
closed, to show how little the Pope had influenced
him.

His arbitrary interference with the usages and
liberties of his states led to revolt. Belgium refused to pay taxes, and declared itself independent.
In Hungary there were risings of the people, and
the emperor was forced to withdraw his orders for
changes in that kingdom. He made war with the
Turks and met with disaster. The hereditary dominions of Austria were in ferment, and revolution
threatened him on all sides. Under these disap-
pointments his health and spirits gave way. Shortly before his death he wrote of himself, " I know
my own heart. I am convinced of the sincerity of
my purposes, and I trust that, when I am gone, I
shall be impartially judged."

That impartial judgment has been arrived at by
all historians. No one doubts the good intentions
of Joseph II.; no one admits that he had the sound
judgment to carry them out prudently. Joseph

died in February, 1790, in his forty-ninth year. As he left no children he was succeeded by his brother Leopold, who had hitherto been Grand Duke of Tuscany.

Leopold ascended the tottering throne to find himself surrounded with dangers. All parts of his vast dominions were agitated by intestine commotions, or were the scene of open rebellion, the fruit of Joseph's ill-considered or premature reforms. Although he reigned only a few years, yet his moderation and his sober judgment succeeded in pacifying the general agitation, and restoring confidence and content. All the good that Joseph had done survived him, and his mistakes were corrected.

LIV.

GENIUS COMES TO THE FRONT.

THE close of the 18th century was a period of great literary waking. In the rococo time the general unreality invaded and pervaded literature; but now a change took place, and men of real genius came to the front who have made themselves imperishable names. The first to break away from the fantastic foppery of the rococo style was Gotthold Lessing (1729–1781), who, though he tried at first to study theology and medicine, was destined to give his life to pure literature. He ridiculed the imitation of French writers, and demanded that German authors should develop originality in thought and style. Calling attention to the genius of Kant and Winckelmann, and opposing the methods of Wieland and Klopstock, he urged that sentimentality should no longer infect religion nor frivolity debase art. He wrote *Minna von Barnhelm*, a comedy not free from the affectations he opposed, and *Emilia Galotti*, a tragedy, in which he retold the story of Virginia but made the characters modern. His Laocöon is a critical dissertation on the limits of poetry and painting which has exerted and still exerts a vast influence everywhere. *Nathan der Weise* is another powerful work of his independent mind, in which, in the guise of a dramatic story, he sets forth the philosophy of his religion.

Before Lessing died he saw the two greatest authors of Germany started on the literary career which has lent its chiefest glory to the period,— John Wolfgang von Goethe (1749–1832) and John Christopher Frederick Schiller (1759–1805). The former stands second only to our Shakespeare as a poet, and was a man of a wonderful genius marred by intense vanity. The son of a gentleman of some fortune, he was educated with remarkable thoroughness, and his personal attainments and manners caused the world to expect great things of him. In spite of this there was much surprise when, in 1773, his drama, *Götz von Berlichingen* appeared. It was followed the next year by *The Sorrows of Young Werther*. The literary world was intoxicated with the spirit of romanticism, and Germany entered upon a season of intellectual convulsion known as the *Sturm und Drang*, or storm and stress period. *Götz* was founded upon the old story of the hero of the Iron hand, a strong and manly but lawless baron of the sixteenth century ; and the *Sorrows of Werther* wove into one texture the unhappy passions of the author and those of a student whose sad story Goethe had learned. With considerable mawkish sentimentality was mingled much admirable description ; the language was wonderful, and the whole so well accorded with the vague longing and discontent of the age, that, as Carlyle says, " the heart and voice of all Europe loudly and at once responded to it." The romance was greedily read by young and old, and some young fools even followed Werther's example and took their own lives, in order to excite for themselves the pity so freely accorded to the hero of the story.

At the invitation of the grand duke, Charles Augustus, Goethe went to Weimar in 1775 ; and there he afterwards made the acquaintance of Schiller, whom he so warmly appreciated for his pure and healthy genius and noble mind, that he called the period a "new spring-tide" in his life. In this little place without trade or manufactures, Goethe was worshipped by everybody, especially by the women ; but the great men of the nation, too, gathered about him, and Weimar became a sort of German Athens. The poet gave himself up at first to social enjoyment, but afterwards he engaged in study, though for several years he published little. His study, travels, and varied experience in life bore fruit, however, and in after years he produced novels, poems, and plays that challenged the admiration of the world. Among his great works are the romantic drama *Egmont*, the tragedy of *Iphigenia von Tauris*, the melancholy reverie *Torquatus Tasso*, and the idyllic epic *Hermann and Dorothea.*

If Goethe's genius did not culminate in his wonderful poem founded upon the fable of *Faust*, in which with melody, wit, pathos, mystery, reverence, and irony he depicted the disenchantment of the intellect, it reached its greatest expression in his songs and ballads, the spontaneous outgushings of his mind in every variety of mood. Charming in sim-

plicity, grotesque, weird, and haughty by turns, they
are certainly human feeling " married to immortal
verse." The genius of Goethe was recognized in
England as well as at home, and on his last birth-
day fifteen representative writers there, including
Scott, Southey, Carlyle, and Procter, united in sending him a greeting accompanied by a seal, on which
were engraved the words from one of his own
poems, *Ohne Hast*, *Ohne Rast*, without haste, without rest. No contemporary had so much influence
upon literature, and no other German author at all
compares with him in this respect. Carlyle said
that he and the first Napoleon were the two greatest men of their day, and that Goethe was " intrin-
sically of much more unquestionable greatness"
than the conquering soldier.

Schiller was at many points a contrast to his
older contemporary. Without the exceptional advantages of Goethe he had prepared himself by
stealth for the career of a poet. As early as his
nineteenth year he had begun to compose a drama,
afterwards published as *The Robbers*, which startled
the literary world by its impassioned and fascinat-
ing eloquence, and is said actually to have induced
some persons of fortune to become amateur outlaws. He did not visit Weimar until his twenty-
eighth year, and when he and Goethe met there
was a mutual repulsion. He wrote to a friend that
between persons of such different views of life no
substantial intimacy was possible. Though each
avoided the other the substantial intimacy grew, as
has been intimated, and was fruitful for Germany.

The one stood for the tyranny of the intellect and the other for the loveliness of the affections.

Among the works of Schiller were the long drama of *Wallenstein*, in three parts, of five acts each, obviously too long for acting; *Mary Stuart*, *The Maid of Orleans*, *The Bride of Messina*, and *William Tell*. Though deservedly renowned as a dramatist Schiller is probably best known by his poems, among which *The Song of the Bell*, *The Diver*, *The Glove*, *The Cranes of Ibycus*, and *Rudolph of Hapsburg* are perhaps the most familiar. Schiller reflected the ideal yearnings of his age, and sought to encourage men to love and be led by the good, the beautiful, and the true. When he died, at the early age of forty-five, Goethe exclaimed, "In losing my friend I have lost half of my being." Thirty-seven years later he calmly breathed away his own life, saying, "More light!" words that have sometimes been thought to express his longing for something better than this life afforded.

While Goethe and Schiller ruled in the kingdom of letters they were surrounded by many disciples and imitators, as well as by original thinkers, who advanced every branch of learning. Humboldt and Ritter cultivated geographical science; Herder and the brothers Schlegel went deep into history and criticism; Fichte, Hegel, Schelling, and Kant carried the fame of German philosophy over the world; Ranke and Niebuhr presented history in new phases; Schleiermacher and Neander discussed deep principles of theology; Jean Paul Richter soared to the mysterious heights of transcendentalism; and Hoffmann, Fouqué, and Tieck revelled in the realms of the imagination. If the rulers were royal the subjects were truly worthy of them.

Music, which began to become a great art in the rococco period, now sprang into full perfection. Some of the greatest musical geniuses of the world belong to this period: Mozart, Glück, Haydn, and Beethoven. All of these wrote church music; Haydn composed the beautiful oratorio *The Creation;* Glück wrote operas on classic themes; Mozart took more popular subjects; Beethoven wrote one opera only, *Leonore* or *Fidelio.* Mozart's music is exquisitely melodious, but lacks the massiveness possessed by that of Beethoven. Mozart died at the age of thirty-five; poor Beethoven became deaf, gloomy, and distrustful in his old age. With these composers the orchestra became of much greater importance than formerly. Handel, the great master of the previous generation, scarcely knew anything of the power and properties of the various instruments; but now they were brought into use, parts were written for each, and all were woven into a whole, blending and governed by one idea, but each acting separately from the others. This may, therefore, be said to be the epoch of the development of orchestral music.

LV.

AN UPTURNING IN FRANCE.

Louis XIV. was succeeded on the throne of France by his great-grandson, Louis XV., aged only five years and a half. On the death of the king the Duke of Orleans, as first prince of the blood, was appointed regent. The duke led a profligate life, and set a bad example, which was only too readily imitated by those at court. By his extravagance he raised the national debt to dangerous proportions. This wretched condition of affairs did not mend when Louis XV. attained his majority. The young king thought of nothing but his pleasures, and left the management of the affairs of state to his ministers and favourites.

At this time it became the fashion to be, or to affect to be, vicious, and to scoff at religion and morality. Many authors took up the pen to write profanities and to turn Christianity, the clergy, and virtue into ridicule.

At the same time writings were distributed among the people showing up the badness of the Government, and urging the abolition of abuses and the introduction of reforms. The vices of the court, its extravagance, the growth of the national debt, the burden of taxation falling on the people made the latter ready to accept these teachings. Both the nobility and the clergy at this time had very extensive privileges. Neither paid taxes, so that the whole burden fell on the farmers and tradesmen. This was a grievous injustice. It had been redressed in England long ago by the nobility, voluntarily. In France and in Germany it remained as an intolerable wrong. Most powerful of all was the example of the English colonies in North America, who, in 1783, separated themselves from their mother country, and founded a republic.

France, intent on weakening her ancient foe, had sent numbers of her sons to America, where they had fought against the English, and these returned to their native land full of the novel ideas of liberty and of enthusiasm for a republican form of government. They contrasted the fresh virtue of the new institutions in the United States with the decrepid corruption of the French crown.

Thus it came about that there grew up in what was called the *Tiers état*, or Third Estate—*i. e.*, the people themselves—an intense anger and bitterness against the nobles and clergy, who paid no taxes, and against the crown, which sanctioned such abuses.

In this time of agitation of spirits Louis XVI. came to the throne of France. He was married to Marie Antoinette, daughter of Maria Theresa, and sister of Joseph II. The accession of Louis XVI. was greeted with great acclamations of joy from the people, for they hoped that with it would come relief from their crushing taxation, and a return to better times. Louis, a well-intentioned, blameless man, with his heart full of love for his people, and desirous to be a just and good ruler, lacked the mental power and the energy of character to grapple with an evil of such long growth, and to take decisive and subversive measures. His queen was fond of gaiety, and by her example countenanced the most lavish extravagance. She was only fifteen when she was married, and at Versailles she was surrounded by frivolous and pleasure-seeking courtiers, who hid from her the truth, so that she probably had no idea of the real condition of affairs. She was only nineteen when her husband became king. She was a good woman, tenderly attached to her children and husband. She was very beautiful, and much flattered, and this perhaps a little turned her head.

The evil condition of affairs increased to a fearful degree. The exchequer was robbed by those who had charge of it; the taxes would not suffice to cover the outlay; and the king, almost reduced to the necessity of declaring the state bankrupt, demanded aid from the nobility and clergy, who, hitherto free from taxation, had amassed great wealth. The aristocracy, blind to their true interest, refused to comply, and by so doing compelled the king to have recourse to the Third Estate.

Accordingly, in 1789, he convoked a general assembly, in which deputies sent by the citizen and peasant classes were not only numerically equal to those of the aristocracy, but were their superiors in ability and energy. When the nobility and clergy refused to share the burden of taxation, and even declined to sit together with the commons, the deputies of the Third Estate separated from the other two houses and declared themselves a competent national assembly. Many of the nobility and the majority of the clergy, feeling the justice of the cause of the people, united with them, and gave up their privileges. The members of this assembly met in the Tennis Court of the palace of Versailles, and there swore not to separate till they had given a new constitution to the realm. The assembly was thenceforth called the Constitutional Assembly. The men who most distinguished themselves at this conjuncture were Count Mirabeau, the Abbé Sieyes, and the Count of Lafayette.

The news of this decided step created violent agitation in Paris, and the people broke loose. On June 14th, 1789, a mob attacked the Bastille, an ancient strong castle in Paris that served as a prison, took it by storm, and levelled its walls with the dust. Soon after, armed bands of men and women rushed off to Versailles, burst into the palace, where they killed several of the guards, and forced the king to come to Paris. The National Assembly also, at the same time, transferred its sessions to Paris. Emboldened by its first successes the Assembly now undertook a thorough transformation of the state, and in order to attain the object for which it had been assembled, that of procuring supplies, declared the aristocracy subject to taxation, and sold the enormous property belonging to

the Church.   All distinctions and privileges were
abolished, and all Frenchmen were pronounced equal.
It went further still.   The people were declared the
only true sovereign, and the king the first servant
of the state.

At the first outbreak of the revolution the two
brothers of the king and many of the nobility fled
the country.   All through France the peasants rose
and set fire to the chateaux, and burned the archives containing the title-deeds of the nobles to
their lands.   The Assembly continued its work.   It
divided France into eighty-three departments.   It
published a list of the rights of men without saying anything about their duties.   Everywhere disturbances became worse.   The royal family, feeling
no longer safe, attempted to fly, but were arrested at
Varennes and brought back as prisoners to Paris
(July 23, 1791).

The rabble had now completely got the upper
hand.   At midnight of the 9th of October they
broke into the Tuilleries, the royal palace, massacred the gallant Swiss guards who defended the
king, and clamoured for his deposition.   That
he and his family might not fall into the hands of
these savages the king, with the queen and his children, escaped to the hall where the National Assembly was collected, at nine o'clock in the morning
of the 10th.   The Assembly declared the king
provisionally deprived of his functions, and con-
signed him and his family to the Temple, one of
the prisons of Paris.   All the adherents of the king
were then secured and thrown into the prisons.

LEOPOLD II. IN THE IMPERIAL ROBES.

Leopold II., Emperor of Austria, and Frederick William II., King of Prussia, now prepared for war. The French forestalled them by declaring war. The King of Prussia, at the head of 50,000 of his own men and 30,000 Austrians, took Longwy, and advanced upon Verdun and Champagne. The news filled the rabble with fury. The Jacobins, as the most extreme of the revolutionists were called, from a club into which they had formed themselves, cried out, " Our most dangerous enemies are not the Germans at Verdun, they are to be found at Paris in our prisons." Thus instigated, the mob burst into one place of detention after another, and for four days in succession massacred all they found in them. The same horrors were perpetrated at Lyons, Rheims, Meaux, and Versailles. The massacre began on Sept. 2d, and the same day Robespierre was elected to the National Convention, as the third national assembly was designated.

To protect the frontiers against the allied sovereigns, and to carry the war into their territories, the Assembly ordered armies to advance. The French at once invaded the Netherlands and defeated the Austrians at Jemmapes. The Republican soldiers entered Brussels, pillaged the Netherland cities of all that was valuable, and after doing this effectually proclaimed liberty and equality and the rights of men. Another French army advanced to the Rhine and secured Mainz.

The alliance of the German sovereigns against the Revolution precipitated the fate of the king. The National Convention condemned him to death, and

FRIDERICUS WILHELMUS. II.
BORUSSORUM REX

FREDERICK WILLIAM II. OF PRUSSIA.
(From the painting by Schröder.)

the execution was fixed for the 21st February, 1793. After a heart-rending parting from his wife and children Louis XVI. mounted the scaffold with dignity and Christian resignation. On reaching the platform he advanced to the breasting to address the people. " Frenchmen," he said, " I am guiltless of the crimes whereof I am accused. I forgive those who have brought me to my death, and I pray God that the blood you are about to shed may not be required of France." His address was cut short by the rattle of drums. He allowed his hands to be bound without an attempt at resistance ; and as the Abbé Edgeworth, his confessor, exclaimed, " Son of S. Louis, mount to heaven ! " the axe fell. Then there was a rush of the people. They burst through the guards to sop their handkerchiefs in the royal blood. Thus died Louis XVI. His prime minister, Necker, a Swiss, said of him, " He was a sovereign good to the heart's core. He loved his people as a father loves his children. He did what was right when he saw what was his duty, and how to discharge it. He was a ready help to all in trouble. He released the peasants from serfdom, and abolished the irksome feudal duties. He put a stop to torture, and had the prisons placed under proper supervision and put into decent order. He restored to the Protestants their citizen rights. His whole life was spent in doing good. He suffered, not for his own sins, but for those of his forefathers. His people were, during the latter years, blinded to his excellence, and allowed his enemies to do what they willed with him. He died a martyr to his virtues."

The execution of Louis was followed by that of the queen in October. She was taken to the scaffold in a cart, with her hands tied behind her. She was scarce 38 years old when she died.

LVI.

THE MAN FROM CORSICA.

THE news of the execution of the king filled all Europe with horror and indignation, and in France several towns and the province of La Vendée rose against the National Convention. Most of the European powers formed an alliance against the French Republic (the 1st Coalition, 1793), and their armies advanced on the frontiers. A very speedy termination to the Republic might have ensued had not the powers been filled with rivalries, and had their forces been led by competent generals. The Duke of Coburg was at the head of the main body of the Austrians in the Netherlands, and he was reinforced by the English and Dutch. With their aid he drove the French out of the Netherlands, but instead of advancing at once on Paris he dawdled in the Low Countries, issuing manifestoes and investing Dunkirk. The Duke of Brunswick, in command of the Prussians, retook Mainz, but owing to the jealousy felt by the King of Prussia at the union of the English with the Austrians was not allowed to go forward.

In the spring of the following year the emperor, Francis II., visited the Netherlands, with the intention of pushing straight upon Paris. This project, practicable in 1793, was now utterly out of the question. The French had massed their armies to protect the frontier, and the Prussians had withdrawn in a sulk. The French sneered, " The allies are always wool-gathering, and wake up a year too late."

In face of the danger that menaced the Republic, on April 6th, a Committee of Public Safety was appointed at Paris, and the lives, the freedom, and the property of all the citizens were placed in the hands of this committee. They could condemn to death whom they would. At the head stood Robespierre, a cold, bloodthirsty man.

Now executions went on without cessation. No one was safe. The more moderate members of the Convention (the Girondists) were sent to the guillotine. Blood poured in streams, not in Paris only, but in all the large towns of France. Any one, on the faintest suspicion, was arrested, and once arrested his fate was sealed.

The Republic then turned its attention to repel the enemies at its doors. The English were beaten at Toulon. The Spanish, who had crossed the Pyrenees, retired over them again. The Prussians were defeated by Hoche and the Austrians by Jourdan The Prussians, full of jealousy of the Austrians, withdrew from the alliance, and concluded peace with the Republic, basely surrendering to France the whole left bank of the Rhine. Belgium was overrun and annexed to France, Holland formed into a republic under its protection. England remained inert. Only Austria abided unshaken. The French crossed the Rhine and invaded Swabia; were encountered by the Archduke Charles, and defeated him. The French took Stuttgart and Frankfort. Then the Austrians succeeded in breaking to pieces the invading army, and as it retreated the peasantry rose in a body and hunted the soldiers down.

In the mean time the Reign of Terror at Paris had come to an end. Robespierre had raged with such frightful bloodthirstiness, putting to death every one whom he considered an opponent, sparing not even Republicans of as advanced views as his own, that at last his own adherents were afraid for their lives, and the more moderate united against him. He was accused, a majority formed to condemn him, and he was dragged to the guillotine, a cowardly, quaking wretch, with a broken jaw, having tried, ineffectually, to shoot himself when sentenced to death.

A fresh constitution was now issued, and five men were appointed as *Directors* of the Republic. Among the many able generals possessed by France at this period Napoleon Bonaparte stood pre-eminent. He was the son of a Corsican lawyer, and was born at Ajaccio. As a boy he had shown a love for military studies. In his sixteenth year he entered the artillery in Paris as sub-lieutenant, and at the age of six-and-twenty he was nominated commander of the army of Italy. He found there that the soldiers were in a pitiable condition, without food, money, or clothing, dissatisfied and disorganized. But Napoleon was not one to be daunted. "Soldiers," he said, "you are badly fed, naked, and miserable among barren rocks. I will lead you down into the richest plains in the world. Great cities full of wealth, whole provinces will fall into your power; in them you will acquire all you want—fame, treasure, repose. Soldiers of the Army of Italy, with this prospect will your hearts fail? No; surely not. Forward!" and, in fact, in a surprisingly short time he conquered the greater part of Italy and converted the provinces that came into his power into republics. The Austrian armies sent against him were led by incompetent generals, who were perfectly incapable of winning success opposed to so consummate a genius as Bonaparte.

In the mean time the Austrian army, under the command of the gallant Archduke Charles, the brother of the emperor, Francis II., had, as you have heard, defeated the French in Würtemberg and the Black Forest, and driven them back across the Rhine.

In January, 1797, the Austrian general, Alvinzi, met a crushing defeat in Italy, with the loss of 20,000 men taken prisoners. At the same time another general, Wurmser, was forced to capitulate at Mantua with 21,000 men.

As soon as the snow began to melt on the Alps Bonaparte prepared to march up the Isonzo, cross the Alps, and penetrate to Vienna. In his alarm the emperor recalled the Archduke Charles from the Rhine, but he had only the fragments of the discouraged troops of Alvinzi to lead. "Hitherto," said Napoleon, "I have been fighting armies without generals, now I have to fight a general without an army."

A battle took place in the mountains at Tarvis, high up on the pass into the Gail Valley, afterwards called "the battle above the clouds." The archduke, with a handful of Hungarian hussars, defended the pass against sixteen thousand French, and did not turn to fly till only eight of his men were left. The archduke retired to Glogau, where he collected five thousand men, and again barred the way against the French, and held his ground with dauntless heroism till only two hundred and fifty of his men remained.

But now the archduke's troops, whom he had led to victory on the Rhine, were coming to his aid. The republic of Venice had made an alliance with Austria, and Napoleon was threatened in his rear. The brave Tyrolean peasants were up in arms, and routed his troops as they tried to push forward. The archduke hoped now to nip Bonaparte in the mountains, and crush him. But, with inconceivable folly, the emperor's advisers at Vienna threw away this unique opportunity. They were so panic-struck at the advance of Bonaparte that when he, conscious of the predicament in which he stood, to gain time, sent overtures of peace, not in the least supposing the Austrian ministers such fools as to accept them, they actually snapped at the proposals, and were in haste to get a treaty concluded. When Bonaparte saw the timorous sort of men with whom he had to deal he assumed a more defiant tone. The plenipotentiary of Austria was Count Cobenzl, who had been much in the service of the Empress of Russia, and had presented Bonaparte a beautiful and costly vase from Catherine, the Empress of Russia. Cobenzl was a witty playwriter, and immediately after some unpleasant piece of state business he produced a comedy full of fun. "I suppose," said the empress, "Cobenzl, you are waiting to kill us with laughing till you hear that the French are in Vienna?" This was the man sent into Udine to treat with Bonaparte. Now the latter was in far greater straits than Cobenzl supposed, for the Directory in Paris were getting jealous of him, and refused him more soldiers, and he knew very well that he could not get any further through the Alps where the passes were guarded by brave mountaineers, ready to roll down rocks on his troops, and excellent shots were lurking behind every stone and tree to pick off his officers. However, he put a bold face on the matter, and when Cobenzl made some demur to one of his demands Napoleon took up the porcelain cup the Empress Catherine had sent him, and dashed it to atoms on the floor. "There," said he, "take my terms, or I will shatter your precious monarchy like this vessel."

Cobenzl was too much frightened at the threat to stand out. A treaty was drawn up and signed, called the TREATY OF CAMPO FORMIO, on October 17, 1797. By this the emperor ceded to France the whole of the west bank of the Rhine, Flanders, and the Lombard provinces, but received in exchange the territory of Venice and the archbishopric of Salz-

burg. Now this concession of Napoleon was part
of his cleverness; he wanted by all means in his
power to rouse up the jealousy of Prussia against
Austria. You know that among children one becomes spiteful if another gets one slice of bread
and jam more than itself,—so is it with nations.
Prussia was consumed with anger and envy when
it heard that Austria was to gain that rich merchant-
city, Venice, and consequently would have nothing more to do with Austria against the common
enemy.

When the news reached Paris the French Republicans liked the idea of the cession of Venice to
Austria almost as little as did the Prussians; but
Napoleon quieted them. "Pshaw!" he said, "it is
only for a bit." The result of this clever stroke soon
became apparent. The Prussians sent an army into
Franconia, and seized Nuremberg and several other
towns. She also entered Westphalia, annexing
it, and stirred up Hesse-Cassel to grasp part
of Schaumburg-Lippe. That same year Frederick
William II. died, and was succeeded by his son,
Frederick William III., who continued the same
shameful and dishonourable policy of playing the
game of France against the only upholder of the
German name and honour, the Emperor of Austria.

Whilst Austria was lulled into peace the French
overran Switzerland and converted it into a republic under their protection; and thus this great
barrier which had protected the Austrian frontiers on
the side next France was thrown down. The peace

concluded by Napoleon at Campo Formio had to be ratified, that is, agreed to by all the powers concerned, and a meeting was appointed to be held at Rastadt, which had been the residence of the margraves of Baden. In it is a red sandstone palace: to this palace the envoys were summoned to meet

KARL WILHELM, BARON VON HUMBOLDT. *
(From a Drawing by P. C. Stroehling.)

in 1797, and there they sat haggling over terms till April, 1799, when the congress was broken up without coming to any agreement, in the way you shall hear.

The French envoys demanded all that had been granted by the treaty of Campo Formio, and agreed that, to indemnify the German princes, these latter should seize on all the remaining ecclesiastical principalities in the land, as the archbishoprics of Salzburg, Mainz, and Cologne, the bishoprics of Münster,

---

* See page 316.

Würzburg, Bamberg, Eichstädt, etc. But they went further. Not content with the west, or left, bank of the Rhine, they now asked for some places on the other bank as well.

Whilst the negotiations were in progress, France was collecting men and material for prosecuting the war. At Rastadt their principal envoy was Talleyrand, a man who had been a bishop, but had cared little for Christianity. He was a man of extraordinary talents, and cunning as a fox. He was able to do without sleep, and when asked how that was, he showed that his pulse throbbed, then stopped for some seconds, and then throbbed again. He said that his nature recruited itself in these pauses. With him were three others, Robert, Bonnies, and De Bry, from the dregs of the people, coarse, insolent, rapacious men. The German princes, all eager to make good terms with the French for themselves, bribed these French envoys to put in a good word for them; these scoundrels pocketed their money and insulted them for their folly. On the 1st of March, however, whilst negotiations were still in progress, the French crossed the Rhine, under Jourdan, and entered Würtemberg. The brave and able Archduke Charles met and defeated them, and Jourdan was obliged to recross the Rhine to Strasburg, where he left his army and returned to Paris. The insolence of the envoys and their outrageous demands at Rastadt had aroused great anger in the people, and a tumult broke out in Vienna, in which the tricolour, floating above the residence of the French ambassador, was torn down and burnt. The Congress of Rastadt broke up in haste. As the envoys were leaving the place some hussars rushed out of a wood upon the carriage and killed two of them.

Against England alone had the French hitherto been unable to deal crippling blows. In order to hurt English trade and to menace her Asiatic possessions Napoleon was sent with an army into Egypt. There he was victorious on land, everywhere; but Nelson, with the English fleet, fought and completely destroyed the French fleet lying in Abukir Bay. Whilst Bonaparte was in Egypt the French armies met some serious disasters on the Rhine and in Switzerland. The Directory at Paris was, moreover, weakened by the various parties squabbling together.

Bonaparte now left his army in Egypt and slipped across the Mediterranean unperceived by the English, landed in France, was appointed generalissimo over all the army, and at once upset, with the aid of his soldiers, the government, and appointed himself and two others as *Consuls*. This was in 1799, when the SECOND COALITION of European powers was formed against France, consisting of England, Russia, and Austria.

Inspired by Napoleon the French troops gained victory after victory. He crossed the Alps at the head of a new army, before the Austrians were aware that he was in motion. With that inconceivable folly which seemed to pervade the counsels of the Austrian ministry the Archduke Charles had been deprived of his generalship and sent into

Bohemia, and the command of the forces given to Marshall Kay. Suddenly Napoleon appeared in Lombardy, and on June 14, 1800, gained such a decisive victory at Marengo that the Austrian army was forced to lay down its arms. The whole of Italy fell once more into the hands of the French. And now, instead of recalling the able Archduke Charles, the command-in-chief was given to the Archduke John, a lad of eighteen, without experience and without genius. On the 3d of December this boy-general with his army was completely routed in the tremendous battle of Hohenlinden, more momentous even than that of Marengo in its military consequences. The shattered remains of the imperial army retreated behind the River Inn, followed by disaster. The Austrians lost 10,000 prisoners and 100 cannon. But now the voice of the nation made itself heard. Where was the Archduke Charles? Let him be recalled. Accordingly, he was ordered back from Bohemia. He flew to the rescue, but when, instead of the proud battalions he had led so often to victory, he found only a confused crowd of infantry, cavalry, and artillery covering the road, filled with panic, lost to discipline, the tears rolled down his furrowed cheeks. In vain did he try to rally them; they were too broken even to obey his voice. The French fell on the rear of the flying Austrians, and routed the rearguard with a loss of twelve hundred men, completing the demoralization of the army. A few days later the news arrived of the defeat of the Austrian army in Italy at the passage of the Mincio. These disasters once more inclined Austria to peace, which was concluded at Luneville (9th Feb., 1801). By this peace the whole of the left bank of the Rhine was again assured to France, and the petty republics established by France in Italy, Switzerland, and Holland were recognized. All but six of the free imperial cities were deprived of their privileges, the spiritual principalities were abolished, and many of the secular princes were "mediatised," that is, lost their sovereign authority, though allowed to retain their titles.

LVII.

NAPOLEON AS EMPEROR.

(1804.)

As Consul, Napoleon governed in France with great vigour and discretion. By wise laws and beneficial measures he endeavoured to give prosperity to the land, and to heal the wounds caused by protracted wars. The Revolution had abolished Christianity, hung or guillotined the priests, and had forbidden the use of the churches for Christian worship. Napoleon, in concert with the Pope, restored the exercise of the Christian religion, and arranged for the organization of the church in France, at the same time that he allowed perfect freedom of conscience to Protestants and Infidels. The bishops were paid by the state instead of from the confiscated estates, and the clergy also, without restoration of the tithe. The monasteries and convents were not re-opened; new schools were founded, and provision made for general education. To encourage traffic, good roads and canals were made. By these means Napoleon won the favour of the people. They were sick of the bloodshed of the Republican tyrants, and they breathed freely under the prudent rule of the First

Consul. Moreover, his victories over the powers opposed to France flattered the vanity of the nation. These circumstances conduced to further his aim for supremacy; but he did not dare take the title of king, which was still abhorrent to the people; therefore he resolved to make France an empire, and renew in himself the splendours of Charles the Great's reign. On the 18th of May, 1804, Bonaparte abolished the French Republic, and was elected hereditary emperor of France. On the 2d of December he was solemnly anointed and crowned by the Pope, Pius VII., whom he forced to come to Paris for the purpose. The ceremonies used at the coronation of Charlemagne were revived on this occasion. In March, 1805, he abolished the Italian republics and crowned himself with the iron crown of Lombardy. He formed the grand and daring scheme of converting the whole of Europe into one vast empire, with kings and princes over the several nations, all subject to himself.

In the mean time he sent an army into Hanover, and overran it. Prussia offered no interference, hoping by her neutrality to secure Hanover as her reward. England now persuaded Austria, Russia, and Sweden to combine again against France. This is called the THIRD COALITION, and was effected in 1805. To her eternal disgrace Prussia kept neutral, and allowed the Fatherland to be ravaged, because of her jealousy of Austria.

Napoleon at once put himself at the head of an army and advanced to Ulm. Sixty thousand Aus-

trians were in the town under General Mack, an incompetent man, who, panic struck at the appearance
of Bonaparte, capitulated without striking a blow.
A body of 12,000, commanded by the Archduke Ferdinand, made a bold attempt to break out, but all
his infantry and the greater part of his cavalry were
slain or captured, and a few hundred men alone succeeded in cutting their way through the enemy into
Bohemia.   Where was the Archduke Charles at this
time? Of course, where he was not specially
wanted, in Italy, through no fault of his, but through
the blundering stupidity of the emperor's council.
After Mack's surrender, Napoleon, with his usual
alacrity, marched with his main body straight upon
Vienna, whilst he sent some detachments into the
Tyrol to hold that in check, and entered the capital
in November, before the Archduke Charles, who
had been recalled, had time to arrive for its defence.   In the mean time the Emperor Alexander
I., of Russia, at the head of an army, approached
through Moravia.   Francis II. gathered together as
many of his scattered troops as he could and joined
Alexander.   Both emperors appealed earnestly
to Prussia to renounce its base alliance with France,
and in this decisive moment to aid in the anni-
hilation of the enemy, not of the Fatherland only,
but of Europe.   But no; the King of Prussia, hun-
gering after Hanover, hoped to buy it by his neutrality.   On December 2, 1805, a famous battle,
in which the three emperors of Christendom were
present, took place at Austerlitz, not far from
Brünn, and terminated in one of Napoleon's most

ALEXANDER, NAPOLEON AND FREDERICK WILLIAM III.
(From a contemporary picture by an unknown Artist.)

glorious victories. Immediately Prussia threw in
her part with France, secured Hanover, and in exchange surrendered Cleves, Anspach, and Neufchâtel
to the French. The Austrians, utterly paralyzed,
were unable to continue the struggle, and were
forced to conclude a peace, called the PEACE OF
PRESSBURG, at enormous sacrifice. Austria lost
Venice, Tyrol, and the Breisgau, a portion of land
between the Black Forest and the Rhine.

On his way east Napoleon had forced the dukes
of Bavaria, Würtemberg, and Baden to unite their
troops with his against the Austrians. Napoleon
now rewarded them by elevating Bavaria and Würtemberg into kingdoms, and by exalting the Duke
of Baden into a grand-duke, and giving him the
Austrian lands adjoining his own.

On the 12th of July, 1806, sixteen German princes,
of which the principal were Bavaria, Baden, Würtemberg, and Hesse - Darmstadt, formally separated
themselves from the German empire and declared
themselves subject to the French emperor. This is
called the Rhein-bund. Napoleon, to increase his
own splendour, now erected the provinces dependent
upon France into kingdoms and principalities, and
bestowed them upon his relatives and favourites.
His brother Joseph he made King of Naples; his
brother Louis, King of Holland; his step-son, Eugene Beauharnais, Viceroy of Italy; his brother-in-
law, Murat, formerly a common soldier, Grand-duke
of Berg; his first adjutant, Berthies, Prince of Neufchâtel.

On the 6th of August, 1806, the Emperor Francis

II. was forced to abdicate the imperial crown of Germany, and announce the dissolution of the empire in a touching address, full of stately sorrow. The last of the German emperors had shown himself, throughout the contest, worthy of his great ancestors, and had, almost alone, sacrificed all in order to preserve the honour and independence of Germany, until, abandoned by the greater part of the princes, he was unable to continue the contest.

Two years before, Francis II. had assumed the title of Emperor of Austria, *i. e.*, of the Eastern Realm, and it remains to the House of Hapsburg.

Now it was the turn of Prussia to be chastised. Now only did she awake to the fact that she had betrayed her best interests by not coming to the front with Austria. Napoleon seized the Prussian fortress of Wesel, and he insisted on the formation of a northern bund, like the Rhein-bund, under the protection of himself. Louisa, the beautiful Queen of Prussia, a Mechlenberg princess, had alone foreseen the inevitable end, and had entreated the king to draw his sword against the conqueror. Now she redoubled her entreaties. The Emperor Alexander, of Russia, visited Berlin and joined his voice to that of the queen. The whole kingdom felt the shame that covered it, and at last war was declared (1806). But the spirit of Frederick the Great no longer animated the army he had created. The Prussians were defeated at Jena, and again at Auerstädt. Russia, which took the field at the same time, met bloody repulses at Eilau and Friedland. Napoleon at once pushed on to Berlin, where he was received, not, as at Vienna, by the citizens with mute rage, but with loud demonstrations of delight. Men of high rank stood behind the crowd and urged them on to cheer, saying, " For Heaven's sake, give a hearty hurrah ! Cry, ' Long live the emperor ! ' or we are done for." Many citizens pressed forward, eager to betray the public money and stores that had been concealed. " I know not," said Napoleon, " whether to rejoice at my success or to feel ashamed for this people." The noble-hearted and beautiful Prussian queen was treated with the grossest inso-lence by Bonaparte. He knew how earnest and ener-getic she had been in stirring up her husband against him. He visited the tomb of Frederick the Great, and gave vent over it to the most unbecoming expressions of contempt against his unfortunate descendant.

The Prussian fortresses fell, one after another, during the autumn and winter, some from utter in-ability to maintain themselves, but the greater part because commanded by incompetent generals.

At last, on July 9, 1807, a conference was held at Tilsit between the sovereigns of France, Russia, and Prussia, whereby peace was concluded. Prussia was deprived of half her territory, which was con-verted by Napoleon into a kingdom of Westphalia, of which he appointed his brother Jerome ruler.

In the year 1809 Austria again took up arms against Napoleon. The Archduke Charles had en-treated, after former disasters, that the army might be put on a better footing. Now, at last, his advice was attended to. But Austria had now opposed to

her France, Bavaria, and the rest of the Rhenish
Bund, and Saxony. In five battles in five consecutive days Napoleon defeated the archduke, and
again the great conqueror entered Vienna. But
now the brave archduke returned to the charge from
Bohemia with fresh levies. A battle was fought at
Aspern which lasted two days, the 21st and 22d of
May, 1809, and for the first time Napoleon was defeated. For some time the two armies continued
watching each other; at last, on the 5th of July, Napoleon attacked the Austrians at Wagram, not far
from Aspern. The fight was desperate, the valour
of the Austrians splendid. They captured twelve
golden eagles and standards of the enemy, and
would have gained a victory had not the reserve
which had been called up failed to arrive, owing to
the dilatoriness of the Archduke John, who commanded it.

Two hours after the battle was over it arrived on
the blood-stained field. Owing to this defeat Austria was again compelled to negociate a peace,
which goes by the title of "THE PEACE OF VI-
ENNA." She had now to make additional sacrifices,
to give up Carniola, Trieste, and Dalmatia to the
French, and Salzburg and other portions of her possessions in the Alps to Bavaria. The Tyrol also became Bavarian. During this heroic struggle of
Austria against the tyrant, Prussia again remained
inert.

LVIII.

THE HEROES OF TYROL.

(1809.)

To this time belongs one of the most heroic and glorious achievements of modern history,—the rising of the Tyrolean patriots against the French and Bavarians, under the leading of Andreas Hofer, an innkeeper, Speckbacher, a hunter, and Haspinger, a friar.

Hofer kept a little tavern in the Passeyr valley that opens into the main valley of the Adige at Meran. The inn is at a place called "Sand," and so he went by the familiar name of the "Sand-host" (Sand-wirth). He was a tall, fine man, with brown, vivacious eyes, black hair, and a long, bushy beard, that reached nearly to his waist. His walk was measured and grave, his voice soft and clear, the expression of his features cheerful and serene. Without any pretence to eloquence, he had the gift of finding his way to the hearts of men and winning their confidence. His dress was the picturesque costume of his native valley,—a dark jacket, a scarlet waistcoat crossed by broad emerald-green braces, black chamois-leather breeches, and a belt of black leather, embroidered over with tiny threads of goose quill. On his head he wore a black goat's-hair steeple cap with broad brim, surrounded by twisted scarlet silk string. His stockings were of blue wool. Around his neck he wore a small crucifix. If ever you go to Meran you will see the peas-

ANDREAS HOFER.
(From a contemporary Engraving.)

ants there on a Sunday and market day wearing the same beautiful costume.

When Austria took up arms again, in 1809, against France and her German allies, she had not many regular soldiers to send into the Tyrol to defend it, and the defence had to be entrusted to the peasants themselves, who had shown what they could do, as you may remember, just before the Treaty of

Campo Formio. In the resistance then offered, Hofer and Speckbacher had distinguished themselves.

On the 7th of April little slips of paper, on which were written only the words "It is time," were circulated through the Tyrol. As the river Inn rushed along it whirled on its milky waters bits of wood with red flags stuck into them. The peasants knew the signal, caught their weapons, and the whole of the mountain region was in insurrection against the enemy. On the south side of the Brenner pass, the main road from Innsbruck to Italy, in the green basin of a dried-up lake, stands the quaint old town of Sterzing. The mountains tower above it, and up the Ridnaun valley the eye looks to glorious ranges of ice peaks. Into this basin marched the Bavarians on their way south to Brixen, where was another Bavarian force. When they were in the plain, the Tyrolese, commanded by Hofer, poured down from the mountain sides around, and attacked them. This was their first battle in the open country. The Bavarians formed square, and poured a shower of lead into their advancing ranks. They hesitated. Then a young girl with a shout drew forward a waggon load of hay towards the enemy. The Tyrolese followed with two others. They threw over the loads in a line, and lying behind the hay fired into the mass of their enemy. The hay had made a wall of shelter for them. The Bavarians wavered, broke, and with a shout the peasants charged them over the hay heaps, and took them prisoners. They were carried to a castle that stands on a height overlooking the plain.

Then every trace of the battle was removed, for the news reached the peasants that the French and Bavarians together were marching up the valley from Brixen. Hofer made the townspeople promise him not to say a word of what had happened; and when the united army arrived and wondered what had become of the Bavarians who had been ordered to meet them there, no one told them what had taken place. Next day they recommenced their march, and were no sooner involved among the rocks and pines than bullets and stones poured down on them, and terrible were their losses as they struggled through, unable to reach and dislodge the enemy.

On the 11th of May a French force, under General Lefebvre, and a Bavarian force, under Devey, invaded the Tyrol; but already had the gallant Tyrolese stormed Innsbruck and taken Hall, where were large stores for the army, and had cleared the Inn Valley of the enemy, led by Speckbacher, and South Tyrol had been freed by Hofer.

On the 11th of May also a Bavarian force, under Wrede, advanced from Salzburg upon the Tyrol through the Strub pass. This is a long and gloomy ravine, shut in between abrupt walls of rock. The road zigzags up among dark pines, around promontories of rock, high above a brawling torrent. The 11th of May, that year, was Ascension Day. It was brilliant with sunshine; the slopes were blue with gentianella and sprinkled with the delicate pink primula.

They were soon to be deepened dark red with blood. Holding the pass were 350 brave peasants with two small cannon, six-pounders. A few miles behind was an Austrian general with regulars, but, like so many of the old generals in the Austrian service at that time, he was half asleep, and so bewildered as not to know what to do when the opportunity of doing anything offered. As Napoleon said of them, "They are asleep when their eyes are open." Wrede had 14,000 well-disciplined soldiers and several cannon. When he saw that the pass was guarded he poured a volley and played on the defenders with his big guns; but they neither heeded nor replied. Then he ordered a charge. At once the two little field-pieces blazed, and the unerring guns of the peasants were discharged. The Bavarians went down in heaps; the rest recoiled, and the wounded staggered to the edge and fell down the gulf into the thundering stream far below. For five hours the fight continued, and then a shell injured one of the little cannon. Eight times did the Bavarians come on and were repulsed, and now their ammunition began to fail. A ninth attack was made, and at the same time a detachment, sent around by a circuitous path, fell on the brave Tyrolese behind. Then the battle was concluded by the enraged Bavarians butchering the wounded peasants who had fallen on the road they had held so heroically. Only a few escaped, but they had killed some 1500 of the enemy. You must remember that at this time Napoleon was at Vienna, and held in his grip the heart of Austria. The Archduke Charles was in Bohemia, whither he had fled after the five battles, on five consecutive days, in which he had tried to arrest the onward roll of Napoleon. Austria was in such distress that she could not help the Tyrol. She was forced to withdraw from it the few regiments of regulars left there. The peasants had only themselves to look to. Innsbruck, their capital, was in the hands of the Bavarians. The Tyrolese were resolved to recover it. On May the 29th was fought one of the most remarkable battles in the war, the battle of Berg Isel, in which the hardy mountaineers defeated, and drove out of the town, the well-trained army of invaders. Due south of Innsbruck the road to Italy runs over a level plain for about a mile and a half, passing a large abbey, called Wilten. Then there rises from the plain a hill, Berg Isel, up which the road winds. On this hill, occupying the Brenner road, were the Tyrolese, and here the three leaders, Hofer, Speckbacher, and Haspinger, united. The Bavarians not only held Innsbruck, but the whole left bank of the Inn as far as Hall and Volders, some 6 or 9 miles down the river. Speckbacher opposed them at this point, that is, he and his men formed the right wing of the patriot army. The Bavarians crossed the Inn at once at Hall and at Volders. Speckbacher immediately fell on them at Volders and drove them back; then, leaving a detachment to destroy the bridge, he flew to Hall, where some Austrian regulars were opposed to the Bavarians, and drove them back again. During the fight here a young woman ran among the Austrians and Tyrolese with a little cask of wine on her head, and a mug in her hand, giving them drink. A bullet struck the cask, entered it, and the wine began to run down her cheek and neck. " Quick, quick ! " cried the brave girl, "drink away, my hearties ! before another ball finishes the wine and waitress." Speckbacher was rushing over the bridge when he found his little boy at his side. In vain did he urge the child to go back ; the gallant little fellow would be in the thick of the fight beside his father. Speckbacher had to box his ears and severely rebuke him before he would retire ; and then he occupied himself in collecting the bullets that fell about him for his father's gun. Three times did the brave Speckbacher lead the charge ; at last a reserve body came up, the Bavarians were beat back, and then Speckbacher led his men to the assistance of Hofer in the centre, at Berg Isel. Here a furious contest was going on ; and here it was that Haspinger, the friar, turned the tide of battle. Father Haspinger wore the snuff-coloured robe of his order, with a cord knotted round his waist, bare feet and sandals. His head was bare ; he had red hair and a long, thick red beard. In his hand he carried a stick, and on his breast a little black cross. He had no weapons. Above Berg Isel are two villages, Mutters and Natters, and these were in the hands of the Bavarians. After two hours hard fighting the enemy was driven from them down the hill towards the plain. But this would not have happened but for Haspinger. Seeing the Tyrolese falter, then break and begin to fly, the brave Capuchin friar

roared to them, as he waved his staff, "Good-bye!
Good-bye! Brothers, I go forwards to the throne of
God to accuse you of cowardice." They were
ashamed and returned to the charge. The bullets
whistled around their leader, but none touched him.
A Bavarian soldier rushed forward with a curse to
run him through with his bayonet; the friar
knocked the gun out of his hands with his alpen-
stock. Next moment he would have fallen, pierced
through, had not a rifleman, perceiving his danger,
fired over his shoulder at the Bavarian, thereby
singeing the Father's beard. Then forward with
shouts of joy rushed the Tyrolese, and drove the
Bavarians down on the Inn. Now that the left
wing had succeeded, as well as the right, Hofer in
the centre pushed forward, and the Bavarians retired precipitously into the town. The ammunition
of the peasants was spent; they were unable to follow up their success, and during the night the Bavarian general slipped away from the town with the
remnant of his army. After the battle of Wagram,
Austria was obliged to consent to a truce, which
was to lead to the Peace of Vienna, by which the
Tyrol was to be given up to Bavaria. This had
been agreed to on July 7th, at Znaym; but the Tyrolese obstinately refused to be transferred to Bavaria, and prosecuted the war.

General Lefebvre, who had been a miller's boy,
and had become a field-marshal of France, and had
been created by Napoleon Duke of Danzig, was
sent, at the head of a large army of French, Bavarians, and Saxons, into the Tyrol, to subdue it thor-

oughly.   He occupied Innsbruck, and then marched
over the Brenner Pass to Sterzing, on his way to
Brixen and Botzen.   He intended to quiet the South
of Tyrol.   At the same time an army was sent up
the valley of the Inn, which was to go through
the Finstermunz Pass above Landeck, descend
the Adige, and meet him at Botzen.

The first to go forward were the Saxons.   They
were allowed to advance as far as a very narrow
defile, called the Sack, where there is a wooden
bridge near a precipice of rock that rises above
the road.   The peasants passed the bridge and set
it on fire as the Saxons came up, and as they
halted, hesitating what to do, suddenly there came
a rumble, then a roar, and an avalanche of rocks
and stones poured down on them from the cliff
overhead.   A thousand men, among them forty-
four officers, were lost in the Sack.   When the
Duke of Danzig heard this he was very angry, and
ordered the rest of his troops forward.   He had
been lodging at the little inn of " the Nail," at Sterzing, and grumbled at the poor breakfast he had received.   " It matters not," he said to the hostess,
" I shall have a famous dinner to-day at Brixen."
But he was met at the Sack by the dauntless peasants, who poured their fire upon his advancing columns, and showered rocks on him from the sides
of the pass, and the army was obliged to fly back to
Sterzing in confusion.   As the duke returned,
angry, humiliated, exhausted to the inn, he found
his hostess at the door.   She courtsied, and with
a twinkling eye, asked, " I hope your Grace has

enjoyed your famous dinner to-day." The army
sent round by the Finstermünz met a like disaster, and the broken fragments of both armies
were forced to retreat into the Inn valley. There, at
Innsbruck, Lefebvre, the duke, concentrated 25,000
infantry, and 1000 horse, and 40 pieces of artillery.
After them, flushed with victory, poured the gallant Tyrolese. Another battle was fought on Berg
Isel; again were the patriots commanded by Hofer,
Speckbacher, and the friar, and again were they
victorious. The Tyrolese lost 132 wounded and 50
killed; they took 6000 prisoners and killed 4000
men, and Lefebvre was obliged to retire.

The Peace of Vienna was signed, and Austria
was forced to abandon the Tyrol. She could not help
herself. Her powers of resistance were exhausted.
But the Tyrolese would not acknowledge it. Accordingly, fresh bodies of men were sent into the
Tyrol to subdue the mountaineers. They continued
the desperate struggle, but against the enormous su-
periority of numbers could not make headway.
The French and Bavarians held the main roads, and
all the towns, and could starve them into submission.
Another battle was fought at Berg Isel, but this
time the valour of the patriots could not win them
victory. At last a former friend betrayed Hofer
to the French, and, to the eternal disgrace of Napoleon, he had the brave man shot in cold blood.
Speckbacher, later, was rewarded by the Austrian
emperor, and Haspinger would have been rewarded
had the humble friar consented to receive anything
at his hands.

LIX.

THE MARCH ON MOSCOW.

(1812.)

THROUGH his defeat of the Prussians and Austrians, Napoleon had reached the highest point of his career. No power but England dared to defy him. The great fleet of England harassed and defeated the French navy. Napoleon tried what he could to hurt England. He forbade all trade with Britain, and the sale of English wares. All the harbours of the continent were closed against the English, so as to kill their trade and manufactures. However, the Emperor Alexander, of Russia, refused to consent to have his ports thus shut; accordingly, the French dictator determined on war with him.

Napoleon strained every effort to make this gigantic undertaking successful. At the head of 600,000 men, in the summer of 1812, he crossed the Russian frontier. But before doing this he convoked all the princes of Germany to Dresden, where he lectured them with such insolence as even to repel his warmest partisans. Tears sprang into the eyes of the Empress of Austria and the Queen of Prussia; the princes and kings bit their lips with rage at the petty humiliations and coarse affronts put on them by their powerful but momentary lord. The army led by Napoleon against Russia was principally composed of German troops, who were skilfully mixed up with the French, so as not to be themselves aware of their numbers. Austrians, Prussians, Saxons, Hessians, Bavarians, Würtembergers, Badeners, Swiss, Flemings, even Portuguese, Spaniards, and Italians, went to make up this great host, which was destined to whiten with its bones the plains of Russia. In order to secure his rear Napoleon garrisoned the Prussian fortresses with French troops, and the Prussians sent forward to fight in Russia were commanded by French officers. Sixty thousand French held Prussia, whilst the sons of Prussia were sent to die in arms for their conqueror. Now bitterly did she feel the consequences of her baseness.

No enemy opposed the invading army. The Russians retired before Napoleon without striking a blow, leading him on deep into their dreary plains.

On the 7th of September, after a march of over two months, the army came in sight of the cupolas and towers of Moscow. A mysterious stillness reigned in the great city of the Czars. None appeared with the keys to lay them at the feet of the invader; no crowd of curious sight-seers poured out of the gates to gaze on the mighty conqueror. The town was deserted. Napoleon took up his quarters in the Kremlin, the ancient palace of the Czars. All at once fire broke out in various quarters of the town. An autumn storm fanned the flames, and in a short time the whole city was a waving, roaring sea of fire. Every attempt to extinguish the conflagration was in vain ; the very Kremlin kindled. The Russians had themselves accumulated the combustibles in their houses and set them on fire, and sacrificed their glorious city so as the more surely to work the destruction of the French army.

Now Napoleon's overwhelming pride proved his ruin. Instead of leading his army south into fertile lands for winter quarters at once, he waited among the ashes of Moscow till the middle of October, in daily expectation that the Emperor of Russia would send humbly to him, entreating peace. Finding that no appeal came ; hearing the winds of winter begin to howl, and seeing the snowflakes begin to fall, he sent overtures of peace to Alexander. No answer came. All at once inaction disappeared. His cavalry were surprised and defeated with great loss. The frosts began to set in, the ice to form over the pools. Faster and faster fell the snow. Now Napoleon found that he had an enemy ranged against him that he was unable to defeat and insult— winter. Now, when too late, he resolved on retreat. The winter of 1811 had been unusually mild ; that of 1812 set in unusually early, and with unwonted severity. Provisions failed. The vast plains were white and deep in snow, and as the army retired the Cossacks hovered around them with their long spears like musquitos, maddening and torturing them. The horses died by thousands. The numbed and weary soldiers flung away their arms. The grand army was reduced to a cowering, starved, frightened wreck. Gaunt forms of famine, wan, hollow-eyed, wrapped in strange garments of misery to keep out the cold—skins and women's clothes— with long beards, dragged their faint limbs along, fought for a dead horse, murdered each other for a morsel of bread, and fell over in the deep snow, never again to rise. Numbers fell into the hands of the Russian boors, who stripped them and drove them out into the snowdrifts. When at last they reached the Beresina, which had to be passed, a thaw had set in, and the river rolled down broken blocks of ice. At the same time the Russians appeared on their flanks, charging them with spears, pouring cannon shot among them, hewing them down with their sabres. Two bridges were hastily built, and over them poured the terrified, flying rabble of soldiers. They crowded on one another, trampled one another down. The railings gave way, and many were precipitated over the sides; others were run down by the horses, and crushed under the wheels of the cannon carriages. Then, to complete the disaster, the bridges themselves broke, and the stream of human beings, forced on by those behind, fell into the ice-cold whirling river to perish in its waves. Those who did not reach the shore were made prisoners.

On the 5th of December Napoleon deserted his army, leaving it to take its chance, escaping on a slide. With his flight all discipline ended; soldiers, and officers, and generals all sought only individual safety. Of the great army led into Russia not one twentieth part returned in safety. The mighty host of the conqueror was totally annihilated.

LX.

NAPOLEON FALLS AND GERMANY RISES.

THIS unexpected disaster of the Emperor Napoleon seemed to Europe a sign from heaven that the hour of emancipation had struck. The first to recognize this was Prussia. In February, 1813, the king met Alexander of Russia and concluded an alliance with him. But Berlin was in the hands of the French. Now, however, the whole Prussian nation, eager to throw off the hated yoke of the foreigner, to wipe away the dishonour of her past, cheerfully hastened to place their lives and property at the service of the impoverished government. The whole of the able-bodied population was put under arms. Every heart bounded with hope and pride. The king and emperor issued a proclamation appealing to all Germany to rise against the common enemy. It found an echo in every German heart. Warning was sent to Napoleon of the menacing temper in the land. "Pah!" he exclaimed, "Germans can't fight like Spaniards." However, he levied a French army 300,000 strong, which so overawed the Rhenish Bund that their princes actually again called together thousands of their subjects to go with Napoleon against their brothers in the North. Mech-

CLEMENS WENZEL, PRINCE VON METTERNICH.
(From a Painting by Th. Lawrence.)

lenburg alone sided with Prussia.   Austria was too
exhausted to lift a hand.   But now was a fight to
be seen calculated to rejoice the heart of one loving
his country.   As sometimes a great distress or humiliation coming on a man with good qualities, who
has lived an inglorious, unworthy life, will spur him
to take a new start, cast aside those infirmities
which have marred his character and rise to true
nobility of life, so was it now with the Prussian people.   As animated by one heart, all responded to
the call. Prussia became a great arsenal. Youths
hardly ripe enough, old men with grey hair, fathers
of families, tradesmen, artisans, professional men,
landed gentry, even young women in men's clothing flew to arms; all wanted to hold a gun and
brandish a sword for Fatherland. He who could
not enter the ranks gave his money. He who had no
money gave his labour. None would hang behind
the others in the great cause. Speedily the whole
of the able male population was converted into an
army. There was the standing army, and there
were the free corps. Among these latter Lützow's
Huntsmen gained a glorious name in these days of
gallantry.   Napoleon advanced into the heart of
Germany, and he was in Saxony before the Prussians
were ready to meet him.   Now the Emperor Alexander of Russia sent help, and the two allies met
Napoleon, and were defeated by him in two bloody
battles at Lützen and Bautzen.

The Emperor of Austria offered to mediate. His
minister, Count Metternich, was sent to Napoleon.
"Hah! come to mediate, have you?" asked Bona-

parte; "if that be so, you are not on my side."
Then, insolently, " Well, Metternich, how much
money have you been bribed with by England to
take this part?" and he threw his hat down on the
floor to see if Count Metternich would stoop to
pick it up. Metternich looked at the hat, then
at Napoleon, and set his lips. He would not stoop.
Napoleon turned his back on him,—and so, war
with Austria also was determined on. Immediately, the combined Prussian and Russian army
entered Bohemia, where they were joined by the
Emperor of Austria at the head of his army. The
army in Bohemia was placed under the command
of Prince Schwarzenberg. Another army to guard
Silesia was under Blücher, a third, the North army
at Berlin, was under the Crown-Prince of Sweden,
who was a Frenchman, Charles Bernadotte, one of
Napoleon's generals, who had been elected to succeed the childless King of Sweden.

On the 23d of August a murderous conflict took
place at Gross-Beeren between a Prussian division
of the North army and the French. The almost
untrained peasantry that composed it rushed upon
the enemy and beat down entire battalions with the
butt-ends of their muskets, whilst the crown-prince
and his Swedes looked on without taking part.
The French lost 2400 prisoners. Blücher in Silesia
also won success three days later. Having drawn
the French across the river Neisse, he drove
them, after a desperate engagement, into the river,
swollen with heavy rains. The muskets of the soldiers had been rendered unserviceable by the wet,

and Blücher, drawing his sabre from beneath his cloak, dashed forward, exclaiming, " Forwards!" Several thousand French were drowned or bayonetted, or had their skulls fractured by the butt-ends of the muskets. They lost 103 guns, 18,000 prisoners, and a greater number were killed. The general in command, Macdonald, escaped almost alone to Napoleon at Dresden. " Sire," said the defeated general, " your army no longer exists." Blücher was given a title of prince from the place where this victory was won, but his soldiers preferred to call him " Marshal Forwards." The place of this battle was Wahlstadt, not far from Liegnitz.

Before Dresden, on the same day, Aug. 26, however, the allies were defeated by Napoleon with great loss ; but this was the last victory obtained by Napoleon on German soil.

LXI.

THE BATTLE OF THE NATIONS.

(1813.)

NAPOLEON'S generals were thrown back in every quarter with great loss on Dresden, where Napoleon remained waiting his opportunity. A fresh disappointment befel him. The Bavarian army refused to fight for him, and went over to the allies, and marched to the Main to stand across Napoleon's path if he attempted to retreat. When the news of this disaffection reached Napoleon's main army at Dresden the German troops in it began to waver, and when he ordered a march on Berlin, broke out in mutiny. A feeling of melancholy foreboding of his approaching fall stole over the great conqueror, and he remained for some days irresolute. Then his spirit revived. On the 16th of October, 1813, began the great battle of Leipzig, which is called by Germans "The Battle of the Nations," because of the various nationalities represented in it, and the number of the troops engaged. It was fought on the 16th, 17th, 18th, and 19th of October, and was one of the longest, sternest, and bloodiest actions of the war, and one of the greatest battles recorded in history. Napoleon had an army of 200,000 men, and the allies 300,000 ; but the allies had not more than 200,000 the first day, as the Northern army was at Halle under Bernadotte, who was little inclined to fight his old master, Napoleon.

Now let me try to give you some idea of this great Battle of the Nations. Leipzig lies in a plain where two rivers, the Elster and the Pleisse, meet, and two smaller streams, the Luppe and the Partha, also meet and unite into one river, which thenceforth flows a short way and falls into the Saale above Halle. From the East comes the high road from Dresden, along which Napoleon marched to Leipzig. From the South comes the road by which the Silesian army was advancing. This road ran along the Pleisse, through coppices of scraggy alders. On the West were two roads, one from the Saale at Weissenfels—*i. e.* S. W.—the other from Halle— N. W. Along this latter the North Army was advancing,—reluctantly indeed,—under Bernadotte, Crown-Prince of Sweden. The Emperor of Austria, the Emperor of Russia, and the King of Prussia were with the main army from Bohemia. With Napoleon was the King of Saxony, and Murat, King of Naples. As the allies drew near they formed a half moon, with the left wing on the Luppe and the right on the east bank of the Pleisse. Moreover, the Silesian army was planted on the road from Leipzig to Halle, and the Northern army, which was at Halle, ordered to come up quickly and unite with it, which it did not do. The object was to cut

off Napoleon's retreat, and drive him either back
on Dresden, or, better still, due north.

The battle began at 8 o'clock in the morning. A
thousand cannon roared; smoke rolled over the
extended field. Napoleon planted himself with his
main body across the south road that enters the

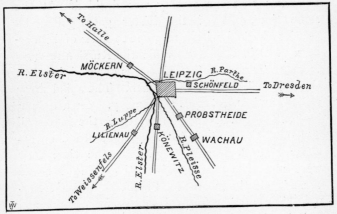

THE BATTLE OF LEIPZIG.

town from Wachau and Probstheide. The Polish
prince, Poniatowski, with his Poles was between the
Elster and the Pleisse. Another division was placed
between the Luppe and the Elster; another again,
under Marmont, was on the Halle road. The battle began with a tremendous fight at Wachau,
which lasted till 2 o'clock in the afternoon, in
which the Russians were principally engaged; but
almost simultaneously it exploded at Lindenau,
Konnewitz, and Möckern; so that Leipzig was surrounded on all sides but N. and E. by the thunder
of war. Nothing decisive was done at Lindenau

and Konnewitz, and Napoleon massed his men to make a crushing rush upon the right wing of the allies, and turn it at Probstheide. They shook and recoiled. Then above the booming of the guns sounded the merry bells of all the churches of Leipzig; Napoleon had ordered them to be rung, believing that the victory was decided. At the same time, out of the Elster gate galloped a courier charged with a message to Paris of his success. But just then up came the Russian reserves from the South. The Cossacks charged down on the advancing wave of French. The allied army rallied, and rolled back the enemy. On a mound beside the road Napoleon watched the battle all day, and the three allied sovereigns stood on another mound near Wachau. At one time they were almost captured, when the tide of battle turned. In the mean time Blücher, "Marshal Forwards," was going forwards at Möckern unable to wait for the Swedes and their dawdling half-hearted leader, and he drove back the French within the walls of Leipzig. Darkness fell, and the roar of the cannons ceased, leaving the allies in possession of the field, and the French retiring behind Leipzig, so as to hold the roads to Dresden and the North. At the moment when victory seemed to have declared for the French, Napoleon shouted exultantly: "The world turns round for us." When darkness settled in he felt that he was a beaten man; but his spirit was not broken.

Next day only desultory fighting ensued; but he saw that he was in peril, and he ordered that at all cost the road to Weissenfels, along which lay his course to France, should be kept clear. He sent to the allies to ask for a truce, but was refused. On the 18th the battle began with renewed fury. But now the Swedes and North army came up from Halle, and another Russian force, and a large Austrian division. The French army, by its losses, had been greatly thinned, and the allies were at the same time reinforced.

Napoleon now resolved on retreat, and concentrated his army on the South. The allies then extended their right wing to the Partha, shutting off the road to Dresden, where they were opposed by the Saxons. The main column of the allies advanced from Wachau to Probstheide, driving the French before them. And now the Saxons went over, then the Würtemberg cavalry, to the side of the allies. The gap was at once filled, and a tremendous struggle took place at Schönewald; but the French held their own. The circle was fast closing in on Leipzig. Only one road was left open, that to Weissenfels. Night settled down again on the bloody field, and Napoleon spent it in the town, into which he withdrew all but the outposts of his army, and prepared to break away home for France on the morrow.

The 19th broke, and with the gathering light the allies advanced. The cannon-balls fell in showers in the streets. Napoleon, finding all was lost, quitted the town as the allies entered it on the other side. Indeed, it is doubtful whether he would have escaped but for the bravery of his generals,

Macdonald and Prince Poniatowski, who covered his retreat. When he had crossed he ordered the bridge by which he had passed to be blown up. This was done whilst his flying army was crossing, leaving 25,000 of his men behind. Prince Poniatowski plunged on horseback into the Elster, in order to swim across, but sank in the deep mud. The King of Saxony, who, to the last, had remained true to Napoleon, was taken prisoner.

The retreat of the great conqueror to the Rhine was a flight. In the " Battle of the Nations " the French lost 78,000 men in killed, wounded, and captives, 300 cannon, and 1000 standards. The loss on the side of the allies was, however, very heavy.

Thus ended this glorious victory. All Germany was filled with rejoicing. The yoke of foreign bondage was broken. Thenceforth Germany was free from the French.

LXII.

NAPOLEON CHECKED.

(1814.)

THE allied princes met at Frankfort to take counsel about a general peace. They agreed to offer Napoleon that the Rhine, the Alps, the Pyrenees, and the sea should form the frontiers of France. But in his still unbroken pride he refused this offer, and the war flared up again. On New Year's night of 1814 Blücher went "forwards" over the Rhine at Mannheim and Coblenz with his army. The main army of the allies had crossed a few days earlier at Basle, as well as a Prussian army under Bulow from Holland. The Rhein-bund dissolved; Holland, Switzerland, Italy fell away from Napoleon. Bavaria had already made terms. Jerome, whom his brother had made King of Westphalia, packed up his valise and ran away. Joseph, who had been made King of Spain, also fled, and the English, under Wellington, threatened Napoleon from the Pyrenees.

Blücher won several battles, and again peace was offered to Napoleon, but in vain. He would not give way. Fortune again seemed to favour him; with his usual celerity he flew from one advancing body

GEBHARD LEBRECHT VON BLÜCHER.
(From a Portrait by T. B. Bock, 1815.)

to another, and beat them separately. However, the host formed against him closed in, and after a short resistance entered Paris. The deposition of the emperor was decreed, and the brother of Louis XVI. was proclaimed king. All the efforts made by Napoleon to save for himself, or his family, some of their former honours were in vain ; his marshals fell away from him. He was forced to sign his renunciation of the crown, but he was allowed to retain the title of Emperor and hold the little isle of Elba as a sovereign principality. For the immeasurable injuries and losses which Germany had suffered from him, with rare generosity no compensation was exacted. This was the FIRST PEACE OF PARIS (1814). A congress was summoned to assemble at Vienna to regulate the relationship of the States of Germany.

From Paris the sovereigns of Prussia and Russia and the victorious generals proceeded to London, where they, more especially Blücher, were received with every demonstration of respect and delight.

In the autumn of 1814 the European princes and their principal ministers and generals assembled in Vienna as had been agreed; but soon the mutual jealousies began to work among them. Talleyrand was there. This utterly unscrupulous man had served under every government ; under the Republic, under Napoleon, and was now under the restored Bourbons. He was there to offer his perfidious advice to the victors, and to sow the seed of discord among them. Soon disputes broke out, and the news reached Napoleon in his banishment.

Suddenly, on the 1st of March, 1815, he set foot on the coast of France. The whole nation received him with acclamations of delight. All the troops sent against him went over to his side. On the 20th of March he entered Paris. Louis XVIII., deserted by his army, fled to the Netherlands. Napoleon's brother-in-law, Murat, at the same time revolted at Naples, and advanced into Upper Italy against the Austrians; but all the rest of Napoleon's ancient allies, persuaded that he must fall, drew closer together in league against him. The allied sovereigns, still assembled at Vienna, let drop their miserable disputes to combine for his overthrow. All his cunning attempts to bribe them were rejected with scorn. Napoleon was proclaimed an outlaw, and they bound themselves to bring a force more than a million strong into the field against him. The French were still faithful to Napoleon. He collected an army of 150,000 men and marched on Belgium, where an English force, under the Duke of Wellington, and a Prussian, under Blücher, were about to cross the frontier.

At Ligny he fought and defeated Blücher on June 16th with great slaughter. On the same day the left wing of the French under Marshal Ney attacked the English at Quatre Bras, and suffered a severe defeat. After this, the Prussians retreated to Havre, pursued by 35,000 French, and Wellington, falling back on the position he had chosen near Waterloo, awaited the approach of Napoleon.

At Brussels, in a picture gallery, by a painter called Wiertz, is a painting representing Waterloo

allegorically. A great black lion is tearing to pieces
an eagle. The eagle represents the French military
power, and the black lion symbolises the power of
the Netherlands. As a matter of fact, all the part
taken by the Belgian soldiers in this memorable
battle was to run away at the first discharge of fire-
arms, and the English opened ranks to allow the
frightened little men to escape through their lines.
In this stupendous conflict of the 18th of June,
the flower of the French soldiery perished in their
desperate efforts against the obdurate valour of the
British. The battle raged from noon till eight
o'clock. Blücher and his Prussians made great
efforts to reach the scene of action, but, marching
over ground rendered almost impassable by the
heavy rains that had fallen, their main body did
not arrive till the victory was already won. They
undertook the pursuit, and so completed the
achievement which the British had begun. The
French army was converted into a helpless mob
of fugitives, incapable of rallying again. Napoleon returned to Paris to abdicate a second time.
Then, failing in an attempt to escape to America, he surrendered himself to Captain Maitland, of
H. M. S. Bellerophon.

With the concurrence of all the powers, he was
conveyed, under the custody of the English, to the
island of S. Helena, where he died on the 5th of
May, 1821. Meanwhile Murat, Napoleon's brother-
in-law, defeated by the Austrians at Tolentino, was
taken and shot, as he was trying to incite the
Italian rabble to insurrection.

After the battle of Waterloo the allies a second time entered Paris. Louis XVIII. returned, and the SECOND PEACE OF PARIS (1815) was concluded. This time the allies did not treat France with as much consideration as before. A large part of the left bank of the Rhine was restored to Germany, and France had to pay an indemnification of seven hundred million francs.

In the new partition of Europe, arranged at the congress of Vienna, Austria received Lombardy and Venice, Dalmatia also, and Tyrol were restored to her. Thus, after three-and-twenty years of war, the monarchy apparently gained a considerable accession of strength, having obtained, in lieu of its remote and unprofitable possessions in the Netherlands, territories which joined in Italy. The ancient German empire was replaced by a German confederation of thirty-nine states, and a permanent diet, or parliament, made up of their representatives, was established at Frankfort. Saxony, Wurtemberg and Bavaria, which had been elevated into kingdoms by Napoleon, were allowed to remain kingdoms; but of all the brothers and field-marshals whom Napoleon had exalted into kings and princes, not one remained in possession of the dignity he had conferred. One only of his marshals, Bernadotte, King of Sweden, whom he had not crowned, and whom he particularly hated, retained his position.

LXIII.

GERMANY STRUGGLES FOR FREEDOM.

AFTER the fall of Napoleon, the relation between the princes and their people went through a great change, a change they themselves were not ready to acknowledge. The French Revolution had greatly influenced men's minds throughout Europe, and men desired more freedom and emancipation from the irksome restraints of mediævalism.

Now, in Germany, in former times, the people had to a very considerable extent governed themselves. Every little state had its houses of parliament, composed of the nobles—that is, the landed gentry, the clergy and representatives of the people. But after the Reformation the great wars, especially the terrible Thirty Years' War, had ruined the small nobles, and the institution of a parliament had fallen into disuse. Thenceforth the princes ruled absolutely; they levied what taxes they chose, and made war on whom they chose, and imposed what religion and what laws they chose, without consulting the people, who had but one duty—to obey and pay. But the freedom which France had fought to establish, the declaration of the rights of men, had set Germans thinking, and they felt that they had these rights, and that they ought to be consulted in matters affecting their welfare. However, the kings, and emperors, and princes, when they recast the map of Europe, had no idea of conceding liberty more than they were obliged. They wanted to restore things as they were before the great European war broke out.

The emperors, Alexander of Russia, Francis of Austria, and King Frederick William III. of Prussia, concluded between them " the Holy Alliance," and promised to stand by each other, and to advance religion, peace and righteousness in their lands, and to rule their people as fathers. Unfortunately, they took a wrong idea of fatherly rule. They thought it meant despotic rule, and accordingly, instead of advancing prosperity and giving more freedom to their people, they treated them like children, devoid of intelligence, or as expecting of them the docility of school-girls.

William, Duke of Hesse-Cassel, said, " I have slept seven years, now we will forget the bad dream," and he tried to put everything exactly on its old footing. In the congress of Vienna, all the princes had promised to give constitutions to their principalities, that is—self-government by means of houses of parliament. But none of them, when settled on their thrones, thought of giving what had been promised. This led to much uneasiness. The people were dissatisfied and clamoured for what had been promised. The students in the universities especially took up the cry for liberty and a constitution, and formed them-

selves into " Bauchenschaften," clubs for the
spread of liberal ideas. The young men dressed in
short black jackets, wore tops boots, long hair, ex-
posed their throats with falling collars, wore dag-
gers in their breast pockets, and drank barrels of
beer in honour of liberty. They assumed a tricolour ribband, red, black and yellow, as their badge.
In October, 1817, they held a great meeting on the
Wartburg in commemoration of Luther, and to express their detestation of the formalism and re-
straint exercised by the government. They lit
a huge bonfire, and burned in it several " pigtails,"
stiff-neck stocks, and other symbols of the 18th
century. This was all very absurd, and the government ought not to have noticed it, but when,
shortly after, Kotzebue, the dramatic author, who
had turned some of the German peculiarities into
ridicule, was assassinated, they took a serious view
of the affair, and proceeded to put the universities
under police supervision, and to break up the
clubs, and make many arrests.

Not only did the people want parliaments, but
also open courts of trial, with juries. Trials were
conducted in secret, and carelessly, and much par-
tiality was shown. Strict justice was not always
dealt. For instance, in 1820, a painter and a carpenter were murdered in Dresden, and the police arrested an innocent man, and racked and tortured
him, to force a confession. To escape the rack he
did at last confess guilt, and only just as he
was about to be executed did his innocence trans-
pire. In 1830 a carpenter at Rostock was accused

by his apprentice of having murdered his wife. He was kept imprisoned for nine years, and only then did it come out that the apprentice was the murderer. In the same year the Danish ambassador in Oldenburg was assassinated, and his two servants, who were perfectly innocent, were kept in prison for six years, and so badly treated as to be broken in health and spirit by their confinement. The people were very dissatisfied, and very justly dissatisfied, with the way in which criminal trials were carried out. Another cause of complaint was the censure on the press. No books might be published and sold, no newspapers issued, which had not passed under the eye of officers appointed to read and approve them. I remember about this time, when I was in Germany, that my father wanted to buy the memoirs of Baron Trenck, who had been imprisoned for many years by the King of Prussia. The bookseller replied that he was not allowed to sell it, but he winked to my father, and when no one else was in the shop led him into a back room, and produced the book from a secret cupboard. So it was, books that were forbidden were sold, but purchasers were put to great inconvenience to get them, and if the bookseller were found out, he was thrown into prison.

Spirits were so agitated, that some of the small princes gave way, and granted constitutions to their subjects. In July, 1830, revolution broke out again in France, and Charles X., who had succeeded Louis XVIII., was driven from his throne, to which succeeded Louis Philippe, his kinsman. This change

was not without effect in Germany, and led to considerable disturbance. The people cried out for
more freedom, for sounder institutions, a healthier
form of government; they refused to be any longer
treated as children; but they did not rise in a
body, and it ended in only the grant of a few more
institutions. Austria and Prussia would not yield.

William IV., of England, died in 1837 without
male issue. Since George I., the kings of England
had been electors of Hanover, but now the union
ceased, and Ernest Augustus, brother of William
IV., succeeded to the kingdom of Hanover. A
constitution had been granted to Hanover in 1833,
and this he proceeded to abolish. This created
general opposition in his land, and an appeal
against him was made to the Diet of the Bund at
Frankfort. The confederation, however, declared it
had no authority to interfere, and this completely
struck down all confidence in the Frankfort Diet.

One good institution, and only one, dates from
this period, and that was the Zoll-verein, or German Customs - Union. Hitherto, things made or
grown in one little principality were subject to duty
if they passed into another. The result was that
smuggling went on very generally, and that every
little state was put to great cost to keep its frontiers guarded. Moreover, trade was terribly crippled
by the arbitrary duties imposed on things exported
and imported. Consequently, several of the German
states agreed with Prussia to unite in one customs-
union; but Austria, and some of the northern
states did not join it.

LXIV.

ANOTHER REVOLUTION.

(1848.)

LOUIS PHILIPPE, who, by the July Revolution, had come to the throne of France, forgot his promises to rule his people through a constitution. The welfare of his own family lay nearer his heart than that of his subjects. Very likely he thought that, as a piece of rare luck had brought him to the throne, luck might desert him, and throw him down again ; and, as he thought this was not very improbable, so he resolved to feather his own nest whilst he had the chance. But this the French people did not acquiesce in, so they rose in revolt against him, as they had against Charles X., in the month of February, 1848. Louis Philippe at once fled to England, and France received a Republican constitution, and Louis Napoleon Bonaparte, a nephew of the late Emperor Napoleon, was elected, in December of the same year, first president of the Republic.

On December 2, 1851, he forcibly dissolved the National Assembly, and assumed absolute power. On the 2d of December, 1852, he had himself proclaimed Emperor, under the title of Napoleon III.

You may perhaps wonder who Napoleon II. was. Napoleon I., at the height of his power, desiring to obscure as much as possible his humble origin, and the ignobility of his family, divorced his wife Josephine, and obliged the Emperor of Austria to give him his daughter, Maria Louisa. By her he had one son, born in 1811. When Napoleon had to abdicate after the battle of Waterloo, he tried hard to get his little son proclaimed as Napoleon II., but, of course, in vain. The son died of decline when he was twenty-one years old. When Napoleon proclaimed himself as the third of that name, he in fact claimed that the poor boy had really been Emperor, and ignored the kings who had actually governed France, and the decision of Europe.

Louis Napoleon, the new Emperor, was the third son of Louis, the brother of the Great Napoleon, who had been created by the conqueror King of Holland.

The Revolution in France, in 1848, was of the greatest importance for all Europe, especially for Germany. In a few days every German state was in commotion, and the people loudly and threateningly demanded four things: 1. Freedom to express their opinions by word or writing, on what was going on in the government of their country (freedom of speech, and freedom of the press). 2. Universal military service, the right of every man to bear arms, and at the same time the right of all to assemble when and where they liked, for political or other purposes. 3. Trial by jury, and open courts. 4. The abolition of the Bund-Diet, and the constitu-

tional re-organization of every state. Most of the
princes gave way in terror, fearing expulsion like
that of Louis Philippe ; the King of Prussia and the
Emperor of Austria only refused to yield. Then
the people flew to arms, and in Vienna and Berlin
bloody fights with the military ensued, which ended
in the success of the latter. However, the Emperor
Ferdinand had to fly his capital, and take refuge in
Innsbruck, and thus to abdicate in favour of his
nephew, Francis Joseph, who promised reforms.
Also in Berlin, after much fighting, a constitution
was granted.

In the mean time the people desired that a
national German parliament should be summoned,
which should recast the institutions of the whole
Fatherland. For this end 600 representatives of
the people assembled at Frankfort to arrange
preliminaries, and to call together a constitutional
Diet, or National Assembly, each member of which
was to represent 50,000 inhabitants. On the
18th of May, 1848, this National Assembly was
opened at Frankfort, when it sat in the Protestant
church of St. Paul. It at once proceeded to appoint
a provisional government, and elected the Archduke
John of Austria to be president and protector ; the
Diet handed over to him its powers and then dissolved itself. The decision arrived at was that a
new law code was to be drawn up applicable to the
whole of Germany ; the German Empire was to
consist of one Federal body, with only one House
of Representatives. Frederick William IV., King of
Prussia, was elected emperor, but he refused to

accept the title thus offered him, and when he heard the decisions of the Assembly, he said, "They forget that there are princes still in Germany, and that I am one of them."

Upon this, great commotions broke out again, especially in the South. The peasants rose and took arms; some wanted one thing, some another. The students claimed liberty of the press, the peasants the burning of the mortgages held by the Jews on their property. All these insurrections were put down by the military. All attempts to give Germany a satisfactory general constitution broke down, and in May, 1851, the old Bund-Diet or Federal Assembly was re-appointed. The governments had got the upper hand, but much more liberty was granted, so that the people had gained a great deal by this revolution. That which they really aimed at was unity, and the time for that was not yet come.

LXV.

A QUARREL ABOUT TWO DUCHIES.

THE two duchies of Schleswig-Holstein were subject to the King of Denmark ; but a portion of the inhabitants were Germans, and the German inhabitants and the Danes were continually quarrelling, and the Germans appealed against their neighbors to the sovereigns of Germany. In 1848 the German residents in the duchies tried to expel the Danes, and to get themselves free from the crown of Denmark, but in vain. There were troubles again in the duchies in 1851. When, in 1863, King Frederick VII., of Denmark, died without issue, the crown passed to Christian X., but the Prussian king would not consent to this arrangement, as far as the duchies were concerned, and insisted that they should go to Prince Frederick of Augustenberg, who was descended from a younger son of the same Alexander, Duke of Sonderburg, ancestor also of Christian IX., the new King of Denmark. Of course this was a mere excuse. The real object of Prussia was to get the two duchies joined on to Germany. However, the Danes had no intention to have a large portion of the kingdom torn from them, and so war broke out. Austria

Christian III.
(K. of Denmark, Duke of Schleswig-Holstein.)
d. 1559.

John of Sonderburg,
d. 1622.

Alexander,
d. 1627.

Ernest Gunther,
d. 1689.

Augustus Philip,
d. 1676.

Frederick of Augusten-
burg.

Christian IX.

Frederick II.
d. 1588.

Frederick V.
d. 1766.

Christian VII.
d. 1808.

Frederick VI.
d. 1839.

Frederick.

Christian VIII.
d. 1848.

Frederick VII.
d. 1863.

joined with Prussia, because the incorporation of
the duchies with Germany was popular, and Austria did not wish Prussia to do a popular thing un-
aided.   Accordingly, these two giants attacked the
poor little dwarf kingdom in 1864 ; but the Danes
fought like heroes, and the war continued in 1865.
Only then, crushed by the enormous preponderance
in wealth and numbers of their mighty foes, did the
Danes yield.

But, no sooner was the war over, than Prussia
showed that it was her intention to annex the
newly acquired duchies to herself.   This Austria
could not endure, and accordingly, in 1866, war
broke out between Austria and Prussia.   Prussia
sought alliance with Italy, which she stirred up to
attack Austria in her Italian possessions.   The Austrian army defeated the Italian at Eustazza ; but
the fortunes of war were against them in Germany.

Allied with the Austrians were the Saxons, the
Bavarians, the Würtembergers, Baden, and Hesse,
and Hanover.   The Prussians advanced with their
chief army into Bohemia with the utmost rapidity,
dreading lest the Southern allies should march north
to Hanover, and cut the kingdom in half, and push
on to Berlin.   The Prussians had three armies, which
were to enter Bohemia and effect a junction.   The
Elbe army under the King, the first army under
Prince Frederick Charles, and the second army under
the Crown Prince.   The Elbe army advanced across
Saxony by Dresden.   The first army was in Lusatia,
at Reichenberg, and the second army in Silesia at
Heisse.   They were all to meet at Gitschin.

The Austrian army under General Benedek was at Königgrätz, in Eastern Bohemia. Now, if you will look at your map, you will see that all the north of Bohemia is walled in by mountains, with only three tolerable passes through them. What the Austrians should have done was to have flung themselves at one army as it entered the mountains, beaten it, or at all events crippled it, then swung about and gone like a hammer at the second army, hurt that, and then battered down the third army. But, as in the wars with Napoleon, so was it now; the Austrian generals were half asleep, and never did the right thing at the right moment. Benedek did indeed march against the first army, but too late, and when he found it was already through the mountain door, he retreated, and so gave time for the three armies to concentrate upon him.

The Elbe army and the first met at Münchengratz, and defeated an Austrian army there, pushed on, and drove them back out of Gitschin on Königgrätz, where Benedek was rubbing his eyes, and thinking it time to begin.

The Prussians pushed on, and now the Elbe army went to Smidar, and the first army to Horzitz, whilst the second army, under the Crown Prince, was pushing on, and had got to Gradlitz.

The little river Bistritz is crossed by the high road to Königgrätz. It runs through swampy ground, and forms little marshy pools or lakes. To the North of Königgrätz a little stream of much the same character dribbles through bogs into the Elbe. But about Chlum, Nedelist and Lippa is terraced high ground, and there Benedek planted his cannon. The Prussians advanced from Smidar against the left wing of the Austrians, from Horzitz against the centre, and the Crown Prince was to attack the right wing. The battle began on the 3d of July, at 7 o'clock in the morning, by the simultaneous advance of the Elbe and the first army upon the Bistritz. At Sadowa is a wood, and there the battle raged most fiercely. The Austrian cannons pounded the Prussians as they advanced, but they would not go back, but held on, and there the Austrians met them, and so exhausted were they at noon that they drew off. As yet the Crown Prince had not arrived; he was floundering through the bogs, unable to make much way. Now was Benedek's second chance. He ought to have gathered up his men, and driven them like a wedge into the panting, pausing Prussians. But he waited, and drew a long breath, and rubbed his hands, and thought things were not looking very bad. To keep him amused, the Prussians thundered with their guns at his positions till they were rested. Thus passed two hours. All at once, boom! boom! then a roar of artillery brought down by the wind from the North. It was the signal that the Crown Prince with the first army had arrived on the scene, was crossing the brook and assailing the right wing and flank of Benedek. Immediately the refreshed Prussians of the other two armies charged. The King called up the reserves to help. At the same time the Crown Prince took Chlum, the key of the Austrian position, and the battle was won.

The battle was fought with the utmost bravery, but two things were against the Austrians ; first, the incompetence of their general, and, secondly, the inferiority of their guns. The Prussians had what are called needle-guns, breech-loaders, which are fired by the prick of a needle, and for rapidity with

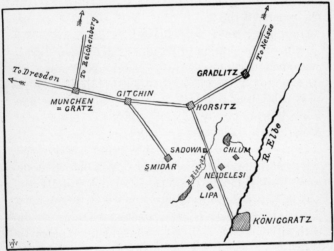

THE BATTLE OF KÖNIGGRÄTZ.

which they can be fired far surpassed the old-fashioned muzzle-loaders used by the Austrians.

After this great battle, which is called by the French and English the battle of Sadowa (Sadŏwa, not Sadōwa, as it is erroneously pronounced), but which the Germans call the battle of Königgrätz, the Prussians marched on Vienna, and reached the Marchfeld before the Emperor Francis Joseph would come to terms.

At last, on the 23d of August, a peace which gave a crushing preponderance in Germany to Prussia, was concluded at Prague.

In the mean time, however, a battle had been fought at Langensalza against the Hanoverians, in which they were defeated, and by rapid marches the Prussians had entered Hesse-Cassel and seized the person of the Duke. By the PEACE OF PRAGUE a complete change was effected in Germany. The Germanic Federation or Bund, was dissolved. Prussia annexed Hanover, Hesse-Cassel, and Nassau, as well as the two duchies of Schleswig-Holstein. Austria, Würtemberg and Baden were required to pay a war indemnity, and in addition to this Bavaria and Hesse-Darmstadt were forced to surrender some of their territories to Prussia. The states north of the River Main were formed into a Northern Federation (Nord-Bund) at the head of which stood Prussia, those south were to form South Germany, and Austria was excluded from having anything to do with either. She had also to surrender Venice to Italy. Thus the war of 1866 led to a division of Germany into three parts ; but Prussia had obtained such power that South Germany could not resist her will ; and everything was ready for the union of the North and South, which was soon to take effect.

LXVI.

A TERRIBLE STRUGGLE WITH FRANCE.

(1870–1871.)

THE throne of Spain was vacant, and Prince Leopold of Hohenzollern was a candidate for it. This created a profound excitement in France. You will remember how Francis I. fought against Charles V. because he was at once King of Germany and King of Spain. Now France was alarmed at the prospect of a German king ruling Spain, fearing a combination against her to crush her, as Prussia had combined with Italy against Austria. The agitation was so great that the Emperor Napoleon III. was forced to proclaim war. The candidature of the Hohenzollern Prince had been withdrawn when it was seen how offensive it was to France, but that did not content the French, and Napoleon was obliged to humour the popular passion and go to war.

At the time King William of Prussia was at Ems for a holiday, and all his principal ministers were in the country enjoying their leisure. The French envoy, Benedetti, visited the king at Ems, and the king, seeing that war was inevitable, hastily returned to Berlin, and called his ministers about him. On the 16th July the North German Federal council

met, and decided to prepare for war. On the 19th
an Imperial diet was called, attended by representatives of all the North and South German states,
and all decided on making common cause with the
King of Prussia.   This was a great surprise to Napoleon, who thought that South Germany would
remain neutral.   By the union of North and South
he had to contend against a vast power, and his
own force was not even equal to that of the
Northern Federation alone.

War was declared, and the fear was lest the French
should cross the frontier before the German army
was " mobilized," that is, got together and fitted for
war. .

According to all the traditions of the French
army, it ought to assume the offensive. It had
been so with the campaigns of Louis XIV. and of
Napoleon I., but it was not so on this occasion,
because the French were not ready.   Here was a
first blunder—they declared war before they were
prepared to begin it.   The French army had
indeed marched to the frontier, but it was without
supplies—the requisite munitions of war.   The plan
adopted was this : 150,000 men were to be placed
at Metz, 100,000 at Strasburg, and 50,000 were to
act as the reserve at Chalons.   Then, the Metz and
Strasburg armies were to cross the Rhine after
passing through the Bavarian palatinate, and to
advance on Frankfort, by Rastadt, where a great
battle was to be fought against the Northern army,
on the defeat of which it was expected that South

Germany, Denmark and Austria would take up arms and become the allies of France.

However, nothing was ready. The soldiers remained inactive, waiting for the military trains a whole fortnight. In the mean time, all the railways of Germany were conveying soldiers to the front ; but no troops were sent forward till they were thoroughly equipped and ready to take the field. After the second week, the German army lined the frontier, prepared at all points for the French.

There were, in fact, three armies : The first, under General Steinmetz, formed the right wing, and was stationed on the Moselle at Trèves. The second, under Prince Frederick Charles, was in the Rhenish palatinate. The third, under the Crown Prince of Prussia was planted on the right bank of the Rhine, from Mannheim to Rastadt. These armies were composed of 447,000 men. Behind, in Germany, remained ready under arms a reserve of 188,000 men to be sent forward later. Behind them, again, a second reserve of 160,000 men, also 226,000 men to be kept to fill up the gaps made by war. On July 28th the French Emperor, along with his son, the Prince Imperial, a boy of fourteen, went to Metz to assume the command. On August 2d he attacked Saarbrücken, which contained only 1300 men, and drove them out, after a fight of three hours, but they retired in good order, and were not pursued, neither was Saarbrücken occupied by the French.

Now the Germans advanced. The leading idea in the mind of Moltke, who directed operations, was, " Let the armies march separately, and concentrate to fight." That was, as you may remember, the way in which the battle of Leipzig was won. It was the way, later, in which the battle of Sadowa was won.

A little below Rastadt the Lauter runs into the Rhine from the west. The third army began its forward march on August 4th and crossed the Lauter, which was then the frontier. It came upon the French at Weissenberg, and after a battle that lasted five hours, drove them back. These French were not the main army, but a division thrown out in front, and MacMahon, the French general, with the army behind ought to have known that the Germans who attacked and took Weissenberg were not a division, but an entire army. He did not. He had no idea how and where the German armies were disposed.

The army of the Crown Prince pushed on, and presently discovered the French in force at Wörth, and routed them on August 6th, with the loss on the German side of 10,642 men. That on the French side is not accurately known, but cannot have been less. The French fought with splendid bravery, but were outnumbered. This victory opened to the Germans the passes of the Vosges, and the road to Nancy.

The very same day a victory was gained at Spicheren, about three miles from Saarbrücken, by the first and second armies, which had united. General Frossard commanded the French, and he had entrenched himself on a height with steep coppice wooded sides. The storming of the heights of Spicheren was one of the most difficult and bloody fights in the whole course of the war. Bad generalship was the cause of the defeat of the French—throughout the battle several divisions of this army were left in inaction. The heights were taken as darkness fell, and Frossard fell back under the protection of the fire of his artillery, towards Oettingen. All three divisions of the German army were now on French soil, and set forward under directions from headquarters, which was in the rear. The third army now crossed the Vosges. On the 10th a telegram from headquarters at Saarbrücken announced, "The French army is retreating on the Moselle at all points, pursued by our cavalry." From this time, the use and importance of the cavalry as a most invaluable branch of the service was recognized. It was sent before the main body of the army, gathering information as to the movements of the enemy, and marking those of the Germans. It swept over large districts, attacked and cut off trains of transport and convoys of provisions, collected food and exacted contributions. When a battle was to be fought it was called in and ready to take part in it with effect.

On the 14th of August the whole of the first army under Steinmetz was east of Metz, and the natives informed the general that the French troops, encamped on the right bank of the Moselle, were leaving their quarters. Marshal Bazaine now commanded in place of the Emperor, who was back in Paris, where great agitation broke out at the news of the successes of the Germans and their forward march.   Napoleon sent orders to Bazaine to retire on Châlons, where was the reserve, and whither the remains of MacMahon's army had retreated.   The marshal accordingly, on the 13th, had thrown bridges over the Moselle, sent some of his trains to Gravelotte the same day, and intended to follow on the morrow with all his army, leaving only sufficient men in Metz to hold the fortress.   When, however, the Germans saw that the French were in retreat they attacked them, at the village of Colombey, on the 14th of August.

I must try to give you some idea of the position of Metz that you may understand the events that followed.   Metz was the capital of old Lotharingia, or Lorraine, and is situated on the river Moselle which here flows through a broad valley from three to four miles wide.   The hills are close to the river on the east side, but stand back from it with ab- rupt fronts on the west.   Just by Metz, however, they draw together.   Metz stands on rising ground on the east side of the river, that is, its right bank, but the ground rises behind it, though not to a great altitude.   On the west side the hills are higher, and one opposite Metz, crowned by a fort, stands up immediately above the river.   The range of hills that runs north and south of the valley of the Mo- selle is broken through at several places by streams. Nine or ten miles south of Metz the Gorze stream flows in from the north-west.   Three miles nearer, another stream, the Mance, enters the Moselle, at Ars-sur-Moselle.

Now the road from Metz to Verdun and Châlons

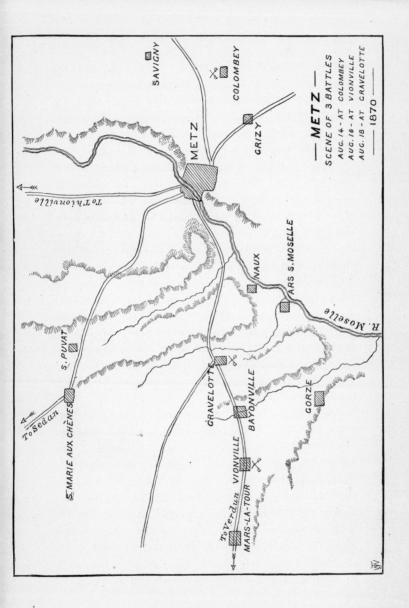

METZ

SAVIGNY

COLOMBEY

GRIZY

METZ

To Thionville

NAUX

ARS S.MOSELLE

R. Moselle

S. PUVAT

GRAVELOTTE

BAYONVILLE

GORZE

To Sedan

S. MARIE AUX CHÊNES

VIONVILLE

To Verdun

MARS-LA-TOUR

— METZ —

SCENE OF 3 BATTLES

AUG. 14 – AT COLOMBEY

AUG. 16 – AT VIONVILLE

AUG. 18 – AT GRAVELOTTE

— 1870 —

is an old Roman road.   It turns under the hill with
Fort S. Quentin, opposite Metz, and then crosses
the highland and the two streams one after the
other.   There is also a third stream, also running
from the north-west, which enters the Moselle just
under the hill and fort of S. Quentin. Now Marshal Bazaine had, as you have heard, received orders
to retire from Metz by Verdun to Châlons, and he
was beginning to do so on the 13th when the cavalry, who flew about spying all the proceedings of
the French, discovered what he was about.   So on
the 14th the Germans attacked his rear guard with
their first army.   The battle lasted seven hours.
The French occupied the ground from Grizy to
Savigny, with their centre at Colombey.   They
were driven back on Metz, and in the evening the
Germans occupied all their line.   The great importance of this battle was that it delayed Bazaine's retreat nearly two days, and gave the second German
army time to come up and cross the Moselle some
miles above Metz.

And now you must try to understand the very
masterly plan and movements that followed, the
later of which have scarce been surpassed in any
war.   Directly the king heard of the victory of
Colombey, he ordered the second army to cross
the Moselle where the Gorze brook enters it, advance up the Gorze valley and occupy the old
Roman road to Verdun, so as to cut off Bazaine's
retreat.   The Moselle was crossed at 3 o'clock in the
evening of the 15th, that is, the day after the battle
of Colombey, and the army advanced on Vion-

ville. The French were discovered to be in force all along the high table-land or terrace from Mars-la-Tour to Rezonville, and to hold the valley of the Gorze and the hill between it and the Mance. On the morning of the 16th the battle began with the advance of the 3d corps between Vionville and Flavigny. For five hours this gallant corps held its own against overwhelming odds till it was relieved by the coming up of the 10th corps and Prince Frederick Charles, "the Red Prince," as he was called, from his red beard. The principal fight was on the left wing, which was mostly composed of cavalry, who tried to turn the flank of the French at Mars-la-Tour. About 5000 horsemen on either side were engaged in the fight, which finally ended in the success of the Germans. The right wing was also successful. It drove the French from their positions and gained the top of the hill between the two streams. By this victory the road was taken and the retreat of the French by it was cut off.

Next day the French retired to the line of hills on the Metz side of the Mance. The position was very strong by nature, and they fortified it by digging trenches, and throwing up embankments. The left wing of the French rested on the Moselle at Vaux, and the right was at S. Marie-aux-Chènes on the main road from Metz to Longuyon and Sedan.

The Germans at once advanced and occupied Gravelotte. The first army was engaged here on the 18th. The Saxons and the guards were sent north to turn the flank of the French at S. Marie. Also the left wing was attacked at Vaux. The centre was at Gravelotte, but opposite this the position of the French was too strong for much to be effected. The hardest fighting and the most life lost was about S. Marie and S. Privat, where the wing of the French was successfully turned and they were driven back in confusion, and fled to Metz in wild rout. The left wing, however, held its own all night, but retired on Metz on the morning following. That same morning the German cavalry cut the railway north to Thionville, so that now the French army was enclosed in Metz.

A new arrangement of the army was at once made. Hitherto there had been three forces, now four were made, the fourth being called the army of the Meuse, and was made up of some of the corps belonging to the others and of the reserves which began to arrive. The first and second armies were left under the Red Prince to hold Bazaine in the trap into which he had been driven, and the third and fourth were sent on to meet MacMahon, who was supposed to be with his broken army and the reserve at Châlons. No time was lost. On the 19th, the day after the battle of Gravelotte, it began its advance.

Presently the cavalry discovered that Châlons had been deserted. MacMahon had gone north. What was his object ? Was he going to retreat to Paris, or was he aiming at a flank movement against the advancing Germans ? Forth went the cavalry, like a cloud of mosquitoes in all directions, and presently they found out where he was. He had not gone to Paris; he had retired on Rheims.

The Germans pushed after him. Next they ascertained that he had gone away with his army to Rethel, north-east. Now his object was clear. He was going to the Moselle, to relieve Bazaine in Metz. If he had been quick in his movements he might have done it, but he wasted ten precious days in crawling from Rheims to Beaumont on the Meuse, which gave the Germans time to catch up with him, and spoil his plan.

Directly the Germans saw what he was after, without losing a moment they marched north, and sent out detachments from the armies enclosing Metz to stop him if he came over from the Meuse to the Moselle valley.

On the 28th of August MacMahon was between Vonziers and Stenay on the Meuse. The Germans came up from the south, to the dismay of the French, and began to advance on them, and drive them back. On the 30th, Beaumont and the heights behind it were stormed, and MacMahon was obliged to retire beyond the river to Carignan, and next day to fall back on Sedan, although by this time he saw that neither in generalship nor in the quality of his soldiers, was he a match for the Germans, yet he would not yield without a blow. As you see, if you look on the map, he had allowed himself to be driven into a corner, and now, as in the battle of Leipzig with the first Napoleon, so was it with Napoleon III. at Sedan. The Germans concentrated on him from all sides except that which was towards the Belgian frontier. Gradually they closed in, driving the French before them. Mac-

Mahon was wounded at the beginning of the battle, and the command was taken by Wimpffen. But it mattered not who commanded ; no general was equal to saving this army driven into a trap, as Bazaine's army had also been driven. The French were crowded about Sedan, unable to make effective resistance, with 500 cannon playing on them. Then the Emperor Napoleon, who was in the town, seeing that everything was lost, hoisted the white flag. One of his adjutants brought King William a letter, in which the Emperor said, "As I have not died at the head of my troops, I hand over my sword to your Majesty."

The king replied that he would accept his sword, and would send an officer with full powers to treat about a capitulation. Next morning (2d Sept.) early, Napoleon left Sedan to meet the German chancellor. Bismarck met him in the house of a poor weaver at Donchery, but no decision was come to, as the Emperor would not treat of the conclusion of peace. Then King William met his prisoner in the little château of Bellevue, near Frenois. The arrangement for the capitulation was concluded between the war minister, Von Moltke, and General Wimpffen. The army was to surrender itself as prisoners of war. Every officer who would pass his word not to take up arms again during the war against Germany was to be set free. All the weapons, standards and war material in Sedan were to be delivered over. Thus fifty generals, 5000 officers, 83,000 men, 558 cannon and 6000 horses fell into the hands of the Germans. About 28,000 prisoners

KARL OTTO, PRINCE VON BISMARCK–SCHOENHAUSEN.

had already been taken ; 14,000 wounded lay in Sedan, 3000 men had escaped over the Belgian frontier,
where they were disarmed.   Thus, an army of 135-
000 men was annihilated.   The Emperor was sent to
the castle of Wilhelmshöhe, near Cassel, the summer
resort of the Dukes of Hesse-Cassel.

And now, consider the rapidity with which these
splendid results had been attained.   On the 4th of
August the German army had made its first onward
movement to the Lauter, and on September 1st
the battle of Sedan was fought.   On August 2d,
Napoleon had directed the first operations against
Saarbrücken,—the first guns had been fired and
the swords drawn.   On the 2d of September he
handed over his sword and his army, and became a
prisoner of the Germans.   The news of the defeat
and surrender of Napoleon caused a revolution to
break out in Paris ; and a republic was proclaimed
on the 4th, with a " Government of National Defence" to conduct the war, composed for the most
part of lawyers who knew nothing about war.
Hopes of peace, founded on the surrender of the
Emperor, fell.   The war must be prosecuted to the
end.   The Germans did not let the grass grow
under their feet.   Next day they entered Rheims,
and on the 15th were before Paris, surrounding it
like a half-moon.   Paris is defended by a number
of forts which crown the hills around it, allowing a
good open space between them and the city walls.
This allowed the French to form and fling themselves
between the forts, in sorties, upon the Germans,
unperceived.   None of these sorties, however,

were successful. Fresh German troops came up and completely encircled the city, so that no provisions could get into it. On October 5th the King of Prussia made the Palace of Versailles his headquarters.

MAP OF THE FRANCO-GERMAN WAR.

The siege of Paris could not be prosecuted with energy, because the Germans had not, at first, a siege train, that is, heavy cannon and other articles necessary for a bombardment; consequently the German army at first assumed a purely defensive attitude, driving back the various sorties attempted by the French.

Now a number of fortified towns in Elsass surrendered; Strasburg had made a gallant defence, and after a terrible bombardment yielded on September 27th. Marsal, Vitry, Toul, Soissons, Schlettstadt, all capitulated. On October 27th Marshal Bazaine surrendered Metz. His army, consisting of three marshals, 6000 generals and officers, 173,000 men, and 1340 cannon, fell into the hands of the victorious Germans. Thus the second French army was annihilated; and the army under Prince Frederick Charles was set free for further operation.

Just before Paris was surrendered some of the members of the new Republican government had fled to Tours. Gambetta, a French-Italian lawyer, with some cleverness, and an overweening opinion of his own abilities, escaped from Paris in a balloon, and joined the members of the government at Tours, where he took on himself the direction of the war, and acted as a dictator to France. He called out all able-bodied men in the country to arms, ordered war material from abroad, and the newly-formed troops to be drilled into order. We can see how absurd it was to suppose that such raw recruits could effect anything against armies of such tried and splendid quality as the Germans, but we must acknowledge the heroism of these men who would not yield when two of their armies had been destroyed. The result was, however, infinitely disastrous to France. It increased the misery fiftyfold, and led to useless loss of life.

A large army was formed on the Loire under General Aurelle de Paladines, which might have effected something if Gambetta had not meddled and tried to override the authority of the general in command. The Germans went at once against it, as it was menacing their army about Paris, and beat it at Orleans and Beaune. General Aurelles had been forced by the dictator Gambetta to fight against his judgment. After his defeat he resigned, and the army of the Loire was divided into two. One, under Bourbaki, was concentrated at Bourges. The other, under Chanzy, was further down the Loire at Beauzency, between Orleans and Blois. The Germans soon found that the latter had the largest army, and the Red Prince went at him and defeated him, and drove him back on Vendôme. The government finding Tours no longer safe, ran away to Bordeaux. Chanzy then retreated to Le Mans. On the last day of that disastrous year Chanzy made an attempt to strike a deadly blow at the army of the Red Prince which pursued him, but this also failed.

In the mean time an army had been formed in the north of France, under General Faidherbe; and against this the first German army, under General Manteuffel, was sent, attacked this army at Amiens on November 27th, and beat it, driving it away in confusion to Arras and Lille.

Another division of the north army was at Rouen, and now Manteuffel turned against that and dispersed it, and occupied Rouen. Then he went back against Faidherbe to finish him off. He defeated him at Hallue and Bapaume. Another battle at S. Quentin completed the ruin of Faidherbe's army. This last battle was on January 18th. The same day General Trochu who commanded in Paris, made an attempt to burst out, but was beaten back with great loss.

Thus every attempt made to relieve Paris by falling on the rear of the besiegers had failed.

Gambetta now formed a new plan of operation. He determined to carry the war into the enemy's country, and so force them to send back their troops to the protection of Germany, and so relieve the pressure on Paris. Between Vesoul and Basle is a very strong fortified place, Belfort, which had not as yet surrendered, though it was closely besieged. Gambetta resolved that Bourbaki should march to the relief of Belfort, and thence cross the Rhine, and fall upon Baden and Würtemberg.

The Germans speedily discovered what was intended, and formed a new army, called the south army, to follow Bourbaki under Manteuffel, who was recalled from the north when he had crippled Faidherbe. The Red Prince was, in the mean while, driving Chanzy back ; and on January 12th he defeated him at Le Mans, taking prisoners 20,000 men, and completely breaking his power. The French army of the west fled in confusion to Laval and Mayenne, pursued by the Germans. Chanzy was never again able to collect an effective force ; so now his army was dissolved, as well as the army of Faidherbe.

In the east was General Werder at the head of

a German army engaged in the sieges of Belfort and Langres. Directly he heard of the march of Bourbaki, he threw himself in his way at Hericourt. He had only 35,000 men at his command, whereas the French army numbered nearly 100,000. Moreover, in the rear of the Germans was Belfort, and they were in danger of an attack thence. However, for three whole days, the 15th, 16th and 17th of January, they held Bourbaki at bay. The weather was bitterly cold, snow was on the ground. On the 18th the French retreated. The little band of Germans had defeated an army three times its size. As King William truly said of this battle, " It is one of the most remarkable feats of arms of all times."

Now Manteuffel was hastening up, and Gambetta again meddled, throwing Bourbaki out of his arrangements. Ashamed of his ill success, maddened by Gambetta, he shot himself, but though severe, the wound did not prove mortal. General Clinchant was appointed in his place, but it was merely the substitution of General Naught for General Nothing. All he could do was to retreat on Bezançon, and from Bezançon on the Swiss frontier, which the defeated army crossed, gave up their arms, and disappeared. Thus another army was annihilated, and France was left without one to defend it, except only that enclosed in Paris. Resistance was impossible. On the 24th February the preliminaries of peace were prepared, and on the 15th March peace was concluded. France was to surrender all Elsass and part of Lorraine (Lothringen) with Metz, and to pay a heavy war indemnity, and till this indemnity was paid the German army was to hold in occupation certain portions of the French territory. Some of the forts about Paris were to be held by the Germans till the money had been paid. A congress was to meet at Brussels to settle particulars.

Thereupon, the greater part of the victorious army returned to Germany, and the Peace congress met at Brussels on March 28th. Proceedings were, however, delayed by the breaking out of a new revolution in Paris. The Commune took possession of the capital and several of the forts vacated by the Germans, and established a government of their own. And now the Republican government had to lay siege to Paris, and bombard it, whilst the Germans looked quietly on from the forts they still held. The Republican government called the remains of its armies together, and so Paris had to undergo a second siege, which left it in a more disastrous condition than the first. When the Communists saw that the place was taken, they tried to set fire to all the public buildings and churches, so as to bury themselves under its ruins.

Only on the 10th of May peace was definitely concluded at Frankfort, which was substantially the same as the preliminary agreement arrived at on March 1st.

LXVII.

THE NEW EMPIRE.

THE war had drawn all the states of Germany together, had broken down the dislike of the South for the North, and had united all German hearts.

The time was come, Providence seemed to have declared it, when at last the lesson of the past, which had been written and rewritten in blood, but which had been unheeded, should be laid to heart and acted upon. That lesson was—Unity. All the miseries of Germany had been due to petty rivalries and jealousies. Now God had given Germany victory over the power that had been her deadliest enemy—the busy hand that had sowed strife in her fields, and that victory had been given only because she had acted unitedly.

The several states took counsel together, and agreed to offer the imperial crown to the King of Prussia. The proclamation declaring the foundation of the restored empire was made on January 1st, 1871, and on the 18th William, King of Prussia, was saluted as Emperor of Germany, in the Palace of Versailles, by the representatives of the states of Germany.

The capitulation of Paris followed on Jan. 28th.

The preliminaries of peace were decided on, on Feb. 26th, and peace was concluded definitely on May 10th, at Frankfort-on-Main. The re-union of Elsass and German Lorraine with Strasburg and Metz was a military necessity, and was in accord with the general wish of the German people.

The first diet of the Empire assembled at Berlin on March 21, 1871.

The present German empire comprises twenty-six states. Of these twenty-two are monarchical, and three (Hamburg, Bremen, and Lubeck) are republican. One, Elsass—Lothringen, is an imperial province, under the sovereignty of the German empire. The other states are kingdoms, grand duchies and duchies.

Formerly, the traveller up the Rhine had to obtain Prussian coins at Aix or Cologne, and change them into South German coins at Mainz. At Cologne he had thalers, groschen, and pfennig. Twelve pfennig made a silver groschen, and thirty silver groschen made a thaler. At Mainz the coinage was different. There one had kreutzers, and gulden or florins. Sixty kreutzers made a gulden. In Hamburg the coinage again was different. There sixteen shillings made a mark, and the value of a shilling was under an English penny. Now throughout Germany (not including Austria) there is but one coinage. Ten pfennig make one mark, the value of which is about one shilling English. This is a great gain. Now also the laws have been simplified and made alike throughout Germany, and these are only some of the many advantages

WILLIAM I., EMPEROR OF GERMANY.

gained by unity. You remember, doubtless, the fable of the old man and his sons and the bundle of sticks. Each stick alone could easily be snapped, but a strong man could do nothing to the bundle when tied tightly together. Now at last that bun- of sticks, the German nation, has been bound together firmly, and ever may it so remain.

There is a favourite German song to this effect:

> " What is the German Fatherland?
>> Is it Prussia?
>> Is it Swabia?
>> Is it the grape-hung Rhine?
>> Is it the Baltic gull-sought strand?
> Greater, O greater, the German Fatherland.

> " What is the German Fatherland?
>> Is it Bavaria?
>> Is it Saxony?
>> Is't where the sedgy marshes spread?
>> Is't where the miners work the ore?
> Greater, O greater, the German Fatherland.

> " What is the German Fatherland?
>> Is it Pomerania?
>> Is it Westphalia?
>> Is't where white sands the blue sea laves?
>> Is't where wild Danube rolls her waves?
> Greater, O Greater, the German Fatherland."

Then the song goes on to say that the German Fatherland is where the German tongue is spoken, and German songs are sung, where German hearts beat true, and foreign falsehood is abhorred, where there is common good, and a common love of all that is great, and noble and right.

I have said that German history shows us the

FREDERICK WILLIAM, IMPERIAL PRINCE, AND HEIR APPARENT TO THE
GERMAN THRONE.

great lesson of unity taught so simply in the fable
of the old man, his sons and the bundle of sticks.
It teaches another lesson also, a lesson illustrated
by a fable. You well recall that of the dog and the
piece of meat and the shadow. The dog, in grasping at the shadow, lost the substance. German emperors, in grasping at that vainest of shadows, the
Roman empire, lost the opportunity of consolidat-
ing the German nation under a firm government.
It was this grasping at a vain shadow which had
made the empire so weak, and Germany so in-
coherent, that Napoleon was able to ruin it almost
hopelessly. It took Germany many centuries to
learn this truth; it did learn it in the end. It has
taken it still longer to learn the truth that in Unity
is Strength.

But it must by no means be supposed that every
problem has been solved, and that Germany now
knows the safe road that leads to prosperity. It
has learned one or two lessons, but it has another to
learn. It has solved certain problems, but there is
another to be solved which is full of difficulty and
menace.

In order to make Germany united and powerful
its manhood has been organized into an army.
Every able-bodied man is a soldier. He has to
drill, and serve for three years actively with the
colours. Only those who are studying for the
learned professions and are capable of passing a
high standard in examination are let off with one
year of active service. Now, this system unques-
tionably is of great advantage, not to the nation

only, but also to the individual soldiers. All the young men receive a discipline which transforms louts and boobies into trim and intelligent men ; for the German military course is not one of drill of the body only, but of mental drill as well. Consequently, all the manhood of the country is brought to discipline, subordination, and to the sense of interdependence. But on the other hand, the cost to the country is enormous and crushing. Some of the best years of a young man's life, the most valuable years for acquiring knowledge of a profession are lost to him. Moreover, the country has to be heavily taxed to feed, clothe, and equip this enormous body of recruits. Many men, rather than serve these three years, run away to America, or England, and the drain in this way of able-bodied men is so serious as to perplex the authorities greatly.

Now, Germany having armed all her male population, France, Austria, Russia, Italy have had to do the same, so that the continent of Europe is burdened with this terrible cost, and one nation cannot withdraw its shoulder from the burden, because it fears to be crushed by the superior force of the others.

Consequently, as you see, though the empire of Germany is a splendid power, it is also a very crushing power to the people, and though the nation has escaped from one set of difficulties, it has plunged into another. What the result will be we cannot tell, but in this world there is no great gain made in one direction without a loss in another. Still.

mankind is teachable, though often terribly slow to learn. Where a mistake has been made, better experience comes to insist on a redress. The great advantage of the study of history is, that it teaches us to look at the mistakes that have been made by preceding generations, and to avoid the like in our own.

INDEX.

28